Sudan on the Eve of Independence 1954-1956

Dr Faisal Abdel Rahman Ali Taha

Ink Press Publications
London

Ink Press Publications Ltd.
21 Grosvenor Crescent
Kingsbury
London NW9 9DB

First published in Arabic as
al-Sūdān ʿala Mashārif al-Istiqlāl al-Thānī

First published in English in 2022

Translated by Osman Nusairi
Edited by Fergus Nicoll

ISBN: 978-1-7397434-9-9

Very slowly, the British and Egyptian flags were lowered and the blue, green, and yellow flag of the new Sudan was hoisted in their stead. As it unfurled in the fresh north wind, the cheers of the multitude broke out in Kitchener Square outside the Palace Wall. ... The band of the Sudan Defence Force struck up a lilting march. The ceremony was over.

With tears streaming from his eyes, Sayed Abdel Rahman El Mahdi rose from his chair in the grip of emotion, and collapsed in a heap on the ground, his flowing robes around him. He had fainted. In the ensuing weeks this indomitable figure looked twenty years younger. There were many other Sudanese friends in tears: the more able they were, the more deeply they felt the significance of this historic moment.

J.S.R. Duncan[1]

---

[1] J.S.R. Duncan, *The Sudan's Path to Independence* (Edinburgh: William Blackwood & Sons, 1957), pp. 206-7.

CONTENTS

ILLUSTRATIONS

PROLOGUE

This book chronicles the period between January 1954 and December 1955. Under the 12 February 1953 Agreement concerning Sudan's self-government and self-determination, concluded between the Condominium partners Egypt and Britain, Sudan went through two stages: the transitional stage and the stage of self-determination.

Under Article 12 of the 1953 Agreement, the Sudanese had, during the latter stage, to choose – via an elected Constituent Assembly – between a link with Egypt in any form or complete independence. It is no surprise that Article 12 of the Statute presented self-determination as outlined above. This was because Sudan's political class had been split since its inception into two trends: one calling for the complete independence of Sudan and the second calling for differing levels of unity with Egypt. Equally, there was disagreement in the visions of Egypt and Britain over Sudan's future.

Under Lord Milner's 1920 recommendations, Britain pursued a policy of Sudan developing independently from Egypt, with its people, on attaining complete self-government, to have the right to self-determination. Egyptian governments under the monarchy had argued that the right to self-determination would not apply to Sudan as it was an inseparable part of Egypt.

The Egyptian revolution of 23 July 1952 should be credited with recognizing the right of the Sudanese to self-determination. That did not mean, however, that Egypt had conceded Sudan: the Government was under the illusion that, by bringing together all Sudanese political parties that supported unity with Egypt into one political party – the National Unionist Party (NUP) – the process of self-determination would be decided in favour of Sudan being linked to Egypt.

Egypt's revolutionary government regarded it as auspicious that the NUP achieved a sweeping electoral victory in internationally-supervised elections held in November/December 1953 thanks to Egyptian financial and media support – and that Ismāʿīl al-Azharī was elected Prime Minister of Sudan on 9 January 1954. There then followed a peaceful and smooth transfer of domestic authority from British hands to a Sudanese government calling for unity with Egypt.

Matters, however, developed in a manner neither expected nor desired by Egypt's revolutionary government: in April 1955, the NUP declared its alignment to the option of Sudan's complete independence.

The period chronicled in this book may seem short but it was replete with momentous events and exciting developments, including:

a) Prime Minister al-Azharī discreetly notifying the Governor-General's adviser, William Luce, in February 1954 that his ultimate aim was the complete independence of Sudan;
b) The bloody and violent events in Khartoum in March 1954;
c) al-Sayyid ʿAbd-al-Raḥman al-Mahdī asking Britain in March 1954 to declare Sudanese independence outright;
d) The 2nd Juba Conference of October 1954 choosing federation within a united Sudan – with the scope of the Conference extending to the Nuba, the Fur, the Funj and non-Arabs in Khartoum;
e) The Government seeking British advice on combatting communism;
f) Splits within the NUP;
g) Drafting of a National Charter;
h) Mutiny of the Southern troops in Torit;
i) Adopting a plebiscite as the means to self-determination;
j) Egypt's Czech arms deal speeding up Sudanese independence;
k) Britain's proposal that self-determination be declared in Parliament;
l) And the failure of the attempt at such a declaration on 3 November 1955.

This book deals with all these issues and more in 16 chapters, as well as this Prologue and the concluding Epilogue.

In preparing this book, the author has relied primarily on British documents available to readers and researchers in The National Archives at Kew. These include telegrams, letters, minutes and reports reaching the Foreign Office from three sources: the Governor-General's Office, the Office of the UK Commercial Commissioner in Khartoum and the British Embassy in Cairo.

These documents are recognised as credible, accurate and objective records. Indeed, it could not be otherwise, as the input of these three sources was the raw material for the formulation of British policy and decision-making processes pertaining to Sudan. The fact that one may sometimes disagree with some projections or deductions contained in some of these resources does not undermine their credibility. It is regrettable that the Egyptian documents for this period have not yet been made available. Had they been accessible, it would have been useful to compare them to their British counterparts.

I was also able to gain access to the Maḥmūd Ṣālih Private Collection, which contains the papers of Sir William Luce relevant to the period and subject of this book. In general, these documents are personal messages exchanged between Luce and the Sudan Government's Agent in London. They contain details, facts, information and impressions which were not mentioned or were mentioned prematurely in the official correspondence.

Some might find this book excessively detailed – but I maintain, as I mentioned earlier, that details help us see events in contexts and judge them according to the circumstances of the time. Details also bring historical events to life.

Finally, I would like to express my appreciation and gratitude to the staff of The National Archives at Kew; the staff of the Readers' and Researchers' Hall of The National Archives in Khartoum; the Egyptian National Library and Archives (*Dār al-Kutub al-Qawmīa*) in Cairo; and to Jane Hogan, formerly Senior Assistant Keeper at the Sudan Archive, University of Durham.

I am indebted to all the friends and colleagues who helped me in the various stages of preparing the original Arabic edition of this book. May I also extend my thanks to Ṣāliḥ Faraḥ 'Abd-al-Raḥman, my wife Bidūr 'Abd-al-Mun'im, 'Abd-al-Jabbār Abū Bakr, my son 'Abd-al-Raḥman who read the draft of this book and offered valuable observations and suggestions, and to my daughter Nawār who carried out the scanning of the photographs.

Throughout, however, I alone take responsibility for what I have written and ask for divine forgiveness for any errors or lapses.

Faisal Abdel Rahman Ali Taha
Abu Dhabi, April 2022

CHAPTER 1

Introduction

i. The Self-Government and Self-Determination Agreement for Sudan (12 February 1953)

a. Outline of the Agreement's provisions[1]

The Agreement stipulated that self-determination was to be preceded by a transitional period which would not exceed three years, during which the Sudanese would exercise complete self-government.[2] This was to be the liquidation of Condominium's administration.[3] Until self-determination was attained, the sovereignty of Sudan was to be held in reserve for the Sudanese.[4]

The transitional period would commence on a day designated as 'the appointed day', namely the day when the Governor-General would certify in writing that the institutions of self-government – i.e. the Council of Ministers, the House of Representatives and the Senate – were formed.[5]

---

[1] 'Agreement Between the Government of the United Kingdom of Great Britain and Northern Ireland and The Egyptian Government Concerning Self-Government and Self-Determination for the Sudan' (London: HMSO, Cmd. 8767 1953), pp. 60-64; see also *al-Sūdān: al-Kitāb al-Akhdar* (*Sudan: The Green Book*) (Cairo: Cabinet Office, 1841-1953), p. 384. The full text of the Agreement is reproduced in Appendix 1.

[2] Agreement Article 1.

[3] Agreement Article 2.

[4] Agreement Article 2.

[5] Agreement Article 9; also Self-Government Statute Article 2.

In order to ensure free voluntary conduct for self-determination, the Agreement provided for a Sudanisation Committee charged, under Annex III of the Agreement, with the Sudanisation of the administration, the police, the Sudan Defence Force, as well as other posts that may have an influence on the free choice of the Sudanese at the point of self-determination.[6] The Annex specified a period of up to three years to complete the Commission's work.[7] We will elaborate on the work of the Commission in Chapter 11.

Under the Agreement, the transitional period would end when Parliament adopted a resolution expressing its desire to take measures necessary for self-determination and notified the Egyptian and British governments of the resolution.[8] The evacuation of Egyptian and British forces from Sudan would commence immediately after the adoption of this resolution. The two governments pledged to complete evacuation within three months.[9]

The existing Sudanese government would then draw up a draft bill for the election of a Constituent Assembly. To become law, the bill would require the approval of the Sudanese Parliament and the consent of both the Governor-General and his Commission.[10]

The Agreement subjected the detailed arrangements for self-determination – including safeguards to assure the impartiality of the elections and any other measures necessary to secure a free and neutral atmosphere – to international supervision. The two governments pledged to accept the recommendations of any international body set up for this purpose.[11]

The Agreement further assigned to the Constituent Assembly a two-fold function: to decide the future of Sudan as one integral whole and to draw up a constitution for Sudan compatible with the decision taken in that respect. The Assembly was also charged with the task of drawing up an electoral law for a permanent Sudanese Parliament. The

---

[6] Agreement Article 8; also Annex iii, Clause 1.

[7] Annex iii, Clause 4.

[8] Agreement Article 9.

[9] Agreement Article 11.

[10] Agreement Article 10.

[11] Agreement Article 10.

future of Sudan would be decided by the Constituent Assembly, choosing any form of linkage with Egypt or complete independence.[12]

b. Powers of the Governor-General

The Agreement stipulated that the Governor-General should remain during the transitional period as the supreme constitutional authority within Sudan. He should discharge his powers under the Self-Government Statute with the aid of a five-member group called the Governor-General's Commission.[13] The Agreement further provided that the Governor-General should remain directly responsible to the two Condominium Governments for matters relating to external affairs.[14]

Article 11 of the Self-Government Statute stipulated that supreme military command should be vested in the Governor-General, who would remain as commander of the Sudan Defence Force. As for the supreme command of the Sudanese armed forces following the evacuation of Egyptian and British forces, the two governments reached an understanding – via memoranda attached to the Agreement – that this would be one of the matters to be considered by the international body to be set up under Article 10 of the Agreement. We shall see in Chapter 14 that the interpretation of this exchange of memoranda created disagreement between the two governments.

Under Clause 2 of the Agreement's Annex 1 and Article 12(3) of the Self-Government Statute, the Governor-General should have 'other discretionary powers' – though they would be subject to the approval of his Commission. Some of these powers will be discussed later in this chapter.

c. The Governor-General's Commission

The Agreement stipulated in Article 4 that the Governor-General's Commission should consist of two Sudanese proposed by the British and Egyptian governments. Their appointment would be subject to the approval of Parliament, once elected. Should there be no

---

[12] Agreement Article 12.

[13] Agreement Article 3.

[14] Agreement Article 6 (a).

parliamentary approval, Parliament would have the right to nominate alternative candidates. The Commission should also include one Egyptian, one British national and a Pakistani – each nominated by his own government.[15] Annex 1 of the Agreement provided that the Commission should be chaired by the Pakistani member.[16]

For membership of the Commission, Egypt nominated Wing Commander Ḥussein Zulfiqār Ṣabrī while Britain nominated Sir Laurence Grafftey-Smith.[17] Pakistan nominated Mian Ziauddin, who, because of his delayed arrival, was temporarily replaced by Tayyib Hussain, the Chargé d'Affaires at the Pakistani Embassy in Cairo.[18]

The nomination and approval of the two Sudanese, however, was no easy matter. The nomination process was conducted by a group called the Coalition Parties' Committee and composed of the three northern political parties: the Umma, the NUP and the Republican Socialist Party. On 25 February 1953, the Committee submitted its nominations to the serving Governor-General, Robert Howe,[19] and to the Chief of Staff of the Egyptian Armed Forces in Sudan. According to the ballot within the Committee, Muḥammad al-Ḥassan Diyāb topped the list with three votes, ahead of Ibrāhīm Aḥmad (two) and Mīrghanī Ḥamza, Ḥammād Ṭawfīq and Muḥammad Aḥmad Abū-Sinn (one apiece). A few days after the vote, Ḥammād Ṭawfīq withdrew and was replaced by al-Dardirī Muḥammad ʿUthmān – but he was supported by Sayyid ʿAlī al-Mīrghanī and the Republican Socialist Party objected to this.

The Governor-General picked the two candidates who had secured the highest votes in the ballot: Muḥammad al-Ḥassan Diyāb and Ibrāhīm Aḥmad. The Egyptian Government picked Ibrāhīm Aḥmad and – following an intervention by Sayyid ʿAlī al-Mīrghanī – al-Dardirī

---

[15] Agreement, Annex I (6).

[16] M.W. Daly, *Imperial Sudan: The Anglo-Egyptian Condominium, 1934-1956* (Cambridge: CUP, 1991), pp. 353-4.

[17] Laurence Grafftey-Smith, *Bright Levant* (London: John Murray, 1970), p. 225.

[18] National Archives, Kew, FO [Foreign Office] 371/108331 (Establishment of the Governor-General's Commission in the Sudan): Minutes by Mavrogordato, 8 January 1954, Minute regarding the Sudanese members of the Governor-General's Commission, 7 January 1954.

[19] A useful guide to colonial appointees in Sudan can be found in M.W. Daly, 'Principal Office-Holders in the Sudan Government, 1895-1955', *International Journal of African Historical Studies* 17/2 (1984), pp. 309-316.

Muḥammad ʿUthmān as well. His name was added to the list of candidates after the withdrawal of Ḥammād Ṭawfīq as mentioned above.

During a visit to Sudan between 21-27 March 1953, a Minister of State in the British Foreign Office, John Selwyn Lloyd, met Sayyid ʿAlī al-Mīrghanī. Mīrghanī Ḥamza was present and he undertook the role of interpreter. When their conversation referred to the Governor-General's Commission, Sayyid ʿAlī expressed his preference for al-Dardirī Muḥammad ʿUthmān over Muḥammad al-Ḥassan Diyāb – although he asked Lloyd not to mention it in public. [20]

Lloyd managed to secure the Republican Socialist Party's agreement to the appointment of al-Dardirī Muḥammad ʿUthmān. Party leaders explained that their objection was not against al-Dardirī personally but the way in which he was included in the list of candidates. [21]

As we shall see later, the ruling NUP blocked the appointment of Ibrāhīm Aḥmad as a Commission member, replacing him with the Southern NUP member Siricio Iro Wani.

It has been mentioned above that the Governor-General had discretionary powers that he could only exercise with the approval of his Commission. These powers – set out in Annex 1 (2) of the Agreement and Article 12 (3) of the Self-Government Statute – included, for instance, choosing members of the Senate and approving the two Chairs nominated for the House of Representatives and for the Senate. Importantly they included the Governor-General's responsibilities under Article 100 of the Self-Government Statute, which provided that he had a special responsibility to secure fair treatment for all the populations of Sudan's different Provinces.

d. Declaration of a state of constitutional emergency

Under Article 102(1) of the Self-Government Statute, the Governor-General was endowed with the power to declare a state of

---

[20] Ibid., FCO 371/102753 (Agreement between Egypt and UK on the Sudan: efforts to achieve implementation): Selwyn Lloyd's Meeting with Sayed Ali, 22 March 1953.

[21] Ibid., Lloyd's meeting with members of the Socialist Republican Party, 23 March 1953.

constitutional emergency if he was satisfied at any time by reason of a political deadlock, non-cooperation or boycott that it would not be possible to carry on administering the country in accordance with the Constitution.

The Governor-General was further empowered under Article 102(2), after consultation with his Commission to the fullest extent possible, to declare a state of constitutional emergency if he was satisfied at any time that a financial crisis was imminent or that the collapse of law and order required his immediate and direct intervention in the interest of the good government of the Sudan.

If the Commission did not consent to the intervention of the Governor-General, it had to refer the matter promptly to the British and Egyptian Governments. In turn they should jointly call on the Governor-General to terminate the state of constitutional emergency which he should do forthwith.

In case either of the two Governments saw no justification for the continuance of the state of constitutional emergency, it should notify the Governor-General of that. The latter would then be obliged to terminate it within 30 days from the date of the referral.

When declared, the state of constitutional emergency would under Article 102 (3) and (4) cause the disruption of Parliament and the relinquishment by the Prime Minister and his ministers of their posts. As long as it remained in force, the administration of the Sudan would be carried out by decrees issued by the Governor-General.

In fact, no Governor-General had ever invoked Article 102 of the Self-Government Statute to declare a state of constitutional emergency, although we shall see later that the question of such a declaration was raised three times: 1 March 1954; on the occasion of Ibrāhīm Aḥmad's likely removal from the Governor-General's Commission; and when Southern troops mutinied at Torit on 18 August 1955.

e. The Sudanese Communist Party (SCP) opposes the 1953 Agreement

Qāsim Amīn, an officer in the Railway Workers' Union and a leading Communist Party figure, wrote a pamphlet entitled 'Weighing up the Agreement'. He reviewed some aspects of the Agreement with criticism and analysis that was, at least in part, exaggerated and alarmist. For instance, the writer criticised both the representation of the United States on the Electoral Commission and the membership of Pakistan on the Governor-General's Commission. The Americans were seen as attempting to sneak into Sudan to control it and its resources at a time when British imperialism was weakening internationally. Pakistan was seen as a satellite of the British Crown, linked to the Western bloc and actively seeking to achieve an imperialist Middle East pact.

Qāsim Amīn, however, was justified in criticising the powers of the Governor-General, in particular his authority to declare a state of constitutional emergency. The pamphlet also criticized the indirect election constituencies, which do not produce members of Parliament directly elected by the people as required by constitutional law. Qāsim Amīn regarded as an expansion of American and British influence over the army, the decision of leaving the question of supreme military command to the International Commission supervising the self-determination process, following the evacuation of British and Egyptian forces. According to Amin, such influence cannot be reconciled with the achievement of a clean national independence.[22]

Kāmil Maḥjūb found further grounds for the Communist Party's opposition to the Agreement: it would not achieve Sudan's freedom because freedom could only be achieved through a bloody revolution. But Kāmil believed that the SCP leadership had completely isolated itself, even as Party members responded positively to the prevailing joy among Sudanese at the Agreement and its achievements in terms of freedom and the removal of foreign influence. [23]

In the prevailing climate of widespread popular acceptance for the Agreement, the Communist Party swiftly reversed its position. ʿAbd-al-Khāliq Maḥjūb stated, by way of justification, that the Party had erred only in viewing the Agreement from one single perspective – that of the "slippery slopes" that might be exploited by the colonial powers as a way of legitimising their own positions and maintaining their own influence. The SCP did not view the Agreement as a product of the struggle of the

---

[22] Qāsim Amīn, *Itifāqīat al-Sūdān fī al-Mīzān* (*Sudan's Agreement in the Balance*) (n.p.), pp. 9-17.

[23] Kāmil Maḥjūb, *Tilk al-Ayyām, al-Juzu' al-Awwal* (*Those Days, Part 1*) (Khartoum: Dār al-Balad, 1999), p. 110.

masses; indeed, better results would have been produced had the middle-class political parties honoured their alliance to the United National Front for the Liberation of Sudan. This, however, was not a denial of the fact that colonialism, under pressure from a popular movement, had been compelled to retreat: the Agreement, then, was a concession on their part, to be used in the interests of the people of Sudan. [24]

f. The position of the South

No Southerners had taken part in the talks conducted by the northern Sudanese parties with Egypt's revolutionary government in Cairo in October 1952. While the Socialist Republican Party was the only northern party to have Southerners as members, no Southerners were represented in the Party's delegation to those talks, nor were they involved in the Agreement that resulted. Nor were Southerners represented in the Agreement reached with Egypt by the political parties on 10 January 1953 – even though the South was one of the five topics covered in the Agreement.

In a communiqué issued on 13 December 1952, a Juba-based group calling itself the Southern Political Committee objected to amendments to the Self-Government Statute introduced by these agreements reached in Cairo. The group was made up of 36 personalities representing Juba, Torit, Yei and Zande; it also included delegates from the Provinces of Upper Nile and Baḥr al-Ghazāl.

The communiqué cast doubt on the goodwill of the northern parties' leadership, who had concluded agreements with the Egyptian Government without bothering to consult the South – and without consideration for the Agreement they had reached with the South back in 1947, which culminated in the Self-Government Statute. The communiqué confirmed the commitment of Southern leaders to that Self-Government Statute, as approved by the Legislative Assembly. They would not accept any modifications introduced to it, unless such modifications were agreed by a fully representative and democratic body.

---

[24] ʿAbd-al-Khāliq Maḥjūb, *Lamahāt min Tārīkh al-Hizb al-Shūʿi al-Sūdānī* (*Glimpses from the History of the Sudanese Communist Party*) (3rd edition) (Khartoum: Dār al-Wasīla Printing and Publishing, 1987), p. 81.

Mr and Mrs Robert Howe with Palace staff

The communiqué objected to the Northern view that self-determination should take place in three years because the South was not yet in a position to enter into an entirely free and democratic union with the North: "The South is, at the present time, well behind the North in terms of education and in all other aspects of development. Southerners desire that the present Civil Service, which has contributed primarily to the level of development reached by the North today, should remain to direct Southerners towards the same goal."

The Southern Political Committee's communiqué concluded by stating that Southerners were looking forward to the day when they could join the North in an independent, united and free Sudan – "but they feel that this would not be realised until they achieve the same level as the North. For this reason there should not be a specific period for self-determination." [25]

---

[25] National Archive, Kew, FO 371/96916 (Anglo-Egyptian negotiations for self-government in the Sudan): Khartoum to Foreign Office, 16 December 1952.
See also Fadwa A.A. Taha, 'The Sudanese Factor in the 1952-53 Anglo-Egyptian Negotiations', Middle Eastern Studies 44/4 (2008), pp. 619-20, and Elias Nyamlell

No political parties were formed in the South until just before the self-government elections, which took place according to Article 7 of the 1953 Agreement. In January 1954 – i.e. after the elections – the United Southern Party merged with the Southern Political League to form the Liberal Party. The declaration of this Party's formation was signed by 16 members of the House of Representatives and seven members of the Senate. The declaration stated that the Party was established "to protect the interests of the South and to avoid entering into factional conflicts." It further asserted that it believed in the complete independence of Sudan and that it would work with any Northern parties that shared that view.

The Liberal Party confirmed the need to establish good relationships with Egypt and other countries but it expressed its strong opposition to any form of unity with Egypt or any foreign hegemony over Sudan. The Party further announced that it was aiming to achieve the economic and social development of backward regions, including the South, the Nuba Mountains, Darfur and the Funj. The Party was chaired by Benjamin Lwoki, with Stanislaus Paysama as his Vice-Chairman, Buth Diu as Secretary-General and Paulo Logali as Treasurer. The Party Committee also included, in different positions, Gordon Ayoum and Alfred Olodo. [26]

We shall see in Chapter 5 that the Liberal Party adopted the call to convene the 2nd Juba Conference in October 1954, which decided on the institution of a federal union between the North and South within a united Sudan.

g. The Governor-General's office

At the time the Agreement was concluded, the post of Governor-General had been occupied since 1947 by Robert Howe, the first diplomat to assume the post. He had served in the British Embassy in Ethiopia and at the Foreign Office in London. Article 103 of the Self-Government Statute authorized the Governor-General to appoint such officials as he

---

Wakoson, 'The Sudanese Dilemma: The South-North Conflict', Northeast African Studies 9/3 (1987), p. 48.

[26] Maḥmūd Ṣāliḥ Private Collection (Bergen), Sir William Luce Papers, 829/8/8-11: 'Summary of Events, No.1. January 1954'.

may consider necessary to assist him in the performance of his responsibilities. Under this Article, he appointed William Luce, Governor of Blue Nile Province, as his adviser in constitutional and foreign affairs, with John Kenrick and John Duncan as assistants. John Mavrogordato was also deputed from the Advocate-General's office to serve as Legal Advisor in the Governor-General's office. It is worth mentioning that Luce had extensive knowledge of the trends and less public aspects of Sudanese politics. Between 1948 and 1950, he had worked for the Civil Secretary's political department, where he was responsible for political intelligence, the press and the Egyptian file. [27]

In November 1954, Governor-General Howe notified the Foreign Secretary, Anthony Eden, of his wish to resign, for personal reasons, at an early date in 1955. His resignation was accepted and the post of Governor-General became vacant on 3 January 1955. Three days later, the Egyptian Council of Ministers issued a decree signed by its Chairman, Gamāl ʿAbd-al-Nāṣir, accepting Howe's resignation and appointing Sir Alexander Knox Helm as his successor. Knox Helm had also been a diplomat, serving in various positions, the latest being as the British Ambassador to Turkey. [28]

ii. The Sudanese political movement

During the period covered by this book, Sudan's political arena was dominated by two trends: a pro-independence faction calling for the complete independence of Sudan and a unionist faction advocating unity with Egypt.

The Umma Party was the most important of the pro-independence parties. It was founded in early 1945 as an alliance between the *Anṣār* – followers of the original Mahdī and his successors – as well as tribal chiefs and a number of graduates who had been calling for the independence of Sudan on the basis of the principle 'Sudan for the Sudanese'. The Umma Party manifesto stipulated its aims as the achievement of independence for Sudan while maintaining cordial

[27] Harold MacMichael, *Sudan Political Service 1899-1956* (Oxford: Oxonian Press, 1958), p. 59.

[28] National Archives, Kew, FO 371/113596 (Departure of Sir R. Howe as Governor-General of Sudan).

relations with Egypt and Britain. The Party cooperated with the British administration in Sudan through the institutions of constitutional development leading up to self-Government and self-Determination.[29]

In November 1945, Maḥmūd Muḥammad Ṭaha and others founded the Republican Party. Its objectives were summed up in six points, the most important of which was the establishment of a free, democratic, republican Sudanese government – while maintaining all the geographical borders of the day intact.[30] In December 1951, the Republican Socialist Party was declared. Item 2 of its constitution stated that the aims of the Party were the complete independence of Sudan within the geographical borders of the day and the establishment of an independent Socialist Republic.[31]

The National Unionist Party, as mentioned earlier, was the leading party calling for unity with Egypt at the time when the Self-Government and Self-Determination Agreement was signed in February 1953. The creation of the NUP was the fruit of the labours of General Muḥammad Nagīb, Prime Minister of Egypt, and Major Ṣalāḥ Sālim, a member of the 23 July Revolutionary Command Council and later both Minister of National Guidance and Minister of State for Sudanese Affairs. These labours included the mediation and, eventually, reconciliation between Sudan's various unionist parties with the purpose of unifying them into a single party. This was because Egypt's revolutionary government believed that such a unification of parties would settle the battle over self-determination in favour of the unity option.

This unification brought together the rival Ismā'īl al-Azharī and Muḥammad Nūr al-Dīn factions of the *Ashiqqā'* (Brothers') Party, the *Itihādiyīn* (Unionists) Party, the Nile Valley Unity Party, the National Front and the Liberal Unionists Party. The birth of the NUP was announced from Nagīb's Cairo residence, following a meeting that began in the evening of 31 October 1952 and lasting until dawn the next day. Chairmanship of the Party was given to al-Azharī, with Nūr al-Dīn as his deputy. Khidir Ḥamad

---

[29] Faisal Abdel Rahman Ali Ṭaha, *al-Ḥaraka al-Sīyāsīa wa al-Ṣirā al-Maṣrī al-Briṭānī bishān al-Sūdān: 1936-1953* (*The Sudanese Political Movement and the Anglo-Egyptian Conflict Over Sudan: 1936-1953*) (Omdurman: 'Abd-al-Karīm Mīrghanī Centre, 2004), pp. 195-8.
[30] Ibid., p. 229.
[31] Ibid., p. 501.

of the Itihādiyīn became Secretary-General; the Treasurer was Khalafallah Khālid of the National Front; al-Ṭayyib Muḥammad Kheir of the Liberal Unionists was the Deputy Secretary-General; while ʿAbd-al-Waḥāb Zein al-ʿAbdīn ʿAbd-al-Tām of the Nile Valley Unity Party held the post of Deputy Treasurer.

The NUP's constitution stated its aims as an end to the *status quo*, the evacuation of foreign colonialism and the formation of a democratic Sudanese government in union with Egypt. The rules of this union were to be specified after self-determination.[32] Obviously, the constitution avoided any definition of the form of the desired union. It deferred such a definition to the period subsequent to self-determination because each of the parties under the NUP banner had their own ideal pattern of union. The Nile Valley Unity Party and the Ashiqqāʾ-Nūr al-Dīn faction both favoured unity via a complete merger. The Liberal Unionists advocated a federal union. The Itihādiyīn wanted a democratic Sudanese government in union with Egypt under the Egyptian crown. The only group that declined to disclose the pattern of union it desired was the Ashiqqāʾ-Azharī faction.[33]

Far away from all these unionist positions stood the National Front, which had been founded by al-Dardirī Muḥammad ʿUthmān, Khalafallah Khālid and Mīrghanī Ḥamza. These three individuals were prominent and trusted members of the Khatmīa community. They were known to lean towards Sudanese independence away from either Egypt or Britain – but they hoped to achieve a positive neighbourly relationship with Egypt that would "block the prospect of a local monarchy with Sayyid ʿAbd-al-Raḥman al-Mahdī as *de facto* king."[34] As we will see in Chapter 7, it was no surprise that the disintegration of the NUP began with the departure of the National Front from the Party.

The differences between unionist parties were not restricted to the kind of union sought but extended even to the sincerity of genuine unionist aspiration. For the Nile Valley Unity Party[35] and the Ashiqqāʾ-Nūr al-Dīn faction,[36] union with Egypt was both political dogma and creed. For

---

[32] Ibid., pp. 599-602.
[33] Ibid., pp. 178-83.
[34] Ibid., p. 385.
[35] Ibid., pp. 225-6.
[36] For details of the split in the Ashiqqāʾ Party, see ibid., p. 431.

the party with most mass support, the Ashiqqā'-Azharī faction, union with Egypt was no more than a tool to get rid of British colonial rule. In Chapter 8, we will see how Ismā'īl al-Azharī informed Luce, the Governor-General's adviser, on 16 February 1954 that, while most people in the country had felt for some time that it was easier and more practicable to be in a temporary alliance with Egypt in order to get rid of the British, that did not mean that they wished to subject themselves to the Egyptians. It will be shown, also in Chapter 8, that the NUP lost three of its component parties – the Nile Valley Unity Party, the Ashiqqā'-Nūr al-Dīn faction and the Liberal Unionists – when it changed track from union with Egypt to a stance advocating complete independence.

The Sudanese Movement for National Liberation (later the Communist Party) raised no such banner for Nile Valley unity.[37] Instead, it adopted a slogan calling for a joint struggle by the Egyptian and Sudanese peoples and the right to self-determination for the Sudanese. 'Abd-al-Khāliq Maḥjūb described the slogan of Nile Valley unity as "an expression of the economic and political deficiency of the Sudanese middle class more than an expression of a wish of the masses to be liberated from the repression of the British colonialism."[38]

The Muslim Brothers, meanwhile, rejected the call for unity with Egypt, describing it as immature and based on wild emotion – and because association with Egypt meant association with a military dictatorship that had made up its mind over the world conflict by standing behind the West.[39]

iii. Elections for self-government

Article 7 of the Self-Government and Self-Determination Agreement (1953) provided for the formation of an Electoral Commission made up of seven members. Three of them would be Sudanese appointed by the Governor-General with the approval of his Commission. The remaining four members would be Egyptian, British, American and Indian

---

[37] Known as HASATU after the Arabic acronym for *al-Ḥaraka al-Sūdānīa li al-Taḥarur al-Waṭanī.*

[38] See Chapter 10.

[39] See Chapter 9.

nationals, appointed by their respective governments, with the Indian national assuming the chairmanship of the Commission.[40]

The Electoral Commission's terms of reference were set out in Annex II of the 1953 Agreement. They included, *inter alia*, supervision of the preparations for and conduct of the elections to ensure their impartiality. To this end, the Commission was required to issue rules for holding the elections as soon as possible and, if practicable, simultaneously throughout Sudan.

On 8 April 1953, the Governor-General announced the formation of the Electoral Commission. In accordance with Article 7 of the 1953 Agreement, he appointed the Indian civil servant Sukumar Sen to be Chairman of the Commission. ʿAbd-al-Fatāḥ Ḥassan, Chief of Staff of the Egyptian Forces in Sudan, was appointed to represent Egypt, while J.C. Penny, a former security supervisor in Sudan, and Warwick Perkins represented the UK and the USA respectively.[41] The three Sudanese appointed to the Commission were: ʿAbd-al-Salām al-Khalīfa ʿAbdullahī, an Umma Party member who served in the Legislative Assembly as Under-Secretary of the Ministry of the Interior; Khalafallah Khālid, the NUP Treasurer; and Gordon Bulli from Southern Sudan.

When the register of voters was closed on 30 September 1953, the number of those registered in provincial constituencies was 1,687,000 out of a population of around 8,271,000 – i.e. around 20% of the census. It is worth mentioning that women had no right to vote at that time except for graduates' constituencies. Lists of voters for those constituencies contained 15 women. When the deadline for nominating candidates passed on 12 October 1953, candidates in provincial constituencies for the House of Representatives totalled 282 – ten of whom won their seats uncontested.

The vote count and declaration of results started on 28 November 1953. By 13 December, all the results had been declared. Thus were Sudan's first parliamentary elections completed, with the following allocation of seats in the House of Representatives:

---

[40] See Appendix 1.

[41] National Archives, Kew: CO [Colonial Office] 1069/14/3 (Sudan Elections for Self-Government).

NUP	51
Umma Party	22
Southern Party	10
Independents	8
Socialist Republicans	3
Southern Party	2
Front Against Colonization[42]	1

In the graduates' constituencies, 1,849 out of 2,247 registered electors cast their votes. Mubārak Zarūq secured the most votes, followed in turn by Muḥammad Aḥmad Maḥjūb, Khidir Ḥamad, Ḥassan al-Ṭāhir Zarūq and Ibrāhīm al-Muftī.

William Luce observed that the relative strength of the Umma Party and the National Unionists was no reflection at all of total sum of votes in the direct ballot constituencies. 229,221 voters opted for NUP candidates, earning them 43 seats, while 190,822 voted for Umma candidates, which secured just 22 seats. Luce attributed this to the fact that the average number of voters in the Khatmīa sphere of influence – i.e. the towns and provincial areas of Kassala and the Northern Province – was less than the average number of voters in other constituencies. It is worth noting that the Electoral Commission pointed in its final report to the vast variation of the size of constituencies and recommended remapping them.[43]

iv. The appointed day: 9 January 1954

As stated earlier, the appointed day was the date when the Governor-General would testify that the institutions of self-government – i.e. the Cabinet, House of Representatives and Senate – had all been formed. Under Article 9 of the Agreement, it was also the day when the transitional period should commence.

The opposition tried in vain to persuade the NUP to choose independent figures to chair the House of Representatives and the Senate. On 1 January 1954, Ibrāhīm al-Muftī was chosen as Chairman of

[42] A proxy for the Sudanese Movement for National Liberation, i.e. effectively a front for the Communist Party.
[43] Taha, *Sudanese Political Movement*, pp. 633 and 647-8.

the House of Representatives, gaining 54 votes against 43 votes for the independent candidate, ʿAbd-al-Fatāḥ al-Maghrabī. In the Senate, the National Unionist candidate for Speaker, Aḥmad Muḥammad Yāsin secured 34 votes against Aḥmad Muḥammad Ṣāliḥ, who won 14 votes.

Ismāʿīl al-Azharī

The Governor-General and his Commission approved the choice of Aḥmad Muḥammad Yāsin but the Governor-General rejected the nomination of Ibrāhīm al-Muftī – overruling the acceptance of his Commission – because he was a prominent member of the NUP. Instead, Bābikr ʿAwaḍallah – then sitting as a judge in al-ʿUbeiḍ - was chosen unanimously for the position.

On 6 January 1954, Ismāʿīl al-Azharī was elected Prime Minister, securing 56 votes against the independent candidate Muḥammad Aḥmad Maḥjūb, who managed 37 votes.[44] It is worth mentioning that Maḥjūb

[44] Khartoum to Foreign Office: Fortnightly Political Summary No. 20 (3-6 January), in Mahmoud Salih (ed.), *The British Documents on the Sudan: 1940-1956* (Omdurman: ʿAbd-al-Karīm Mīrghanī Cultural Centre, 2002) (11 vols.) vol. 9/1, p.

had cooperated with the Umma Party within the wider Independence Front but he did not join as a member until after Sudan's independence in January 1956.[45] In the evening of 8 January, al-Azharī introduced the members of his Cabinet to the Governor-General:

Ismā'īl al-Azharī: Prime Minister and Minister of the Interior
Muḥammad Nūr al-Dīn: Works
Mīrghanī Ḥamza: Education, Agriculture and Irrigation
'Alī 'Abd-al-Raḥman: Justice
Ḥammād Ṭawfīq: Finance
Khalafallah Khālid: Defence
Ibrāhīm al-Muftī: Economy and Trade
Muḥammad Amīn al-Sayyid: Health
Mubārak Zarūq: Transport
Bullen Alier, Santino Deng Teng and Dak Dei: Ministers without Portfolio[46]

It is worth noting that the new government could find no room for Khidir Ḥamad, the NUP Secretary-General, nor for two prominent figures in al-Azharī's faction: Yaḥya al Faḍlī and Muḥammad Aḥmad al-Marḍī.

v. Special Affairs Agency

In an agreed minute attached to the 1953 Agreement, the British and Egyptian Governments agreed to create a post for a Sudanese Under-secretary to act as liaison between the Governor-General and the Council of Ministers, and to prepare for the representation of the Sudan in International technical conferences only. 'Uqeil Aḥmad 'Uqeil, a member of the editorial board of *al-'Alam*, the NUP organ, was appointed to this

---

20. See also Sir William Luce Papers, Summary of Events No.1: January 1954, and National Archives, Kew, FO 371/108320 (Political Developments in Sudan during 1954), Riches [UK Trade Commissioner] to Morris, 15 January 1954.

45 Muḥammad Aḥmad Maḥjūb, *al-Dimūqrātīa fī al-Mīzān* (*Democacy in the Balance*) (n.p.) (2nd edition), p. 178.

46 Sudan Political Intelligence Summary No. 1 1954: December 1953-January 1954, in Salih, *British Documents*, vol. 9/1, p. 43.

position. His assistant was Khalīfa Abbās al-ʿUbeiḍ, who had been a railway director in Khartoum. A dispatch from Philip Adams, the new British Trade Commissioner in Khartoum, described Khalīfa Abbās as a 'good functionary' who would be sent to England in August 1955 to attend, as an observer, a training course for new Foreign Office recruits.[47]

The Special Affairs Agency was the forerunner of the Sudanese Foreign Ministry. At that time, there was no Sudanese representation abroad except for agencies in London and Cairo run by British nationals with the assistance of Sudanese seconded from the civil service and the police force. In the early Fifties, the government had set up two unofficial liaison offices: one in Jedda to cater for Sudanese pilgrims, the other in Asmara.[48] Muḥammad ʿUthmān Yāsin, charged with running the Asmara office, was described as a man of 'significant measure of intelligence and adaptability', who sent annual reports that were 'balanced and useful'.[49]

Egypt's agreement for the Sudanese to be represented in technical conferences was a significant change in the Egyptian position in this respect. The Annex to Article 11 of the 1936 Treaty provided for the manner in which international documents would become enforceable in Sudan but it was completely devoid of any provision regarding the representation of the Sudan in technical conferences. For a number of years, this was a source of disagreement between Egypt and Britain. The Egyptian Government held the view that Sudan on its own – being an integral part of Egypt – had no right to represent itself in either diplomatic or technical conferences. As for the British Government, it held that Sudan had the right to send representatives to technical conferences and

---

[47] National Archive, Kew, FO 371/113583 (Political developments in the Sudan during 1955): Adams, UK Trade Commissioner, to Thomas Bromley, Foreign Office, 12 August 1955. See Colin Mackie, 'A Directory of British Diplomats', p. 13, for details of Adams' further diplomatic career: http://www.gulabin.com/britishdiplomatsdirectory/pdf/britishdiplomatsdirectory.pdf.

[48] National Archive, Kew, FO 371/102925 (Proposed establishment of liaison officers of foreign governments in Khartoum): Minute by Morris, 25 June 1953.

[49] Ibid., FO 371/108311 (Annual political reviews for 1953 on Egypt by HM Ambassador, and on Sudan by UK Trade Commissioner in Khartoum): Riches, UK Trade Commission, to Eden, 22 January 1954. See also Najda Fatḥī Ṣafwa, *Min Nāfidhat al-Safāra: al-ʿArab fī Dhūʾ al-Wathāʾiq al-Briṭānīa* (*From the Embassy Window: The Arabs as Shown in British Documents*) (Riyadh: n.p., 1992), pp. 113-23.

to have a separate delegation, distinct from the two Condominium governments, to international organisations such as the World Health Organisation and the Food and Agriculture Organisation – just like other countries that did not enjoy self-government. This disagreement forced Sudan to miss out on the benefits that it could have gained from such international relations.[50]

vi. Foreign consular representation in Sudan

Article 10 of the Condominium Agreement of 19 January 1899 between Egypt and Britain for the administration of Sudan provided that 'No Consuls, Vice-Consuls, or Consular Agents shall be accredited in respect of nor allowed to reside in the Sudan, without the previous consent of her Britannic Majesty's Government.'[51]

Lord Cromer, the British Agent and Consul-General in Egypt and the engineer of the Condominium Agreement, expected that this provision would be challenged by those who believed that the status of Sudan was not different from other Ottoman domains. He also expected that this Article would create hardship for any European who was married or buried in Sudan. He therefore advised any European who considered essential that his marriage or burial be attested by a consular representative of his country to remain in the territory lying north of the 22nd parallel of latitude, meaning Egypt.

Until Independence Day on 1 January 1956, no foreign consul was accredited or allowed to reside in Sudan. The prime obstacle was the anomalous status of the Sudan as a Condominium, and the allied technical difficulty of who would issue the exequatur i.e. the recognition to carry out consular functions.

In 1945 because of the second World War, there were stationed in the Sudan a number of American servicemen. That prompted the United States Embassy in Cairo to explore with its British counterpart the

---

[50] Faisal Abdel Rahman Ali Taha, 'Some Legal Aspects of the Anglo-Egyptian Condominium Over the Sudan 1899-1954', *British Yearbook of International Law* 76/1 (2005), pp. 337 and 370-82.

[51] For the full text of the agreement, see Muddathir ʿAbd al-Raḥīm, *Imperialism and Nationalism in the Sudan: A Study in Constitutional and Political Development 1899–1956* (Oxford: Clarendon Press, 1969), Appendix II, pp. 233-5.

possibility of establishing United States consular representation in the Sudan. But both the British Cairo Embassy and the Governor-General were in agreement that the time was inauspicious for the appointment of a United States or any other foreign consul.

The Governor-General had two more reasons. Firstly, the tiny number of the United States nationals residing in the Sudan and its negligible commercial interests in the country. Secondly, even in the case of larger communities like the Greek community, there were no sufficient commercial or other interests that keep consuls busy, and they would become engaged in political intrigue. He then summed up the whole matter of foreign consular representation in the Sudan, in the following terms:

> Because of the precariousness of the political future of the Sudan and the Anglo-Egyptian relations, there was little to be said for upsetting a system which had worked well in the past in favour of a system which would introduce new practical complications. Among the many anomalies of the Sudan, the maintenance of the anomaly of having no consular representation in Sudan need cause no undue concern.[52]

vii. Appointment of Foreign liaison officers[53]

The Governor-General began to grant approval for the establishment of foreign liaison offices in Sudan only after 1950. In July 1949, France applied to be allowed to appoint a French representative in the Sudan. As France did not have adequate trade with the Sudan, a liaison officer was appointed in February 1950. His main function was to deal with the administrative matters arising out of the annual movement of pilgrims between French African territories and the Red Sea, and the currency problems arising therefrom. But the British Government expected that he would also send reports to his Government.

The application for the appointment of the French Liaison Officer was made direct to the Governor-General who gave his consent direct to the French Government. The Governor-General did not seek the approval

---

[52] Taha, 'Legal Aspects of the Anglo-Egyptian Condominium', pp. 355-8.
[53] Ibid., pp. 358-61.

of the Egyptian Government. Nor was the appointment officially approved by the British Government. The British Government was of course aware of the French application and agreed 'unofficially' to the appointment.

A United States Liaison Officer was appointed in September 1952. The object of his appointment was to put the State Department more fully in the picture with regard to political developments in the Sudan. The appointment of the United States Liaison Officer had been dealt with in the same way as that of the French Liaison Officer. The Egyptian Government was, however, consulted by the United States Government and when the appointment was made it was announced publicly by the United States Ambassador in Cairo.

The first United States Liaison Officer, Joseph Sweeny, did not leave a good impression in British circles in Sudan because of his continuous criticism of the way things were run. He was also prone to exaggeration when portraying the situation in Sudan in his reports to the State Department. British official documents described him as adopting "the stance of the anti-colonial force" on every issue and that he was "playing the role of a witness for prosecution against the British Administration".[54]

The British Trade Commissioner in Sudan wrote to the Foreign Secretary, Anthony Eden, that "it was interesting to observe that neither the admirable work of the American member of the Electoral Commission nor the activities of the American liaison officer succeeded in securing a sympathetic attitude towards America, which was regarded merely as a combination of imperialist accomplice of Britain and fount of free Point Four and other assistance."[55]

---

[54] National Archives, Kew, FO 371/102753: Selwyn Lloyd's Conversation on 25 March 1953 with Count de Lesseps, French Liaison Officer in Khartoum. See also ibid., FO 371/108321 (Political developments in Sudan during 1954): Riches to Foreign Office, 17 March 1954, and ibid., FO 371/108320: Leward, Foreign Office, to Baily British Embassy, Washington, 9 February 1954.

[55] National Archives, Kew, FO 371/108311: Riches to Eden, 22 January 1954. The Point Four Program was so named because American economic aid and technical assistance for underdeveloped countries was the fourth foreign policy objective announced by President Harry Truman in his inaugural speech in 1949.

We noted earlier that Article 6 (a) of the 1953 Self-Government and Self-Determination Agreement stipulated that the Governor-General would remain directly answerable to the two Condominium Governments with respect to external affairs. A similar stipulation was provided for in Article 12 (2) of the Self-Government Statute. Despite these two provisions, the Governor-General continued granting licenses for the establishment of liaison offices – among them Ethiopia and Greece – without recourse to either Egyptian or British governments.

On the basis of legal opinion, the Foreign Office ruled that the two articles referred to above did not mean that the Governor-General "could not carry out an act in relation to external affairs without seeking the prior approval of the two domini, but merely that he was responsible to both of them to what in fact he had done." If there was an established practice according to which the Governor-General was accustomed to performing certain limited functions having bearing on external affairs on his own authority, he would continue to do so – although he would of course remain responsible to London and Cairo for his actions. Thus, while he could agree to the establishment of unofficial missions analogous to the French and US missions without specific authority from the co-domini, "the appointment of consuls would clearly go beyond anything the Governor-General had hitherto been accustomed to do on his own." Accordingly, he would require the consent of the Co-Domini before he could agree to the establishment of foreign consuls in Sudan.[56]

viii. Office of the UK Trade Commissioner

In March 1953, the UK set up a Trade Commission in Khartoum. At a press conference held in Khartoum on 25 March, the British Secretary of State for Foreign Affairs, Selwyn Lloyd, said that the establishment of the Commission "showed a recognition of the changing relationship between the British Government and the Sudan resulting from the 1953 Self-Government Agreement, which made it no longer appropriate that purely British questions should be dealt with by the Sudan Government."

The Commission was staffed by British Foreign Office personnel and its function was to serve British trade and other interests. Setting up the Commission put the British Government on roughly equal footing

[56] Taha, 'Legal Aspects of the Anglo-Egyptian Condominium', pp. 359-60.

with its Egyptian counterpart: since 1936, Cairo had been allowed to appoint an economic expert to work in Sudan. Still, the Egyptian Government viewed the establishment of the Commission with grave suspicion.[57]

Despite its name, the Trade Commission was in fact a diplomatic mission linked to – and reporting to – the Foreign Office. Derek Riches was the first British diplomat to hold the job; towards the end of 1954, he was succeeded by Philip Adams. As will be seen throughout this book, the Commissioner regularly met senior government and opposition figures and sent regular updates about Sudan, supported with thorough analysis of the political situation and the trends in public opinion.

ix. New British policy in Sudan

In a long letter dated 1 January 1954 to Governor-General Howe, Eden outlined the British Government's policy in respect of the Sudan in the aftermath of the parliamentary elections:

> First: The election has demonstrated the strength of the Khatmia Sect and the danger of any policy which would drive them united in hostility to us. I do not, however, think that we should be in a hurry to throw over Sayed Abdel Rahman el Mahdi as part of our effort to establish better relations with Sayyid Ali el Mirghani. ... Although the Ansar Sect had shown itself to be regrettably weak, they are still and in the foreseeable future will remain the only solid core for an independence movement. The situation would be changed if the Khatmia ever came out as a united force in favour of independence.
>
> Second: The immediate British policy should be to encourage Sayed Abdel Rahman and the Umma Party to form an effective party and opposition by drawing together pro-independence elements outside the Mahdist Sect. Also we should point out to them that our friendship with the independence cause is secure. ... At the same time, we want to make it clear to them that we must cultivate relations with Sayed Ali el-Mirghani and the new government: both because it is the

[57] Ibid., p. 361.

only constitutional way of proceeding and because we must not drive them irrevocably into the arms of the Egyptians.

Third: Against this background, we should undertake a cautious policy of building bridges with the National Unionist Party and of promoting any tendencies in that Party to move away from the Egyptian camp. It is the question of relations of the Sudan with Egypt which may either cause such a movement or break up the Party. The Egyptians will try to prevent that issue arising for as long as they can; and our interests will therefore lie to the same extent in encouraging that it does arise and that the Egyptians and the National Unionist Party are not able to evade it or shelve it.

Fourth: The Government realizes that in the new situation, the extent to which you [the Governor-General] and British officials will be able to influence the course of events will be limited. ... Establishing relations of confidence with the incoming government will depend on the extent to which you are able to convince them that you, as Governor-General, are acting as a strictly constitutional head of the Administration and that British officials are loyal servants of the government in power. Any actions which appear to be directed towards the service of British interests, or which smack of intrigue with the opposition party, will obviously endanger the policy.

Fifth: ... Under the new constitution, the Governor-General and his advisers will have regular contact with the new Ministers and be entitled to the fullest information. The position of Governor-General does not preclude you from offering advice on what is in the best interests of the Sudan. As between the co-domini, you will be bound to appear as far as possible as a neutral figure, but that neutrality must not, I think, extend to the situation in which the rights or interests of the Sudan are threatened by some intervention or other action by one of the co-domini. The Governor-General would have a duty to resist [the co-dominus] so far as you are able. There might also be occasions when you have to defend what could be described as purely British interests. The intention is not only the protection of the rights of British officials but also of a case such as a claim by Egyptians to share in the working of your office.

Sixth: British officials in the administration must keep clear of politics and be loyal and neutral servants of the new government. But, without departing from neutrality or loyalty, they will in fact be in a position to exert a positive influence on policy. ... They should be given some form of guidance on the directions in which their advice should tend. We suggest that a committee of senior British officials should meet informally to discuss this sort of question and decide on the guidance to be passed down orally to their British subordinates.

Seventh: It will be increasingly difficult for the Governor-General and his advisers to maintain contacts with Sudanese of all parties. It is more essential than ever that the British Government should have a representative in the Sudan separate from the Governor-General and his staff. ... National Unionist Party leaders and Egyptian propaganda have attacked the UK Trade Commission's Office during recent months and it is therefore possible that some attempt may be made to dislodge it. ... The Governor-General must resist any such attempt ... and be prepared to use the special responsibility to the Co-Domini for external affairs."[58]

Howe agreed with this general outline about future British policy for Sudan but set out certain difficulties. He explained that, since the elections, the administration had been doing its best to maintain friendly relations with the Umma Party and unobtrusively to encourage them and other pro-independence groups to form a strong opposition, while simultaneously building confidence between the administration and the NUP. The Governor-General recognized, of course, the contradictory nature of these two aims. Then he highlighted the following points:

The Sudanese, whether National Unionist Party or Umma or other plain 'man in the street', have hardly yet woken up to the fact that effective power in this country has now been transferred from the British to a purely Sudanese government.

---

[58] Eden to Howe, 1 January 1954, in Douglas Johnson (ed.), *British Documents on the End of the Empire: Sudan* (Series B, Volume 5, 2 Parts) (London: Institute of Commonwealth Studies, 1998), Part II (1951-1956), p. 299.

The awakening will be painful to all but the NUP. The Umma were showing resentment at our inability to curb the pro-Egyptian tendencies of the NUP Government and are blaming us for the misfortunes which they largely brought upon themselves, while the ordinary people are bewildered by the first signs that the British no longer have the last word in the control of affairs.

The awakening will be rudest in the South, where the rapid replacement of British by Northern Sudanese administrators will be the outward and visible sign of the ending of our power and prestige. As in most oriental countries, it is power that counts, whatever its corrupting influence, and when it is fully realized that British officials are servants and no longer masters, our power to influence affairs will wane rapidly.

Our first duty here is to make the new constitution work, and to do this we must co-operate with the Sudanese Government which means the NUP. If this aim conflicts, as it probably will, with the retention of the confidence and friendship of the Umma and other pro-independence Sudanese, it must nevertheless prevail, so long as the policies and actions of the Government keep within the Constitution and the Agreement.

The most effective way to realize the policy of preventing the eventual domination of Sudan by Egypt is to show the NUP and in particular the Khatmia that they have nothing to fear from the British and so to reduce their professed need to rely on Egyptian support.

Giving advice to the Government must be preceded by creating the atmosphere in which such advice can be freely given and considered, by overcoming the suspicion and inexperience of NUP Ministers. This task is made doubly difficult by the fact that the NUP already have another set of advisers, the Egyptians, with whom they have been in regular contact for many years and now will spare no effort to maintain their role of guide and counsellor to the new government.[59]

---

[59] Howe to Eden, 4 February 1954, Ibid., p. 307.

We shall see in Chapter 4 that William Luce, adviser to the Governor-General on constitutional and external affairs, raised the issue of this contradiction between the two aims of the new British policy on Sudan, i.e. maintaining good relations with the Umma Party and building confidence with the NUP. This evolved in the context of Luce's proposals for positive rapprochement with the NUP.

x. Substitution of Ibrāhīm Aḥmad for NUP supporter

It has been mentioned earlier that Ibrāhīm Aḥmad and al-Dardirī Muḥammad ʿUthmān were proposed by the Condominium Governments to be members of the Governor-General's Commission. Under Article 4 of the Agreement, however, their appointment was subject to the subsequent approval of the Sudanese Parliament. It was inevitable that the NUP would use its parliamentary majority to block the appointment of Ibrāhīm Aḥmad – an Umma Party supporter – to the Commission and appoint a unionist party member in his place. This would mean that the NUP would have two members on the Commission. Given the presence of the Egyptian member, unionists would constitute a majority on the Commission, leaving the Pakistani chairman and the British member totally powerless. The opposition, for its part, considered that to be inconsistent with the spirit of the Agreement and argued that it would eliminate the Commissions' neutrality and lead to a very serious situation.[60]

Whilst still in Khartoum during the first week of March 1954, Secretary of State Selwyn Lloyd warned that if the replacement of Ibrāhīm Aḥmad did occur, there would be a danger of opposition boycotting Parliament which would be a disastrous beginning for parliamentary institution. [61]

Then subsequently on receipt of telegram of instructions from his Foreign Secretary, Lloyd informed the Governor-General that replacement of Ibrāhīm Aḥmad could result in further disturbances and

[60] Minutes regarding the Sudanese members of the Governor-General's Commission, 7 January 1954, FO 371/108331. Also Khartoum to Foreign Office, 6 March 1954, transmitting letter of 6 March 1954 from M.A. Mahjoub, Leader of the Opposition, to the Governor-General, FO 371/108321.

[61] Khartoum to Foreign Office, March 6, 1954, ibid (From Minister of State).

render the orderly government of the Sudan impossible. If the Prime Minister declined to give an undertaking that the desired replacement would not take place, the Governor-General should declare a state of constitutional emergency under Article 102 of the Self-Government Statute. He would then be free to summon British troops to keep law and order. [62]

Ibrāhīm Aḥmad

At a meeting with William Luce in the final week of March 1954, al-Azharī initially appeared to accept the need for a compromise – but he soon came back with the view that the NUP was determined to remove Ibrāhīm Aḥmad. He then put forward the name of Yāqūb ʿUthmān as an alternative but Luce replied that the Umma Party would not accept that because Yāqūb ʿUthmān had resigned from the Umma in 1953 and could not be considered independent. When al-Azharī suggested Siricio Iro, a member of the Senate, Luce replied that he would be a disaster: if the alternative to Ibrāhīm Aḥmad had to be a Southerner, he added, Gordon

[62] PREM [Prime Minister's Office] 11/777, CC15(54) 3, 5 March 1954, (Instructions to be sent to Selwyn Lloyd in Khartoum). See Douglas Johnson, loc. cit., p. 317.

Bulli – a former member of the Electoral Commission with no known party affiliation – could be considered.[63]

On 21 April 1954, the House of Representatives approved the appointment of al-Dardirī Muḥammad ʿUthmān but blocked Ibrāhīm Aḥmad with a 52-42 majority. Siricio Iro was approved in his place. Southerners welcomed the appointment of one of their own to the Commission – although they argued that he should have been a Southerner who was explicitly pro-independence.[64]

The Governor-General did not declare a state of constitutional emergency. His view was that destabilising the balance on the Commission was not, on its own, enough ground for such a declaration: a state of constitutional emergency would only be required to avoid an imminent breakdown of law and order.[65] Nor did the Umma Party carry out its threat of withdrawing from or boycotting Parliament, as such a move would have deprived the opposition of its Southern component, i.e. the Liberal Party. But Ṣiddīq al-Mahdī – son of ʿAbd-al-Raḥman al-Mahdī and Chairman of the Umma Party – wrote to the Condominium Governments stating that the National Unionist Government had, in nominating Iro, an NUP member, violated the constitution in letter and in spirit. As a result, it had become impossible to create the 'free and neutral atmosphere' stipulated in the Agreement. The letter added that the composition of the Commission – with one Egyptian delegate and two pro-union Sudanese in the majority – would give the pro-unity side complete hegemony over the supreme authority in the country. The idea of independence would find no expression in a Commission whose chairman had lost both authority and legitimacy. Ṣiddīq al-Mahdī concluded by appealing to the Condominium Governments to intervene and put a stop to the measure taken by the Khartoum administration so that the Agreement would not be rendered pointless.[66]

---

[63] National Archives, Kew, FO 371/108332, Khartoum to Foreign Office, 24 March 1954.

[64] *al-Ahrām*, 22 April 1954.

[65] National Archives, Kew, FO 371/108332, Howe to Foreign Office, 24 and 26 March 1954, on reasons for declaring a constitutional emergency.

[66] *al-Sūdān al-Jadīd*, 14 May 1954.

CHAPTER 2

Events of 1 March 1954

The Government decided to make the opening of the second Parliamentary session on Monday 1 March 1954 a celebratory occasion to which representatives of foreign countries would be invited.[1] Particular attention was paid to countries involved in the international commissions provided for in the 1953 Self-Government and Self-Determination Agreement, including the Electoral Commission, the Governor-General's Commission and the Sudanisation Committee. Invitations were also extended to the British and Egyptian negotiators of the 1953 Agreement and to other Arab and foreign dignitaries.

Selwyn Lloyd arrived to represent Britain, as did Professor ʿAbd-al-Razzāq al-Sanhūrī, Chair of the Egyptian Council of State. Delegations arrived from Libya, Saudi Arabia, Yemen and Iraq, as well as ʿAbd-al-Khāliq Ḥassūna, Secretary-General of the League of Arab States.[2] Among the most prominent invitees was Muḥammad Nagīb, President of Egypt – but during the last week of February 1954, it was decided that Egypt would instead be represented by Aḥmad Ḥassan al-Bāqūri, Egypt's Minister for Religious Endowments.[3] During that week, acute differences broke out between Nagīb and the other members of the Revolutionary Command Council. As a result, on 22 February, Nagīb resigned from all his posts and

---

[1] UK Trade Commissioner's Office to FO, London: Bimonthly Political Summary No. 23 (14-27 February 1954), in Ṣālih, *British Documents on the Sudan*, vol. 9/1, p. 66.

[2] *al-Ayyām*, 28 February 1954, and *al-Ahrām*, 12 January 1954.

[3] UK Trade Commissioner's Office to FO, London: Bimonthly Political Summary No. 23 (14-27 February 1954), in Ṣālih, *British Documents on the Sudan*, vol. 9/1, p. 66.

Gamāl ʿAbd-al-Nāṣir was appointed Prime Minister. However, after pressure from mass demonstrations and the expressions of support from some army units, Nagīb returned as President of the Republic.[4]

Nagīb arrived in Khartoum, accompanied by Major Ṣalāḥ Sālim, on the morning of 1 March. Nagīb's resignation had aroused anti-Egyptian feelings among the Sudanese: he was immensely popular in Sudan thanks to the role he had played in the conclusion of the 1953 Sudan Agreement.

The Umma Party considered Nagīb's resignation to be proof of the instability of the Egyptian administration. A statement issued by the Party in this respect declared that Sudan's link with an unstable Egypt was harmful to the interests of Sudan and the Sudanese. The statement appealed to the Sudanese to cut matters short and agree upon self-determination, and for the present Parliament to declare the immediate independence of Sudan and the evacuation of foreign troops.[5]

The festivities did not take place as had been arranged because of bloody clashes between the police and the Anṣār youth at the plaza that used to be called Kitchener Square or Secretariat Square. This large open space was situated north of the building now occupied by the Ministry of Finance and to the west of the Governor-General's palace. In the middle of that plaza was Kitchener's statue. The clashes claimed the lives of 34 policemen – including Khartoum's Police Commandant, Colonel Hugh McGuigan, and his deputy, Superintendent Muṣṭafa al-Mahdī – as well as Anṣār and other citizens.

The events caused a state of confusion in the Governor-General's palace, where a meeting was hastily called by Howe and his staff. The meeting was also attended by Selwyn Lloyd and Muḥammad Nagīb, who remained gloomy and depressed throughout the meeting. According to Mavrogordato, the Governor-General's legal advisor, both Selwyn Lloyd and William Lindsay, the Chief Justice of Sudan, put pressure on the Governor-General to declare a state of constitutional emergency under Article 102 of the Self-Government Statute. Mavrogordato strongly opposed this approach and he managed to persuade Howe to declare an

---

[4] Aḥmad Ḥamrūsh, *Qiṣṣat Thawrat 23 Yūlyū, al-Juzuʾ al-Thālith: ʿAbd-al-Nāṣir wa al-ʿArab* (*An Account of the 23 July Revolution, Part 3: ʿAbd-al-Nāṣir and the Arabs*) (Cairo: Arab Institute for Studies and Publishing, 1976), pp. 311-13.

[5] *al-Ayyām*, 27 February 1954.

ordinary state of emergency – and only in Khartoum Province – under the provisions of the 1939 Sudan Defence Force Ordinance because the collapse that had occurred was one of security, not of the constitution. Furthermore, he argued, declaring a state of constitutional emergency would lead to disastrous consequences for relations between the Governor-General and his Cabinet.[6]

Howe then contacted Muḥammad Aḥmad Maḥjūb, the Leader of the Opposition, and delivered to him a *Note Verbale* in which he stated that he would use his authority to declare a state of constitutional emergency if the independence movement were dissatisfied with the way affairs were conducted. Maḥjūb conveyed the content of the Note to Ṣiddīq al-Mahdī, who agreed that they should both ignore it. The following day, i.e. 2 March, Maḥjūb informed the Governor-General that the pro-independence bloc would not agree to any suspension of the constitution.[7]

During the ensuing Cabinet meeting – convened in the evening of 1 March and lasting late into the night – some ministers insisted that Ismā'īl al-Azharī should issue orders for the arrest of Ṣiddīq al-Mahdī, Chairman of the Umma Party, 'Abdallah Khalīl, the Party's Secretary-General, Muḥammad Aḥmad Maḥjūb, Leader of the Opposition and 'Abdallah 'Abd-al-Raḥman Nugdallah, Secretary of the Anṣār youth wing. al-Azharī flatly refused, insisting that he had no proof or even suspicion – let alone personal conviction – that those individuals had played any role in inciting the violence; nor did he have the authority to do so.[8]

Nagīb and Ṣalāḥ Sālim left Khartoum in the early hours of Tuesday 2 March, along with other Egyptian guests. Back in Cairo, Nagīb complained to the US Ambassador to Egypt, Jefferson Caffery, about the action of the Governor-General in not taking him from airport at Khartoum by usual road to the Palace, thus disappointing the Ansar, and that he was not allowed to get in touch with people in Khartoum on 1 March by telephone or otherwise. Nagīb further complained that Howe was not even going to come and see him off at the airport when he left

---

[6] Jack Mavrogordato, *Behind the Scenes: An Autobiography* (Tisbury: Element Books, 1982), pp. 108-10.

[7] Maḥjūb, *al-Dimūqrātīa fī al-Mīzān*, p. 56.

[8] Aḥmad Muḥammad Yāsin, *Mudhakkirāt* (*Memoirs*) (Omdurman: Muḥammad 'Umar Bashīr Centre, 2001), pp. 266-7.

on the morning of March 2, but he finally agreed to do so after representations had been made to him.[9]

Aḥmad Ḥamrūsh, the leftist Egyptian writer, believed that the events of 1 March negated the impact of Nagīb's victory over the Revolutionary Command Council the previous month and undermined Nagīb's stature which depended largely on his popularity amongst the Sudanese and their adherence to him.[10]

We shall now address the various accounts of what happened on 1 March 1954, before considering the judicial rulings on these events. The last of these rulings was that of the Court of Appeal, which held that the events were not premeditated but were, to a great extent, a result of a series of regrettable incidents culminating at Kitchener's Square where chaos broke out spontaneously. The Court of Appeal blamed the Government for the inadequacy of its preparations, for allowing the situation to develop and for failing to control it in a way that would maintain peace. We shall see later how the Cabinet considered this ruling to be far beyond the Court's competence and, worse, an infringement of the authority of the executive. At the end of this chapter, we shall examine the extent to which lessons were learned. The Governor-General said that, though it was no more than a brief demonstration that missed its aim, its impact would be profound and far-reaching.[11]

i. The Governor-General's version of events[12]

According to the Governor-General's own account, in the days preceding 28 February, huge numbers of the Anṣār youth wing sneaked into Khartoum despite the curfew imposed by the Minister of the Interior. On 28 February itself, around 6,000 Anṣār Youth took to the streets in a rally, beginning at the home Ṣiddīq al-Mahdī in Khartoum South to the palace of his father, ʿAbd-al-Raḥman al-Mahdī, carrying banners and chanting slogans. In the evening of the same day, a police officer met

[9] National Archives, Kew, FO 371/108322 (Political developments in Sudan during 1954): Sir Ralph Stevenson, UK Ambassador to Cairo, to Allen, 15 March 1954.
[10] Ḥamrūsh, *Qiṣṣat Thawrat 23 Yūlyū*, p. 313.
[11] Sir William Luce Papers, 828/6/54: Kenrick to Davies, 5 March 1954. See also National Archives, Kew, FO 371/108322: Governor-General's Office G/36.2.15/2, 4 March 1954, Summary of Events No. 2.
[12] Ibid.

Sayyid ʿAbd-al-Raḥman, who promised him that, though his men were determined to be seen at Nagīb's reception, they would be unarmed and would maintain peace and order.

The crowds – estimated to number around 20,000 men – began assembling from 9 a.m. on 1 March at Khartoum Airport, which was surrounded by a large police presence. Government supporters ringed the terminal, while the Anṣār Youth lined the road leading to Gezira Street. Nagīb's plane landed just before 10 a.m., prompting the government supporters to force their way through police lines. The convoy carrying Nagīb and the Governor-General, however, managed to leave the airport via an alternative route. When Nagīb reached the Governor-General's palace, a large group of government supporters was already there to greet him; some had even tried to climb over the palace walls but were brought down by the police.

At about 10.30, a large number of the Anṣār Youth who had been at the airport reached the palace. By this stage, they numbered around 6,000 individuals under the leadership of ʿAbdallah ʿAbd-al-Raḥman Nugdallah, Amīn al-Tūm, ʿAlī Faraḥ and ʿAwaḍ Ṣāliḥ. They were chanting "Independence, O Nagīb!", "Independence, O Howe!" and "Let us go for jihad!". The Governor-General's official account stated that the Anṣār approached the western gate of the palace, guarded by the police. The Anṣār killed several policemen before storming through the gate. Meanwhile, numerous clashes broke out in which policemen using batons and tear gas were handled violently before being forced to retreat towards the palace. According to the Governor-General's office, that was the moment when Col. McGuigan and Superintendent Muṣṭafa al-Mahdī were killed. Live ammunition was then used – with the police now reinforced by units of the Sudan Defence Force (SDF) – and by 12.30 the crowd had been dispersed.

The Governor-General's official account added that the Anṣār had been determined to demonstrate in favour of Sudan's independence and that they had assembled at the airport and on the main road so that their chanted slogans would be heard as Nagīb's convoy was passing. Enraged by the decision to change the convoy's route course, they had rushed from the airport to the palace to make themselves heard. The account noted that the gravest error committed by the demonstration organisers was their failure to disarm villagers who had descended on

Khartoum *en masse*: had it not been for the knives, the police would have been able to suppress the demonstration with tear gas.

It is also worth noting, however, that Sayyid ʿAbd-al-Raḥman has stated on numerous occasions that the Anṣār were in fact disarmed before the demonstration. Confiscated knives were kept in a storeroom but more trucks carrying Anṣār protestors arrived late, leaving insufficient time to disarm them all.[13] This was confirmed by ʿAbd-al-Raḥman ʿAlī Ṭaha, who said it was simply impossible to be certain that every individual in a gathering of thousands had been stripped of his weapon – especially when the lorries carrying the Anṣār kept arriving in Khartoum during the clashes and even after it was all over.[14]

ʿAbd-al-Raḥman ʿAlī Ṭaha believed that matters would have ended peacefully had the Government not switched the convoy route at the last minute. Even after the switch, the escalation would not have occurred had the Government allowed the multitude of independence advocates to reach the Governor-General's palace and continue chanting their traditional slogans instead of forcibly pushing them back and using tear gas – just as, in fact, the Government did permit unionists to reach the palace and chant their slogans to their hearts' content.[15]

There is no question that the Governor-General himself was behind both the convoy route switch and the security arrangements. He wanted the convoy to leave the airport via a side road, passing through the Royal Air Force facility. He proposed this idea to a number of officials at the airport and they accepted it. Among them were Ḥussein Ẓulfiqār Ṣabrī, the Egyptian member of the Governor-General's Commission; Bābikr ʿAwaḍallah, Chairman of the House of Representatives; Aḥmad Muḥammad Yāsin, Chairman of the Senate; and Bābikr al-Dīb, the officer in charge of airport security on the day. The same proposal was discussed with Ismāʿīl al-Azharī, who made no objection to the idea.[16]

The British Minister of State for Foreign Affairs Selwyn Lloyd – still in Khartoum – informed his Government on 4 March that fear of a

---

[13] National Archives, Kew, FO 371/108322: Report by the Police Magistrate on the Events of 1 March.

[14] ʿAbd-al-Raḥman ʿAlī Ṭaha, *al-Sūdān li al-Sūdānīn* (*Sudan for the Sudanese*) (Khartoum: Khartoum University Press, 1992), p. 188.

[15] Ibid., p.188.

[16] Yāsin, *Mudhakkirāt*, p. 260.

resurgent Mahdism had been renewed and that the Umma Party's opportunity to gain power through conventional constitutional means might have been damaged. He added that creating disturbances was the most effective weapon in the hands of the Anṣār – and they had achieved their objective during Nagīb's visit. The relation between the Umma and the police, he added, was tainted with bitterness. Lloyd believed, however, that the events could have been even graver. In his estimate, the Anṣār were strong, brave and stood firm in the face of firearms. After Col. McGuigan was killed, there was a moment of indecision on the part the police force: had the Anṣār pushed decisively at that moment, they could have penetrated the Governor-General's palace.

Selwyn Lloyd attributed the events of 1 March 1954 to Egyptian interference. When Umma Party supporters saw scores of Egyptians travelling to and fro, heard Ṣalāḥ Sālim's fiery speeches and witnessed Egypt's systematic penetration of Sudanese life via charitable work, arms deals and training facilities, he argued, their mood was bound to become increasingly agitated. Selwyn Lloyd concluded by stating that Nagīb's visit, coupled with the Government's determination to make it a victory tour, was the straw that broke the camel's back.[17]

ii. Report of the Khartoum Police Magistrate

In the prelude to his report, Derek Wilson, the Khartoum Police Magistrate, wrote that Col. McGuigan had asked him to be at the airport an hour before Nagīb's arrival and he did just that. He stated that, despite the heavy presence of the crowds and their boiling fiery mood, there had been no requirement for the use of force as the police were in control and succeeded in keeping the streets free for traffic. Besides, the Anṣār leadership was helping to organize the crowds.

Wilson left the airport and followed McGuigan back to his office in the Khartoum Municipality building. Up till that point, Wilson believed, matters seemed to be under control. There was no sense that there were serious disturbances brewing – nor was there any information forthcoming that the crowds were armed. In this regard, Wilson disclosed

---

[17] Selwyn Lloyd to Foreign Office, 4 March 1954, in Ṣāliḥ, *British Documents on the Sudan*, vol. 10/2, p. 114.

an important fact: he had seen no weapons at the airport and no one had told him that any weapons had been seen there.

Kitchener Square, Khartoum

However, shortly after Wilson's arrival at the Municipality building, McGuigan received a message to the effect that disturbances had occurred in Kitchener Square. At that, Commandant and Magistrate set out for the square, accompanied by three lorries carrying reserve policemen, who carried no more than batons and tear gas. According to Wilson, that was the first time that the police reserves had been called up without their rifles.

According to the Magistrate's report, following a request from Col. McGuigan, Wilson authorised the use of tear gas to release several of Superintendent Muṣṭafa al-Mahdī's men who had been surrounded and beaten by the crowds. On this particular detail, Wilson wrote that he could not be certain how and why the Superintendent and his men had become entangled with those rioters.

When McGuigan sustained grievous wounds in the rioting, Wilson accompanied him to the River Hospital, where he subsequently learned that the Commandant, among others, had died.[18] Wilson remained at the hospital until he was sure that all the wounded had been attended to. When he returned to Kitchener Square, Bābikr al-Dīb and a group of angry police officers tried to pressurise him into letting them attack the crowds concentrated around the Secretariat but he refused.

In the final section of his report, Wilson dealt at length with what he saw as mistakes in both police preparations and their management of the disturbances. These included the lack of suitable training to cope with the situation as it escalated in Kitchener Square; the absence of intelligence; the lack of an overall comprehensive plan or integral command structure; as well as equipment malfunctions. It seemed that Wilson was highly embarrassed to have to make these observations: that was why he said that the catalogue of errors should not be taken as criticism of the two brave officers whose loss had saddened everyone but merely as a clear factual analysis to prevent such errors being repeated in the future.

Examining Magistrate Wilson's report, it is immediately remarkable that it fails to mention anything about the police opening fire on the crowds – particularly the source of the firearms used by the police or the identity of the entity that authorized their use or when. One explanation might lie in Wilson's hint that he was narrating only events as he had seen them; those that he had not personally witnessed were to be omitted. Another explanation may lie in the paragraph in which he stated that, as time passed during the day, he had begun to realize increasingly the inadequacy of official preparations and his own inability to do anything to improve them. He should have been more actively involved in making the preparations from the beginning, he wrote, not least because he bore the ultimate responsibility for public security. "It is intolerable," he added, "for a magistrate to have to go along with the police and say, Go in and shoot, or whatever may be required, if he feels that the action is being run in a way which he disapproves of and about which, at that last moment, he can do nothing."[19]

---

[18] The River Hospital, founded in 1826, was the first hospital in Khartoum; it closed in 1959 and the Ministry of Health now stands on its site.

[19] National Archives, Kew, FO 371/108322: Report by the Police Magistrate on the Events of 1 March.

iii. The Umma Party's version of events

A statement issued by the Umma Party stressed that the impact of the 1 March events was painful to the Party's Management Council, its executive body and its followers. The statement explained the purpose of the demonstration and how it transformed into a bloody confrontation. Some of the main points raised were as follows:

a) Masses of pro-independence activists, both resident in Khartoum and from rural areas, came with the aim of taking part in a celebration for the opening of Parliament – just as they had previously celebrated the passing of a year since the signing of the 1953 Sudan Agreement;
b) By receiving the guests, the Umma Party aimed, via governments and media representatives, to make the world aware of the justice of their demand for independence and that the Sudanese did not want their autonomous identity to be erased by merger with either Egypt or Britain. That was why their chanted slogans were restricted to demanding total and complete independence for Sudan;
c) The gathering of pro-independence supporters at the airport occurred by prior agreement with the police authorities. The last-minute change of the convoy's route, however, forced those independence supporters already lining the streets for welcoming the visitors to rush to where the visitors were staying to get their voices heard.
d) The march had been orderly and peaceful as the demonstrators chanted slogans calling for an independent Sudan, up till the point where they reached the street leading to Kitchener Square from Gordon Street, between the Governor-General's Palace and the Post Office building. There the police interrupted the course of the procession, stopping the car at the head of the march and directing the demonstrators to take the northern road situated between the Treasury building and Kitchener's Statue. The demonstrators heeded those instructions but when the procession was well advanced along that road the police had attacked them with tear gas and then live ammunition. The police, both officers and men, had instigated physical contact with the procession without reason or any provocation on the

part of peaceful unarmed independence supporters. Thus came the sad conclusion that took the lives of many citizens, both from the police and the pro-independence march.

e) The authorities had permitted anti-independence campaigners to enter the airport while denying access to pro-independence supporters. The authorities had allowed other demonstrators to occupy both Kitchener Square and Gordon Square and to chant their fill of slogans – even permitting them to scale the walls of the palace itself before being turned back by the police, who did not resort to batons, tear gas or bullets.

f) On the evening of Monday 1 March, after the Umma Party's supporters returned to their base, rifle wielding policemen embarked on a revenge spree in Khartoum and Omdurman, during which they shot several Party members who had not been on the march nor in any demonstration or unlawful gathering.[20]

iv. Ismā'īl al-Azharī meets Imām 'Abd-al-Raḥman al-Mahdī

To clear the air after the tension that prevailed in the aftermath of the 1 March events, al-Azharī met Imām 'Abd-al-Raḥman on 26 March at his residence in Omdurman. The meeting took place at al-Azharī's request, with the mediation of Aḥmad Yūsuf Hāshim, President of the Sudanese Press Association and Editor-in-Chief of *al-Sūdān al-Jadīd*. Imām 'Abd-al-Raḥman al-Mahdī was greatly displeased with the claim made by the Unionist press that it had been al-Mahdī who sought to meet al-Azharī. The meeting was also attended by the Minister of Justice, 'Alī 'Abd-al-Raḥman, as well as Mā'mūn Ḥussein Sharīf and Aḥmad Yūsuf Hāshim.

At the start of the meeting, al-Azharī expressed his anxiety over the situation in the Provinces since the events of 1 March. He asked Imām 'Abd-al-Raḥman to issue one statement to calm people and a second to express support for the government of the day. The Imām retorted that the reason behind the situation in the Provinces was the partisan policies espoused by the Government and its encouragement of Egyptian interference in Sudan. For the sake of good order, however, he would

[20] *al-Ayyām*, 2 March 1954.

consider a calming statement if Mā'mūn Ḥussein Sharīf and Aḥmad Yūsuf Hāshim would agree on a draft – but he would not issue any statement supporting al-Azharī before receiving confirmation that the Government was aimed for Sudanese independence. Likewise, he wanted real proof that the Government intended to pursue a national rather than a partisan policy. The meeting ended with assertions from al-Azharī of his goodwill and positive intentions.

It seems that a draft statement was indeed prepared for Imām ʿAbd-al-Raḥman but his advisers within the Umma Party recommended that he should issue no statement without receiving specific assurances from al-Azharī that he would follow national, non-partisan policies.[21] That was why the meeting resulted in no more than a terse statement reporting, *inter alia*, that the meeting took about two hours and the exchange was "saturated with high nationalist spirits and aimed at the interests of the country and its progress in a climate of calm and stability."[22]

v. Promise by Government to hold a commission of inquiry

In its own statement, the Cabinet pledged to conduct a thorough investigation into the events: motives, causes and circumstances that triggered them, as well all those who acted to incite, abet or participate in violence.[23] The Governor-General appointed Donald Hawley, Chief Registrar of the Sudan Judiciary, as Chairman of a commission of inquiry.[24] It seems that this appointment was made without consulting the Council of Ministers, giving rise to disagreement between them as to who should form the Commission, name its members and set out its terms of reference.

---

[21] National Archives, Kew, FO 371/108322: Khartoum to Foreign Office, 28 March 1954 in 'Political developments in Sudan during 1954'. See also Sir William Luce Papers, 828/6/87-9: Luce to Davies, 3 April 1954.

[22] *al-Ayyām*, 27 March 1954.

[23] Ibid., 2 March 1954.

[24] UK Trade Commissioner's office to FO, London: Bimonthly Political Summary No.24 (28 February-13 March 1954), in Ṣālih, *British Documents on the Sudan*, vol. 9/1, p. 91. Hawley's own memoir was published as Donald Hawley, *Sandtracks in the Sudan* (Norwich: Michael Russell, 1955).

The Governor-General's intention was to form a commission of inquiry with wide-ranging authority, capable of investigating the role of the Minister of the Interior and the wider Cabinet in the events. al-Azharī, however, informed Howe that what was required was merely a low-level commission to investigate the causes of the events and the conduct of the police and civil servants. As the Cabinet was answerable to Parliament, any inquiries or information relating to ministerial work and responsibility should be addressed there.[25] So the question of a commission of inquiry was postponed pending the promulgation in Parliament of a new Commissions of Inquiry Ordinance – and the matter was ultimately dropped altogether.

This was a regrettable outcome: had there been a neutral commission of enquiry, chaired by a competent judge, it might have arrived at an account of the events which had taken place at Kitchener Square on 1 March 1954 that was accurate and objective, replacing the considerable vagueness and contradiction that tainted both official and partisan accounts of these events.

vi. Trials of Anṣār and Umma Party supporters

A magisterial inquiry into the events of 1 March ended on 31 May 1954. Forty-six defendants, charged with minor offences, were tried by police magistrates. Four of the 46 accused were committed to trial by a Major Court under the presidency of Justice James Watson, with Justice Magzūb ʿAlī Ḥassib and District Judge ʿAbd-al-Majīd Imām also sitting. The prosecution was represented by Aḥmad Mutawallī al-ʿAtabānī.

The Major Court hearing began on 19 June and concluded 15 days later. Of the four defendants, ʿAlī Muḥammad Habboia was found guilty of attempting to commit culpable homicide not amounting to murder and was sentenced to five years in jail. The other three – ʿAbdallah ʿAbd-al-Raḥman Nugdalla, ʿAwaḍ Ṣāliḥ and ʿAlī Faraḥ – were all convicted of instigating and abetting acts of violence arising in Kitchener Square.

[25] Sir William Luce Papers, 828/6/87-9: Luce to Davies, 3 April 1954.

Awaḍ Ṣāliḥ was sentenced to death, ʿAlī Faraḥ to life imprisonment and Nugdalla to four years in prison.[26]

vii. The Appeal Court ruling

The judgement of the Court of Appeal was delivered by Chief Justice William Lindsay, who sat alongside Justices Muḥammad Aḥmad Abū-Rannāt and ʿAbd-al-Raḥman al-Nūr. Habboia's five-year sentence was found to be appropriate and his appeal was dismissed. Nugdalla's four-year term was determined by the Court to be on the lenient side because, in the words of the judgment:

> He took the very grave security risk of marshalling these tumultuous crowds and taking them, in their pent-up, excited state, on to the Palace. The main responsibility for the results of the clash which occurred between the Ansar and the Police must rest on his shoulders and on the shoulder of any person of higher authority from whom he took orders.[27]

As a result, Nugdalla's appeal was also dismissed. The Court of Appeal noted that both ʿAwaḍ Ṣāliḥ and ʿAlī Faraḥ had been convicted of the same offence but had received different sentences. As their acts of instigation were broadly similar – with Faraḥ's activities marginally less prominent – the death sentence previously handed down to ʿAwaḍ Ṣāliḥ was commuted to 14 years' imprisonment, while ʿAlī Faraḥ's life sentence was reduced to a ten-year term.

The Court stated that, as a general consideration, sentencing needed to be sufficiently rigorous as to emphasise that the authority of a government established by democratic methods had to be respected. The police, as servants of that Government, had the authority to regulate crowds to protect lives and property, and to prevent breaches of the

[26] *al-Ayyām,* 4 and 5 July 1954. See also National Archives, Kew, FO 371/108324 (Political developments in Sudan during 1954): Khartoum to Foreign Office, 5 July 1954.

[27] ʿAbdallah ʿAbd-al-Raḥman Nugdallah and others (Appellants) vs. Sudan Government (Respondent): Court of Criminal Appeal, Law Reports (1954), pp. 61 and 78.

peace. The Court of Appeal blamed the Government for the events of 1 March in the following terms:

> The Government itself cannot escape all blame for the events of the first of March. It had allowed a situation to develop which at the end it was incapable of controlling with any certainty of preserving the public peace. The security measures taken to deal with the situation were utterly inadequate, and hastily improvised.

'Abdallah 'Abd-al-Raḥman Nugdallah

The Court attributed those shortcomings of the Government to its inexperience on "how to govern and how to make the most effective use of departmental machinery to enforce law and order." But the Court noted that:

> ... since the early days of March, there had been a marked general improvement in the state of security, and the new Government has gained in experience and stability, supported in national issues by the opposition.

In the closing paragraph of the Judgement, the Court of Appeal decided that:

The clash which resulted in such a serious loss of life and injury to persons was not proved to have been premeditated and was to a great extent the result of an unfortunate chain of events which culminated at Kitchener Square in almost spontaneous outburst of lawlessness.

'Awaḍ Ṣāliḥ

viii. The Cabinet response

Shortly after the judgement of the Court of appeal was handed down, the Cabinet published a statement in rebuttal of the criticism and blameworthiness for the events of 1 March 1954. The statement was prepared by the Cabinet's legal adviser, Aḥmad Mutawallī al-ʿAtabānī. In reply to its accusation of dereliction of duty by the court, the Cabinet retorted that the Court had transcended the limits of its jurisdiction by arrogating to itself a power which belongs exclusively to the Parliament. The Cabinet considered that by the involvement in political controversy, and meddling into highly sensitive matters, the Court departed from the constitutional principles established in democratic countries. Below are some of the salient points in the Cabinet's statement:

1. The responsibility of the Government was not a matter of dispute before the Court so that the Government was required to submit to the Court all the measures and precautions taken to cope with the situation, and thereby enable it to decide on their adequacy or otherwise.
2. The Court has no right to hold the Government accountable to it on this matter because the Self-Government Statute is based on the principle of separation of the three powers: the legislative, the executive and the judicial. The Constitution defined the jurisdiction of each power. This would guarantee that no power would encroach upon, or exercise jurisdiction belonging to another power. For otherwise the affairs of the state would be disrupted and its vital interests affected. Therefore Article 19 of the Self-Government Statute provided for the establishment of a Council of Ministers to be responsible to Parliament for the administrative and executive functions of the Government. Whereas Article 76 provided for the establishment of an independent judiciary that would be responsible directly to the Governor-General. Thus pursuant to the Self-Government Statute, the Cabinet would be responsible to Parliament for the stability of law and security and all other administrative functions.
3. The duty of the Court is confined to the interpretation and application of the law to certain facts. It has no control or supervision over the functions assigned to the Government by the Constitution. The sole instance where the Government would be subject to the judiciary would arise in respect of the civil rights of the individual against the state.[28]

ix. Events of 1 March 1954: Lessons and consequences

The events of 1 March did not pass without leaving lessons to be learned, traces or consequences. The events illustrated to the Government that excluding the opposition would not lead to any positive outcome; involving it was important and indeed obligatory at this critical stage of Sudan's history.

---

[28] *al-Rāyī al-ʿAm*, 1 September 1954.

Derek Riches, the British Trade Commissioner, was among those who commented on lessons to be learned from the events of 1 March, asserting that the incident had proven to the Government that its pursuance of total unity with Egypt would be a form of suicide: the Anṣār would oppose it and this might open the door to foreign intervention. Riches added that many new National Unionist Party members had joined the Party out of fear of the Anṣār. The 1 March disturbances might have suggested to them that the safest route was staying away from Egypt. This way, the risk of the Anṣār carrying out a revolution would vanish.[29]

The Governor-General, Robert Howe, described the Anṣār's demonstrations of 1 March as a 'unilateral declaration of independence' on the part of the Umma Party. Thus, the only way to neutralize the Party – apart from intensive security measures – would be an early declaration of Sudan's independence by the governments of the Condominium.[30]

Aḥmad Muḥammad Yāsin wrote in his memoirs that the 1 March events, despite their tragic aspects, were among the leading factors driving the NUP to head towards independence. He said that the Party considered what might happen if Sudan, after the transitional period, entered into the whirlwind of a Constituent Assembly and tabled a simple choice between the conflicting principles of independence and/or unity with Egypt.[31]

---

[29] National Archives, Kew, FO 371/108324: UK Trade Commissioner, Khartoum, to Foreign Office, 24 July 1954.

[30] Khartoum to Foreign Office, 3 March 1954, in Ṣālih, *British Documents on the Sudan*, vol. 10/2, p. 111.

[31] Yāsin, *Mudhakkirāt*, p. 266.

CHAPTER 3

Sayyid ʿAbd-al-Raḥman Calls on Britain to Declare Outright Sudanese Independence: 4 March 1954

i. Selwyn Lloyd meets Sayyid ʿAbd-al-Raḥman

Sayyid ʿAbd-al-Raḥman al-Mahdī, accompanied by his son Ṣiddīq, met the British Minister of State for Foreign Affairs, Selwyn Lloyd, in Khartoum on 4 March 1954. At the start of the meeting, Selwyn Lloyd stated that he fully realised that it was Nagīb's visit that had triggered the demonstration – and that the current atmosphere had been caused by the constant Egyptian interference. He wondered whether Sayyid ʿAbd-al-Raḥman had any idea how to stop that interference. Sayyid ʿAbd-al-Raḥman responded that what Britain ought to do was to immediately declare the independence of Sudan. Asked what he meant by that, Sayyid ʿAbd-al-Raḥman replied that the 1953 Self-Government and Self-Determination Agreement should be torn up.

Selwyn Lloyd drew the Sayyid's attention to the fact that, were Britain to tear up the Agreement, it might have to stay in Sudan for another two or three years – during which period it would be essential to find some solution to satisfy nationalist aspirations. One solution might be to make use of the United Nations, as had been done in the case of Libya.[32] Selwyn Lloyd added that a possible sequence of events in such a case would be: repudiation of the Agreement; ejection of the Egyptians; continuation of the existing constitution; holding fresh elections after

[32] In 1949, the UN had charged a Commissioner, Adriaan Pelt of the Netherlands, to draft a new constitution and prepare the former Italian colony for independence. The United Nations Tribunal in Libya continued to decide disputes in Libya until 1955.

three or four years under UN auspices; a handover of power to the government resulting from those elections.

Responding to this outline proposal, ʿAbd-al-Raḥman al-Mahdī said he would consider it carefully – though he noted that there would be no way of guaranteeing that the Egyptians would not continue to interfere. A shorter and better route, he added, might be for the Sudanese themselves to declare their independence and for the British to support them by repudiating the Agreement. This course of events would serve as a temporary stopgap measure until elections – held under international supervision – produced a new indigenous government.

Selwyn Lloyd enquired whether the Umma Party would win a majority in the new elections under international supervision. Sayyid ʿAbd-al-Raḥman replied that with no Egyptian interference and with a little help from British officials the Umma Party would indeed secure a majority. He indicated that in the previous election pro-independence parties had received 45,000 more votes than the pro-unity parties.

Sayyid ʿAbd-al-Raḥman al-Mahdī

Lloyd pressed al-Mahdī to say what he thought if the elections resulted in a pro-Egyptian government. He doubted this possibility, but he said that if it should happen, he would, with support of the British, establish independence in the country. When asked whether he meant a civil war, he said he would not wish to go so far as that, although it might be necessary, but that he would have the means of bringing pressure to bear temporarily.

In his official report, Selwyn Lloyd summarised ʿAbd-al-Raḥman al-Mahdī's views in five points that he himself promised to consider:

a) Egyptian interference was making the 1953 Agreement unworkable;
b) Egyptian interference must therefore cease, either they must stop voluntarily or the British would have to take action to stop it;
c) Since a voluntary cessation of interference was unlikely, the British Government should be led to denouncing the 1953 Agreement;
d) If the British denounced the Agreement they must put something in its place;
e) Free elections to be held next November, followed by transfer of power to the resulting government. Ṣiddīq al-Mahdī added that, during this period, the British Government would resume control and would arrange for the United Nations to be brought in.[33]

ii. The Umma Party accuses Egypt of violating the Agreement

On 4 May 1954, Ṣiddīq al-Mahdī, in his capacity as leader of the Umma Party, addressed letters to the signatories of the 1953 Agreement, Egypt and Britain.[34] He accused Egypt of breach of the letter and spirit the 1953 Agreement, which "necessitates the free and neutral atmosphere during the transitional period." In effect that brought about the "destruction of the Agreement".

Britain was accused of indifference and failure to take strong measures in this respect, and thereby encouraged the Egyptian

---

[33] Archives, Kew, FO 371/108321: Telegram No. 11 from Riches, Khartoum, to Foreign Office, 6 March 1954, transmitting record of meeting between Al Mahdi and Selwyn Lloyd on 4 March 1954.

[34] Ṣāliḥ, *British Documents on the Sudan*, vol. 9/1, p. 105.

intervention. The letter gave the following as examples of this intervention:

a) During the election campaign, Egypt had openly thrown its lot in favour of the pro-Unity elements by putting under their control all its visible and invisible potentialities, regardless of all considerations. The Umma Party protested to the Electoral Commission at the time and had it not been for our earnest desire to preserve the national cause, we would have withdrawn and self-Government would have vanished.
b) Major Salah Salim and General Abdel Hakim Amir, accompanied by a group of Egyptian journalists and specialised propagandists equipped with propaganda films and the like, toured the different parts of the Sudan by aeroplane especially set for this purpose. The National Unionist Party prepared for them political meetings in which Major Salim delivered political speeches in favour of the Unionists' point of view. In one his speeches in Port Sudan, he attacked the Agreement and described it as a useless piece of paper.
c) Egypt had sent a number of military men to the Southern Sudan under the cover of aviational training; whose real purpose was to spread Unionist propaganda and look for strategic positions.
d) Large groups of Egyptian students from different institutions and secondary schools were also sent to the Sudan for propaganda purposes.
e) A special daily programme from the Egyptian Broadcasting Station was started to attack the cause of independence and defame its champions. For this purpose, they have exploited prominent figures like the Grand Sheikh of al-Azhar University and its learned men and the outstanding politicians. This programme has been very active ever since.
f) The Egyptian propaganda was culminated by the visit of the President of the Egyptian Republic, General Neguib, to Khartoum on 1st March, 1954.
g) Egypt recently sent a gift of fire arms and ammunition to the Sudan and promised to send aeroplanes and other similar gifts, and to accept a number of Sudanese in its military institutes to train for aviation and other military activities.

h) Egypt also sent a number of its Sudanese civil servants to spread Unionist propaganda in the Sudan. These include Sayed Dardiri Ahmed Ismail, Under Secretary for the Egyptian Ministry of Sudanese Affairs, and Sheikh Muhammed Nur il Hassan the Under Secretary for the Egyptian Ministry of National Guidance, who had visited a number of towns and villages in the Sudan, offering, in the name of Egypt, financial aid for different religious institutions.

i) Egypt had allotted a large part of her budget for expenditure in the Sudan for the purpose of opening a University, for religious institutes, Secondary Schools, Hospitals etc.

j) The Egyptian Government had started a special fund, to help the Sudan Government to pay compensation to the foreign Government Officials whose contracts are to be terminated for Sudanisation measures."

Ṣiddīq al-Mahdī

The Umma Party memorandum indicated that pro-independence opinion constituted the majority in Sudan. They were working towards the achievement of Sudanese independence relying solely on Sudanese assets, not on any external foreign aid. According to official figures, it argued, 275,000 Sudanese had voted for pro-independence candidates, against 230,000 votes for unity candidates. However, Egyptian breaches of the Agreement made the pursuit by pro-independence activists of their goal in a democratic atmosphere extremely difficult – especially as they were completely reliant on limited Sudanese resources in the face of limitless Egyptian resources.

In conclusion, the Umma Party argued, the situation was extremely serious. Strong measures need to be taken towards the cause of independence for which the Party had been fighting over recent years – and an urgent reply to the memorandum was expected.

iii. Letter of Sayyid ʿAbd-al-Raḥman to Selwyn Lloyd

In June 1954, Selwyn Lloyd received a letter from Sayyid ʿAbd-al-Raḥman, in which he asked Lloyd to review the suggestion which he put to him in Khartoum "so that the country may be spared the results which will be in the interest of no one."[35] ʿAbd-al-Raḥman al-Mahdī's letter included the following points:

a) Egyptian interference in the Sudan had increased;
b) the establishment of the Unionist Government in the Sudan had allowed the Egyptians wide interference in a manner inconsistent with the free and neutral atmosphere required for this period;
c) In practice the future of the Sudan had been decided in favour of the Union with Egypt;
d) removal of Ibrāhīm Aḥmad from the Governor-General's Commission made the Commission unrepresentative of the two points of view and
e) since Britain is a party to the Agreement, it must see to it that the free and neutral atmosphere would be established to allow the country to decide its future freely.

[35] Archives, Kew, FO 371/108323 (Political developments in Sudan during 1954): Enclosure in Riches, Khartoum, to Thomas Bromley (Head of African Department), 5 June 1954. It is not known whether the original letter has survived in Arabic.

Sayyid ʿAbd-al-Raḥman's letter and the proposals it contained were discussed in three meetings at the British Foreign Office in London.[36] The meetings were attended by Ṣiddīq al-Mahdī, Ibrāhīm Aḥmad and Muḥammad Aḥmad ʿUmar. Selwyn Lloyd was accompanied by Douglas Dodds-Parker, Parliamentary Under-Secretary of State for Foreign Affairs,[37] and Willie Morris, a junior diplomat in the FO's Africa department. Of the three meetings, the most important was the one that took place on 11 June, as Selwyn Lloyd used it to announce his rejection of Sayyid ʿAbd-al-Raḥman's plan as unworkable. His reasons were given in a formal written response to the Sayyid's original letter.

iv. Selwyn Lloyd's reply to Sayyid ʿAbd-al-Raḥman

The response was conveyed via a letter to Philip Adams, the UK Trade Commissioner, who was instructed to relay it to ʿAbd-al-Raḥman al-Mahdī in person.[38] Right at the beginning, Selwyn Lloyd asserted that his priority was reaching the best policy to help the Sudanese so that Egyptian domination would not be imposed upon them unwillingly. Sayyid ʿAbd-al-Raḥman's proposals to take strong measures against matters arising from the present situation were not practicable for the following reasons:

a) If we repudiated the Agreement, the Egyptians would be able to revive their claim to sole sovereignty over Sudan. Legally, Britain could not grant independence to Sudan: we could only renounce our own rights.
b) It is extremely difficult if any international commission could be got together in the circumstances envisaged. We could not get the United Nations to intervene without Egyptian consent.
c) We have to reckon with opposition by the Egyptians and a section of Sudanese opinion. It is difficult to predict what form this opposition could take. We have to plan for it. But it would

---

[36] Ibid. contains minutes of all three meetings.

[37] Dodds-Parker had served in the Sudan Political Service for five years in the 1930s, as a provincial official in Kordofan and as private secretary to the then Governor-General, Sir Stewart Symes.

[38] Archives, Kew, FO 371/108323: Selwyn Lloyd to Adams, 24 June 1954.

be impossible to put a plan into operation and at the same time carry out a British withdrawal. The Governor-General cannot undertake the plan without support by British troops and officials to keep the administration going.

d) If the Umma Party blessed this course of action it would forfeit sympathy and support of the Sudanese nationalist opinion.

Lloyd added the opinion that, in politics, it was a mistake to overestimate the strength of one's opponents. Even with a parliamentary majority, the unionists would be faced with serious difficulties – and relations between the Egyptians and the NUP had experienced many difficulties. Selwyn Lloyd thought that the Umma Party should keep up the fight by constitutional means, making the best of the situation as it developed.

For Selwyn Lloyd, the vital stage would come when the withdrawal of British administrators really began. It would then be possible for the pro-independence lobby to persuade the Sudanese people that anti- colonial slogans were no longer relevant for the British: it would be Egypt that remained the only threat to independence.

Concluding his reply, he said he realised that these ideas might not be palatable to ʿAbd-al-Raḥman al-Mahdī. It is difficult, he wrote, to continue fighting against heavy burdens with insufficient means. He expressed his view that the cause of independence, of which the Umma Party's supporters were the solid base, was swimming with the tide of nationalism in the long run – and that tide would sweep away Egyptian interference in Sudan's affairs. But the measure proposed by Sayyid ʿAbd-al-Raḥman would reverse this tide, putting nationalist forces on a collision course with both the British and the Umma Party.

Adams relayed Selwyn Lloyd's letter verbally on 28 June 1954. He noted that Sayyid ʿAbd-al-Raḥman had not fully absorbed the difficulty of securing UN approval for any intervention in Sudan. He also recorded the Sayyid's general Agreement to pursue the struggle through peaceful means – although one problem was that several of his best men were not members of Parliament. Sayyid ʿAbd-al-Raḥman accepted Lloyd's view of making the most of the departure of British employees from Sudan to establish the fact that the colonial threat now came from Egypt alone and no longer from Britain.[39]

v. Lloyd proposes a plan to secure Sudanese independence

On 26 July 1954, Selwyn Lloyd circulated a note to the Cabinet summarising Sayyid ʿAbd-al-Raḥman's views on Sudan's constitutional position. Twelve days later, he followed that with a memorandum to the Cabinet on the strategy to be followed to secure Sudan's independence, containing the following points:[40]

a) Many of the allegations made about Egyptian pressure and interference were true. It was not true, however, that Britain had made no attempt to stop such interference: the UK Government made numerous protests, while the Governor-General had taken steps to reduce and control this interference. Moreover, London had made its views clear to Egypt in the final round of the Suez negotiations – and the Egyptians had promised that there would be an improvement.
b) Egypt was unlikely to end such pressure and interference, "in view of the long-standing Egyptian policy of the unity of the Nile Valley."
c) It was important that the Governor-General and others believed that "Egyptian propaganda was beginning to outreach itself." The pro-unity faction had tasted power and were becoming less willing to receive orders from the Egyptians – and, as British officials began to depart and power to be transferred, "the Sudanese Government is likely to become more friendly and to rely on the British to protect them from Egyptian domination."
d) In respect of the Umma Party's desire that Britain repudiate the Agreement and declare early independence, such a move would be likely to produce an effect contrary to what Britain desired. It might also be interpreted by the current Government either as an attempt to restore British rule or to place the opposition in

[39] Ibid., FO 371/108324: Adams to Selwyn Lloyd, 29 June 1954.
[40] Cabinet Memorandum by Selwyn Lloyd, 7 August 1954, in Johnson, *British Documents*, Part II, p. 358.

power: either interpretation might force them into the arms of the Egyptians. Such a measure might provoke disorder, forcing Howe to declare a constitutional emergency – in which case there was no guarantee that Sayyid ʿAbd-al-Raḥman or the Umma Party would support the Governor-General.

e) While the Sayyid himself would not personally advocate against Britain, there was a considerable section of his followers who would not hesitate to do so. In the debate on compensation for foreign officials, for example, the only speaker to say derogatory things about Britain was the Leader of the Opposition.

Selwyn Lloyd believed that the biggest contribution to the success of the independence movement could be made by the opposition – a factor not mentioned in ʿAbd-al-Raḥman al-Mahdī's earlier letter. Selwyn Lloyd further argued that the primary obstacle to the success of the independence movement was the fear among the leadership of the Khatmīa of an eventual Mahdist domination of Sudan. The riot on 1 March had only increased that fear.

Selwyn Lloyd revealed that, during the previous 18 months, the British had been urging the Umma leadership to broaden the base of their party and to include non-Anṣār elements. The Socialist Republican Party – pro-independence but not Anṣār – was ready-made for that purpose. But the Umma leaders had failed, during the election and since, to make any effort in that direction. Until they did, Selwyn Lloyd believed, they would not be an electoral majority.

In this memorandum, Selwyn Lloyd noted that Howe himself felt more hopeful about constitutional developments in Sudan and, were the Government to continue to exercise patience in the implementation of the Agreement, its position would be stronger. Howe was reported to feel that Sudanese of all parties were fully aware of the danger posed by Egypt – and as their resentment of Egyptian pressure increased, they were likely to look increasingly to London for help and advice.

In conclusion, Selwyn Lloyd suggested that nationalism would be the dominant force and the British Government should profit from it. He outlined a few steps to be taken immediately:

a) An invitation to Prime Minister Ismāʿīl al-Azharī to visit Britain. He had proven himself to be an ardent supporter of Sudanese independence and had established good relations with the Governor-General. An official visit would strengthen his feeling that Britain could be relied upon to help achieve an independent Sudan.
b) An invitation to a group of Sudanese parliamentarians to London early next year.
c) Continuing to emphasize Sudan's independent identity, 'unobtrusively but firmly', in matters such as foreign representation and the national flag.

We shall see in the next chapter how Selwyn Lloyd's analysis would mesh with the analysis and recommendations stated in a memorandum prepared by William Luce in August 1954. Luce called for a positive rapprochement with the NUP Government – and the first practical step in that respect would be an invitation to the Sudanese Prime Minister to visit Britain.

CHAPTER 4

Luce Calls for Positive Rapprochement with the National Unionist Party: 13 August 1954

i. Luce's analysis of the political situation in Sudan

We saw in Chapter 1 how Anthony Eden – at the time still Foreign Secretary – had outlined to Governor-General Howe the main themes of British policy on Sudan during the transitional period preceding self-determination. Eden had advised, *inter alia*, that a policy be adopted which did not rush to throw over Sayyid ʿAbd-al-Raḥman al-Mahdī of the Anṣār/Umma Party as part of an attempt to establish better relations with his main sectarian rival, Sayyid ʿAlī al-Mīrghanī of the Khatmīa/National Unionist Party. The advice also aimed at building bridges with the NUP and promoting any tendencies in that Party to move away from the Egyptian camp. However, the Governor-General had warned in his reply of 4 February 1954 that those two targets might be contradictory.

On 13 August, William Luce, Howe's advisor on constitutional and external affairs, wrote a detailed analysis on the political situation in Sudan and British policy there.[1] Given the difficulty in reconciling Eden's two objectives – i.e. maintaining friendly relations with Sayyid ʿAbd-al-Raḥman and the Umma Party while building bridges with the NUP – Luce called for this policy to be revisited, beginning with an attempt at rapprochement with the NUP Government and an invitation to Ismāʿīl al-Azharī to visit London.

[1] National Archives, Kew, FO 371/108324: Note by Luce, dated 13 August 1954, enclosed in G. Lampen (Sudan Agent in London) to Bromley (African Department), 20 August 1954. Graham Lampen had previously served in Sudan for 27 years, rising to become Governor of Darfur.

At the start of his analysis, Luce defined the British Government's objectives in Sudan in these terms: that a reasonably stable and well-governed Sudan should emerge, independent of Egypt, in friendly relations with Britain – and subject to British influence. He itemised the main threats to this objective as follows:

a) That the NUP would link Sudan with Egypt in such a way as to lead to Egyptian political and economic domination;
b) That there would be a serious deterioration in security and standards of administration owing to rapid Sudanisation;
c) That economic development would be badly set back by any such deterioration in security and by the departure in 1955 of most of the British technical staff.
d) That the followers of ʿAbd-al-Raḥman al-Mahdī would try to foment a state of civil war; and
e) That inaction would lead to British influence withering away.

William Luce

In terms of his first point, Luce believed that the minds of the NUP and the Khatmīa were moving towards independence. It would be against all precedent and logic, he argued, if they were not nationalists before they were unionists – and "as they savour power and their strength grows their nationalism would become increasingly ascendant." However, Luce added, "we can expect no overt discarding of Egyptian support and influence until the NUP are satisfied that they have laid the bogey of Mahdism."

Luce proposed that it was of no concern to the British Government whether Sudanese independence was brought about by the NUP or the Umma Party. The British had been supporting the Umma because they represented most of those Sudanese who had declared openly for independence. There were, he added, several arguments to support the thesis that independence via the NUP would be more likely to achieve the British Government's aim for Sudan than independence via the Umma Party:

a) If the aim of NUP were independence, they could rely on the support of a large majority of both Sudan Defence Force (SDF) and police officers and a smaller majority of other ranks. On these grounds, the Mahdists and the Umma Party could not hope to dominate the Khatmīa and the NUP, whereas the latter could dominate the Mahdists – and in this might lie the best hope of avoiding civil war.
b) The Umma Party could not run the administration of the country without the support of the educated class, the majority of whom were Khatmīa and NUP supporters.
c) An independent Sudan dominated by the Mahdists would be the 'victim of intrigue' between Egypt and the Khatmīa, resulting in a state of chronic instability and permanent enmity between the two countries.

Luce continued by stating that, if the above arguments were valid and it were to be accepted that the NUP, having gained power, would probably hold it through the period of self-determination – and that in the end they were likely to decide on the independence of Sudan – then it would be time to reconsider the policy of 'building bridges' to the NUP while maintaining friendship with Sayyid ʿAbd-al-Raḥman and the Umma Party. This policy, however, amounted to "little more than sitting on the fence."

As evidence that the two objectives were mutually contradictory, Luce pointed to the fact that British officials in Sudan itself had emphasised the bridge building, while London was concentrated on the maintenance of friendly relations with the Umma and the Mahdists. The series of meetings between the Minister of State and Ṣiddīq al-Mahdī – coupled with fears expressed in the press about the ability of the Sudanese to govern themselves – were taken by the NUP as an indication that the British Government was hostile to them and was determined, come what may, to bring Sayyid ʿAbd-al-Raḥman and the Umma Party to power. "Until this belief is removed," Luce wrote, "the NUP will continue to insure themselves with the Egyptians."

The time, therefore, had come for London to play down the connection with Sayyid ʿAbd-al-Raḥman and the Umma Party and to make a more positive move towards the NUP – but it would have to be done "in an unobtrusive manner if it were not to defeat its own ends." The first move, Luce suggested, might be an invitation to al-Azharī to visit London in the Autumn or the following Spring.

As regards a possible attempt by the Anṣār to stage a civil war, Luce said that the isolation of Sayyid ʿAbd-al-Raḥman and his supporters would increase with the passage of time. Nonetheless, Luce believed that it was likely that the Sayyid might attempt a civil war but he doubted its success, given the superiority that modern weapons gave the SDF in a possible fight with the Anṣār of Sayyid ʿAbd-al-Raḥman, who were, to all intents and purposes, unarmed. Civil war and/or serious disturbances might occur, Luce believed, in the more fanatical regions to the west of the country – but enthusiasm was unlikely to be stirred up in central Sudan as most of Sayyid ʿAbd-al-Raḥman's followers had established interests that required peace and security to maintain. "Nothing must be said or done," he added, "to give the Sayyed the idea that the British Government would regard violence on his part with anything but the greatest disfavour." British influence should be used to prevent such action – even in the knowledge that, in so doing, "we may be sealing his political fate." Luce expected the Sayyid to call this a betrayal but the realities of the situation had to be faced and Britain was in no way in debt to either ʿAbd-al-Raḥman al-Mahdī or the Umma Party.

Luce's note concluded by stressing that British influence in Sudan would not be retained merely by stating policy: "Statements should be followed by action and by positive evidence of British interest in the future well-being of Sudan." To this end, Luce proposed that British technical staff be encouraged to remain in Sudan after July 1955 to help keep technical services going and continue training their Sudanese replacements. Furthermore, Luce noted, the country would need about £50 million over and above Sudan's own resources over the next decade to maintain major projects that were vital for future economic development and financial stability: the Roseires Dam; the Manāqil extension of the Gezira Scheme; extensions of the railway network to the west and south-west; and the large-scale development of underground water supplies in the arid areas of western Sudan.

Luce attributed the obstacles facing the NUP Government in securing finance for these projects from the World Bank or global money markets to its constitutional status, the absence of a separate Sudanese currency and the desire of the Government not to accept during the transitional period any assistance that came with political strings attached. Luce envisaged an alternative source of financing from London's money markets, underpinned by British Government guarantees.

ii. al-Azharī in London

al-Azharī left Khartoum for London in the evening of 7 November 1954, accompanied by the Minister of Justice, ʿAlī ʿAbd-al-Raḥman, the Minister of Social Affairs, Yaḥya al Faḍlī, and the Governor of Upper Nile Province, Muḥammad ʿUthmān Yassīn.

Before his departure, al-Azharī stated that he had agreed to the visit because he had been invited by the British Government and that it was a courtesy visit. He was received in London by the new queen, Queen Elizabeth II, Prime Minister Winston Churchill and Foreign Secretary Anthony Eden.[2]

Eden spoke to al-Azharī about possible future links with Egypt, telling his guest that the British method had always been to start quite modestly and not to be over-ambitious. This was the best method; one could see afterwards how things went. Eden also expressed his hope that al-Azharī would not forget about the opposition, as it was important to carry the country with you, particularly in foreign policy. He informed al-

[2] *al-Ahrām*, 8 November 1954.

Azharī that the Anglo-Persian Oil Company was planning to send representatives to Sudan: modern discoveries, he added, had greatly improved oil prospecting techniques. al-Azharī took note of that, adding that the best prospects were probably along the Red Sea Coast and perhaps in Sudan's western and southern regions. For his part, al-Azharī raised the issue of posting former British employees in Sudan to jobs in Kenya and Uganda: his concern was that such deployments so close to Sudan's southern borders might create some difficulties. Eden responded that he had not heard of this problem but he would take note of it.[3]

Ismā'īl al-Azharī and entourage on his return from London

In Chapter 8, we shall see how al-Azharī told a reception organised by the Sudanese Students' Union in the UK on 15 November 1954 that the NUP had not yet decided its political programme – but that any form of independence chosen by the Party would have to come with adequate guarantees for Sudan's total independence, identity and sovereignty. Also, in Chapter 10, we shall see how Yaḥya al Faḍlī requested British aid in promulgating legislation to countering communism in the context of al-Azharī's Government labour laws.

[3] Archives, Kew, FO 371/96913 (Anglo-Egyptian negotiations for self-government in the Sudan): Eden to Adams, 17 November 1954.

CHAPTER 5

The 2nd Juba Conference Decides on Federation: 18 October 1954

i. Background: The 1st Juba Conference: 12 June 1947

Hubert Huddlestone, then Governor-General of Sudan, announced at the inauguration of the 5th Session of the Advisory Council on 17 April 1946 that a conference would be convened at the end of the session to consider the steps necessary to involve the Sudanese more comprehensively in the running of their country. The Conference subsequently became known as the Sudan Administration Conference.

It was chaired by the Civil Secretary, James Robertson, and was composed of representatives of the Advisory Council for the Northern Sudan, together with representatives of the parties that had agreed to participate: the Umma Party, the Liberal Party and the Nationalists. All these groups were in favour of independence. Those parties that favoured unification with Egypt boycotted the Conference, as did the Graduates' Congress, over which the Ashiqqā' Unionists had exercised control since 1944.

The South of Sudan was represented neither in the Advisory Council nor the Sudan Administration Conference. Robertson justified this by citing the distance that Southerners had to travel from their homes to attend, as well as the unfamiliarity of most Southerners with such large gatherings.

Agreement was reached in the Conference that the best way to improve the Advisory Council, make it more representative of the people and endow it with more responsibility was to form a Legislative Assembly made up of elected Sudanese members representing the whole of Sudan.

The assembly would have legislative, financial and administrative functions, conducted in collaboration with an Executive Council to be set up to replace the Governor-General's Council.

The Sudan Administration Conference put forward a resolution stipulating that Sudan shall be managed as one whole country, as the future of Sudan was dependent on its peoples coming together and merging to make up a single nation. There was a consensus in the Conference that the powers of the Legislative Assembly should cover the whole of the country, North and South, because bringing the South into a national legislative assembly would unify the country. The well-being of all Sudanese ultimately depended on this unification. While the Conference recognised that the Southern Provinces were not Arabic in origin, as were many other parts of Northern Sudan, it demonstrated that the Southern Provinces would not achieve economic and social progress unless they turned towards other parts of Sudan.

A majority of delegates tabled a motion calling for the abolition of the 1928 Permits to Trade Order, the adoption of a single education system for the entire country, the teaching of Arabic in Southern schools, the improvement of communication between North and South, the encouragement of transfers of Sudanese officials between North and South and the unification of administrative systems. All these would greatly assist the unification of the Sudanese.

To explore the views of Southerners – as well as British officials working in the South – a document entitled 'Recommendations of Sudan Administration Conference as regards the South of Sudan' were presented to another conference, convened in Juba on 12 June 1947. Chaired, again, by Robertson, it was attended by the Governor of Equatoria, B.V. Marwood, the Governor of Upper Nile, Frank Kingdon, and the Deputy Governor of Bahr al Ghazal, Thomas Owen.[1] Seventeen Southerners – chosen by the Governors of Equatoria and Bahr al Ghazal as representatives of specific Southern tribes and of the educated class – also participated. These included Chief Buth Diu, Chief Hassan Fertak, Siricio Iro, Chief Lolik Lado, Philemon Majok, Clement Mboro, Chief Cier Rehan and James Tambura. Northern members included Muḥammad

---

[1] Daly, 'Principal Office-Holders', pp. 311-12. See also Sudan Archive, University of Durham, T.R.H. Owen Papers: SAD.350/10/1-192.

Ṣaliḥ al-Shinqittī, Ibrāhīm Badrī, Ḥassan Aḥmad Osman al-Kid, Chief Sarūr Ramlī and Ḥabīb ʿAbdallah.[2]

The Juba Conference recommended that the South should be integrated with the North and be represented in the proposed Legislative Assembly. The Southern members of the Conference had no objection to the principle of unifying educational policy in North and South or to the teaching of Arabic in the schools of the South.[3]

ii. Calls for a second Juba Conference[4]

The Liberal Party organised a conference at Juba on 18-21 October 1954. As indicated in Chapter 1, the Liberal Party had been formed in January of that year and had chosen Benjamin Lwoki as its Chairman and Buth Diu as its Secretary-General. Also on the Party executive were Stanislaus Paysama, Paulo Logali and Gordon Ayoum. It was announced that the Conference would discuss the following questions:

a) The attitude of the present Government to the South;
b) The possibility of forming a united Southern parliamentary bloc;
c) The future of Sudan.

The influential newspaper *al-Ayyām* criticised the proposal for a second Juba Conference, describing it as "blatantly racist" as it involved only Southerners and because its objectives were designed specifically to benefit the South alone – exactly as if North and South were *not* one integral country and as if the affairs of the North were of no concern to

---

[2] Detailed minutes from the Juba Conference (12-13 June 1947), including a full list of participants, can be found online at https://web.archive.org/web/20070311041121/http://madingaweil.com/conference.htm.

[3] For further details see Ṭaha, *al-Ḥaraka al-Sīyāsīa*, p. 301.

[4] National Archives, Kew, FO 371/108328 (Sudan: Two-monthly political intelligence summaries covering period November 1953 to September 1954): Sudan Political Intelligence Summary No. 8 (August-September 1954), 14 October 1954.

Southerners in any way.[5] The paper expressed concern about a possible disintegration and collapse of the unity of Sudan if conferences were to take place in such a manner: "It is enough for our country to have sectarianism threatening its unity. Do we want to incite racism to add to our woes?"

The suspicion of *al-Ayyām* was that one of the Conference's objectives was to bring pressure to bear on the government of the day – and any future government running Sudan – to treat Southerners differently to Northerners, especially in the civil service. The paper added that Southerners would like administrative jobs in the South to be Sudanised by giving them to Southerners but that would destroy the principles upon which the Sudanese civil service had been built. All employees of the civil service in Sudan, be they Southerners or Northerners, were filed under one list – and the only criteria by which one may be assessed for promotion were merit and/or seniority. Introducing racial distinctions, the paper concluded, would expose the civil service to danger and collapse.

iii. The Government pre-empts the Conference resolutions

On 13 October 1954 – just a few days before the 2nd Juba Conference was due to be convened and two days before his own first visit to the Southern Provinces – Prime Minister Ismāʿīl al-Azharī read a message to the people of Southern Sudan over the radio.[6] One of his Government's key objectives, he said, was the introduction of essential reforms that would raise standards in comparatively backward areas, particularly the three Southern Provinces and the Nuba Mountains. al-Azharī conceded that these areas had not received the care and attention they should have, leading to the present differences in both the general standard of living and the wage rates in Northern and Southern Provinces. It was the duty of any government that was alive to its responsibilities to remove such inequalities for the sake of achieving unity and coherence in the nation's social, cultural and intellectual structures.

---

[5] *al-Ayyām*, 13 September 1954.

[6] National Archives, Kew, FO 371/108325 (Political developments in Sudan during 1954): Broadcast Statement by Prime Minister, 14 October 1954.

The Prime Minister quoted a letter that he had written on 14 July 1954 to Southern chiefs, in which he had stressed that his Government condemned racial discrimination of any sort and looked upon Southerners and Northerners as fellow citizens with equal rights and responsibilities. He added that an individual's qualities, qualifications and capabilities were the only decisive factors that would determine the career prospects of a Sudanese citizen, Northerner or Southerner. As evidence, he referred to the composition of his Government, in which Southerners had been given a fair share in shouldering the responsibilities of ruling the country. He asserted his Government's determination to rectify all past mistakes so that the South would catch up with the North as quickly as possible.

To honour the promise that he had made to the Chiefs in July – and to implement the declared policy of his Government before – he listed the decisions taken by his Cabinet in a meeting on 12 October 1954:

a) Southern school graduates shall be adjusted in line with colleagues in the North with equivalent qualifications; their wages should be adjusted accordingly;
b) Southerners with the rank of executive officer or sub-*ma'mūr* to be treated in the same way as corresponding Northern colleagues;[7]
c) Salaries of chiefs, their deputies, heads of courts and their clerks to be increased by 50 per cent;[8]
d) Wages of Southern police, soldiers and prison warders to be made equal with Northern colleagues;
e) Minimum wages for Southern labourers to be raised as follows: in Zande and Maridi, 150 piastre a month; in Bahr al-Ghazal and Equatoria (except for Zande and Maridi), 205 piastre a month; in Upper Nile, 250 piastre a month;

---

[7] Richard Hill, *A Biographical Dictionary of the Anglo-Egyptian Sudan* (Oxford: Clarendon Press, 1951), pp. ix-xvi, has a useful 'Glossary of Ranks, Titles, and Other Designations'.
[8] Sudan Archive, University of Durham (J. Carmichael Papers), SAD.993/1/33-5: Memorandum by John Carmichael on 'The increase in salaries and wages of Southerners announced in the Prime Minister's statement of 13 October [1954]'.

f) Creation of three training posts for junior administrators and three *ma'mūr* posts in the South;
g) Representing Upper Nile Province on the Nile Pumps Control Board;
h) Improving the wages of workers on the Zande Scheme appointed by the Equatoria Schemes Board, establishing minimum daily and monthly wages for those in specified earnings brackets.[9]

The Prime Minister's broadcast was severely criticised for not mentioning development in the South or the Government's plan in this respect. So the Minister of Finance issued a statement, in which he stated that the Prime Minister's announcement had been limited to those matters that needed addressing most urgently. As for development planning, it needed patient thinking. Moreover, development of the South should be considered in the context of the whole of Sudan. The Minister added that development in the South had not been ignored: the Government had allocated one million pounds for the Equatoria Projects Board. The Board's Production Section had encouraged the plantation of cotton on Zande land and had set up weaving mills and factories for textiles, sugar, cooking oil and soap. This had constituted the beginning of industrial development in the South.

The statement indicated that Government policy was directed towards reviewing the aims and activities of this project, to channel them towards a higher standard of living for the Southern population. The Minister added that, beside the Equatoria Schemes Board, wide-ranging experimental work was being carried out under the auspices of the Sudan Development Programmes for 1946-51 and 1951-6. The objective of these experiments was to test the possibility of growing rice in Malakal and Aweil, sugar in Mongalla and Saburi, and coffee and tobacco in Amadi. This policy would decide the most suitable agricultural product for each region to increase production and national income.

The Minister further indicated that a team investigating Southern development was on the verge of completing an initial report

---

[9] National Archives, Kew, FO 371/108325: Enclosure in Adams, UK Trade Commissioner, to Eden, 16 October 1954.

on natural resources in the South. He expressed his hope that the report would contribute to the determination of developmental trends in the South. The Minister did not specify the amount of money spent on the South – instead, he limited himself to stating that it might reach "millions of pounds" and that it would increase when the potential resources of the South were known.[10]

Benjamin Lwoki

iv. Resolutions of the 2nd Juba Conference[11]

Invitees to the 2nd Juba Conference included representatives of the three Southern Provinces, several Chiefs and Sultans, as well as a number of Southerners residing in Khartoum. One of those attending, Mūsa Bashīr, was described as the 'representative of the blacks of Khartoum'. In an intervention before the third session of the Conference, he explained that he did not represent a tribe but simply a colour: he was speaking on behalf of 25,000 Southerners in the North who supported

[10] Ibid., Enclosure in Chancery, Office of the UK Trade Commissioner, to Foreign Office, 23 October 1954.
[11] Ibid., FO 371/108326: Enclosure in Governor-General to Eden, 14 December 1954.

the idea of federation, among them the Nuba of Kordofan, the Fur of Darfur and the Funj of Blue Nile.[12]

The Conference held four sessions between 18 and 21 October 1954. The first was procedural and confirmed Benjamin Lwoki as Chairman, Deng Chol as Deputy Chairman and Marco Morgan as Secretary. Arabic, Bari, Lotuko, Zande and Dinka interpreters were appointed. An agenda was also drawn up to include:

a) The political future of Sudan;
b) The political future of Sudan under a unified administration;
c) Union with Egypt, as advocated by the NUP;
d) Economy and education in the South.

In its first vote, the Conference chose independence for Sudan, under a presidential system of government. Not one delegate voted for union with Egypt. When the political future of the South was put to the vote, 217 participants voted for federation within a unified Sudan. No-one voted against the proposition, although 7 NUP members of Parliament abstained. The session debating federation featured numerous interventions, of which we shall examine two here.

In the first intervention, Faḥal Yūkāndā, a delegate from Bahr al Ghazal, said that North and South had agreed back in 1947 on the unity of Sudan and on equality between Northerners and Southerners in education, training and pay. But since that date, no Southerners had been trained to take up positions in administration, health, education, the military, agriculture or technical jobs. The reason for holding a second Juba Conference was precisely the failure of Northerners to realise what Southerners had demanded in the first Juba Conference. Southerners were still neglected and given no responsibility for managing their country.

Yūkāndā explained that one of his reasons for supporting federation was the Cairo Agreement of 1953, on which Southerners were not consulted and which had led to the formation of the present Government. "The flood of Northerners continues to flow towards the

---

[12] Douglas Johnson, *Federalism in the History of South Sudanese Political Thought* (London: Rift Valley Institute, 2014), p. 11.

South to grab our land," he continued. "On behalf of Bahr al Ghazal, I reject this policy which replaces foreign employees with Northerners, because it can only lead to disturbances and chaos in the South. To save Sudan, the South has to have a federal system of government." He demanded that the South should secede if federation were denied; otherwise the South would be lost.

Buth Diu

In the second intervention, Chief ʿAbdallah of Torit-Katire in Equatoria Province said that the Condominium states had failed to develop the South. The demand for self-government by Northerners was aimed at controlling Southerners – at being their masters instead of their brothers. Chief ʿAbdallah demanded federation as the only way of saving his black comrades in the North. Blacks all over Sudan, he argued, were passing through a decisive stage under the present regime – and as Southerners had rectified their own situation it was up to them to rescue their poor friends, i.e. the Nuba, Fur and Funj.

The concluding session of the Conference was devoted to a debate on the economy and education. Opening the session, the Chairman said that the Condominium had offered the South nothing in terms of education: it had preferred the North and had offered it better education. The present Government, he added, had committed a grievous mistake in including the South among Sudan's 'underdeveloped regions', because the South was far more developed in comparison with the Beja, Hadendawa or Baqqāra tribes – so the South should be treated separately.

There was little actual debate among delegates on economics; indeed, there were few interventions on education. Some speakers suggested that the current schools were inadequate and hardly any Southern school graduates were able to progress to Khartoum University College. One participant demanded the appointment of a Minister of Education for the South, while another called for extra emphasis on technical education.

v. Communicating the resolution on federation

Following the formal Conference closing, Benjamin Lwoki sent a letter to the British Foreign Secretary, the Egyptian Foreign Minister, the Governor-General and the Prime Minister of Sudan notifying them that the Conference had voted in favour of a federal union between North and South Sudan.[13] Lwoki called upon Northerners to recognize the ethnic, cultural and religious differences between North and South: Northerners had to recognize that these natural and essential differences could only lead to either the formation of a federal union or, if this were unacceptable to Northerners, Sudan had to be divided into two independent nations, just as Pakistan had split from India.

Lwoki stated in his letter that the desire of Southerners to see the end of the Condominium was just as strong as their desire to see an end to the increasingly obvious Northern colonial encroachment into the South. Southerners, he asserted, were not bound by the unity of Sudan provided for in the Self-Government Statute, because the Northerners had made their alterations to the Statute in Cairo without considering the opinion of the South. He added that the Statute did not represent fully the aspirations of the South: just because Southerners were sitting in Parliament alongside Northerners did not alter or weaken the Southern viewpoint on the partiality of the Statute. As the South entered Parliament on its own volition, so it could also choose to walk out. Last but not least, Lwoki wrote:

---

[13] National Archives, Kew, FO 371/108326: Letter dated 15 November 1954.

> We firmly believe in our rights as a race distinct from the people of the Northern Sudan. We must determine the future of the South in the way we think suits us and our aspirations. Should a situation arise in which the self-determination of Southerners is denied by anyone, we have the right to apply for an international hearing.

vi. The 3rd Juba Conference: 6-7 July 1955

Benjamin Lwoki chaired a third conference, held in Juba in July the following year, attended by most leading MPs from Upper Nile and Equatoria Provinces. This Conference criticised the main political parties and decided that Southerners should support the Northern party that offered them the best deal – and they should maintain their cohesion so as to retain a casting vote in Parliament. Furthermore, the Conference decided to send a delegation to Khartoum, headed by Benjamin Lwoki. The delegation was authorised to prepare a specific plan for the educational, social and economic development of the Southern Provinces and to draft a Southern National Charter over the political future of South of Sudan.

Evaluating the Conference, the UK Trade Commissioner thought that it had passed without creating a major shake-up. He attached no significance to the decision to form a Southern bloc to hold a casting vote in Parliament: this had been discussed before and nothing had come of it. But the Commissioner did note that both Government and opposition had promised their Southern MPs serious consideration of any economic plan that they brought forward.[14]

We shall see in Chapter 8 that, in April 1955, a section of the Liberal Party breached the resolution of the 2nd Juba Conference by demanding formal constitutional links between Egypt and Sudan. Prominent among these were Buth Diu, the MP for Wadi al-Zaraf and the Secretary-General of the Party.

---

[14] Ibid., FO 371/108582 (Political development in the Sudan during 1955): UK Trade Commissioner to Foreign Office, 15 July 1955.

CHAPTER 6

Egypt Seeks British Support for a Loose Sudanese-Egyptian Union: 21 October 1954

The cordial atmosphere that dominated Anglo-Egyptian relations following the signing of the evacuation Agreement on 19 October 1954 seems to have encouraged the Government in Cairo to seek Britain's support for a loose, rather than total union or merger with Sudan. After the signing of the Agreement, Egypt's Prime Minister, Gamāl ʿAbd-al-Nāṣir, and Foreign Minister, Maḥmūd Fawzī, expressed their wish to have an informal general discussion with the Minister of State, Sir Anthony Nutting, and the British delegation before its return to the UK.

The discussions took place over luncheon at the Nile Barrage Rest House on 21 October. In addition to Nāṣir and Fawzī, the Egyptian side was represented by the Minister of State for Sudanese Affairs, Major Ṣalāḥ Sālim, who had just returned from Sudan and who seemed unhappy about the situation there, the Minister of Defence and Commander-in-Chief, General ʿAbd-al-Ḥakīm ʿAmir, and the Minister for Municipal and Rural Affairs, Wing-Commander ʿAbd-al-Laṭīf al-Baghdādī.

i. Major Ṣalāḥ Sālim's appraisal of the situation in Sudan[1]

Ṣalāḥ Sālim undertook to present his evaluation of the situation in Sudan to the British delegation, while Nāṣir confined himself to listening. Sālim's view was that the issue no longer turned upon the relative merits of independence or unity with Egypt – because there was

[1] National Archives, Kew, FO 371/108381 (Political relations between Egypt, Sudan and UK: fears of chaos or administrative breakdown in Sudan): Terence Garvey, Cairo, to Eden, 25 October 1954.

barely any difference between the two conceptions. If the Sudanese opted for unity, that could mean little more than a loose union, covering perhaps defence and foreign affairs, and particularly foreign representation abroad. Sālim played down the chances of cooperation in the defence arena: the Sudan Defence Force was small and unsophisticated and could not be amalgamated with the Egyptian army. The best that could be expected was an understanding over common objectives and contacts at the staff level. There might be a case for a symbolic union between the two countries, he argued, under a common presidency but separate legislative and administrative systems. Otherwise, Cairo would find that Nile Valley unity would cost Egypt something like £30 million per annum, instead of the £2 million now being spent by Egypt on hospitals, schools and mosques in Sudan.

It was Sālim's contention that there was really no basis for closer union with a country which was so backward and had so little to offer. Much had been said in the past about Egypt's reliance upon the Nile waters but when the Aswan High Dam had been completed, Egypt would finally be free from the danger of losing its water supply.[2] After that, it was immaterial to Egypt what the Sudanese did with the existing irrigation facilities and dams further up the river. The most that the Egyptian Government hoped or indeed wished to achieve was a limited degree of co-ordination between Egypt and Sudan.

Major Sālim spoke in tones of frustration about the 'awful' situation in Sudan; indeed, he was reported to have repeated this adjective three times. He predicted that the situation would reach a crisis point in six or seven months' time. Sudan was riven with strife and hatred. The South hated the North and the Anṣār hated the Khatmīa – animosities more deeply rooted than even the mutual loathing between Arabs and Jews. He expressed his surprise that the British authorities had permitted the communists to "implant their doctrines, which were making considerable headway among the intelligentsia and among farmers in the

---

[2] While construction did not start until 9 January 1960, preparations for a new dam, higher than the 'Low Dam' finished by the British in 1902, had intensified after the overthrow of King Fārūq by Gen. Muḥammad Nagīb, Lt.-Col. Gamāl ʿAbd-al-Nāṣir and their fellow 'Free Officers' in 1952.

Gezira." No fewer than 40 communist clubs were currently operating and their influence was making itself felt in the daily newspapers.[3]

Ṣalāḥ Sālim described the NUP Government as 'weak' and saw no prospect of a strong administration in the foreseeable future – something he attributed to the 'endless quarrels' between Sudan's political elements. Sudanisation, he believed, was proceeding far too rapidly and he saw the country facing the clear possibility of administrative breakdown and chaos when the process was complete. He reckoned that 99 per cent of the Sudanese were "quite incapable of playing any useful part in the administration of their country". As for the parallel process of 'Southernisation' in the South, that was equally pernicious in its effects: the risk of trouble from three million uneducated tribesmen, most of them still going about naked, was of the greatest gravity.

Major Ṣalāḥ Sālim

---

[3] At the time of Major Ṣalāḥ Sālim's statement, the communist movement had a legitimate cover, namely the Front Against Colonialization, a group founded during the 1953 election campaign. The leftist Egyptian writer Aḥmad Ḥamrush wrote that, after Ismāʿīl al-Azharī changed his mind over union with Egypt, Ṣalāḥ Sālim contacted ʿAbd-al-Khāliq Maḥjūb, Secretary-General of the Communist Party and al-Shāfī Aḥmad al-Sheikh, Secretary-General of the Sudanese Workers' Federation, trying in vain to persuade them to accept union with Egypt: Ḥamrūsh, *Qiṣṣat Thawrat 23 Yūlyū*, pp. 316-19.

Major Sālim predicted that 'bloodshed and disorder' seemed inevitable; indeed, Egypt had strong grounds for fearing that, when trouble came, anti-Egyptian factions in Sudan would sabotage the Jabal Awliyyā' Dam, rendering two million acres of Egyptian land uncultivatable and leading to the prospect of a starving countryside and political disturbances in Egypt. There was but one possible stabilising factor: 'co-ordination' with Egypt – and he appealed to Britain to refrain from acting against unity. It is worth noting that Terence Garvey, Counsellor at the British Embassy in Cairo who prepared these minutes for Eden in London, noted of Major Sālim that "as the conversation passed, his mind was turning more and more towards the idea that Egypt might find itself obliged to intervene by force to restore order in the event of a collapse of authority in Sudan."[4]

ii. Gamāl 'Abd-al-Nāṣir and the attempts to secure a form of union

Anthony Nutting, Minister of State for Foreign Affairs, sent Eden formal minutes of his own conversation with Lt.-Col. Gamāl 'Abd-al-Nāṣir, covering Israel, economic and military aid, the Suez Canal and various defence questions as well as Sudan. Nutting quoted Nāṣir as admitting to him outright that – having abandoned his predecessor's insistence on the Nile Valley unity as a precondition of any negotiations with Britain– he was now obliged to try to 'secure' some form of union as a result. Nutting told him that it was not for Egypt to 'secure' anything but for the Sudanese to decide whether they wanted to be united with Egypt or independent. Egypt must respect the Agreement. He explained to Nāṣir that Sudan was a very sore point in Britain, where there was a feeling that Egypt had not honoured its bond and was bringing pressure and influence to bear on the Sudanese.[5]

---

[4] National Archives, Kew, FO 371/108381: Garvey, Cairo, to Eden, 25 October 1954. Terence Garvey had a distinguished career in the diplomatic corps, later serving as High Commissioner to India and Ambassador to the USSR.

[5] Ibid., FO 371/108380 (Conversations on political matters affecting relations between UK, Egypt and Sudan): Nutting to Eden, 28 October 1954.

iii. The British Embassy supports Egypt's demand for a constitutional link with Sudan

In the light of the conversation which took place on 21 October 1954, between Minister Nutting and the Egyptian leaders, Ralph Murray, a Minister at the Cairo Embassy, suggested the re-examination by the British Government of its policy towards the Sudan, with a view to reaching an understanding with Egypt. The object of the re-examination would be to align the British policy with the views and policies propounded by Major Ṣalāḥ Sālim.[6]

Murray argued that Egypt's claim to some sort of special relationship with the Sudan is defensible on the ground of physical, economic, racial and religious links between the two countries. He claimed that recognition by the British Government of the special Egyptian interests in the Sudan and its approval to some form of constitutional link between the two countries, would enable it to exercise an effective influence on Egyptian policy towards the Sudan. Murray stressed the urgency of the re-examination in order to take advantage of the improved political atmosphere brought about by the conclusion of the 19 October 1954 Evacuation Agreement.

iv. Howe criticises Ṣalāḥ Sālim's appraisal and the Embassy's intervention

In Khartoum itself, Governor-General Howe summarily rejected Murray's proposal to realign British policy on Sudan with the views and policies advanced by Major Sālim.[7] In the course of his criticism of Sālim's views, Howe pointed out that Ṣalāḥ Sālim believed that Sudan was heading for chaos and internal strife; and that the only way to avoid this perilous situation was through co-ordination between Egypt and Sudan, in the form of a loose union, under a common president, that covered only external affairs and defence. Howe noted that Major Sālim had not clarified how such co-ordination would contribute towards internal stability in Sudan, though presumably he had in mind that it would

[6] Ibid., FO 371/108381: Murray, Cairo, to Eden, 8 November 1954.
[7] Ibid., Howe, Khartoum, to Eden, 8 December 1954.

facilitate Egyptian intervention should conditions in Sudan deteriorate to the detriment of Egyptian interests.

Howe made it clear that the only hope of future stability in the Sudan lay in the Sudanese choosing independence. Nothing less than that would satisfy either the people of the South or the Umma Party that represented a large proportion of Northern Sudanese. Howe referred back to November 1946, when the Umma Party had vehemently opposed the concept of 'symbolic Egyptian sovereignty' devised in the Sidky-Bevin Protocol.[8] Again, in April 1953, the Umma Party had scornfully rejected Gen. Muḥammad Nagīb's definition of independence for Sudan, which was almost identical to Major Sālim's current definition of 'co-ordination'.[9] And on 1 March this very year, Howe continued, we saw the violence of the Umma Party's feelings against Egyptian interference in Sudan.

Howe warned that the Egyptian aim of imposing on Sudan what he described as "some form of constitutional association by bribery and propaganda through one section of the Sudanese" was, in his opinion, the surest way to create the very conditions in Sudan that Major Sālim had depicted so graphically. And he added:

> One wonders, moreover, whether when he speaks of Egyptian intervention, presumably military, he has seriously considered the practical difficulties of such an operation in this country. The desert barrier between the two countries, the vulnerability of lines of communication and the great distances involved are obstacles which might make a more efficient and determined army than the Egyptian pause before undertaking such an enterprise.

---

[8] The British Foreign Secretary, Ernest Bevin, briefed the House of Commons on his recent talks with the Egyptian Prime Minister, Ismāʿīl Ṣidqī, on 'the texts of a treaty of mutual assistance, an evacuation protocol, and a Sudan protocol': *Hansard*, 27 January 1947, vol. 432, cc. 616-20.

[9] A reference to the letter sent by Nagīb to Sayyid ʿAbd-al-Raḥman al-Mahdī on 19 May 1953, to which he attached a second letter to the Chairman of the Umma Party expressing his views on union vs. independence: Ṭaha, *al-Ḥaraka al-Sīyāsīa*, pp. 695-702.

The Governor-General rejected the argument that Egypt's claim to some sort of special relationship with Sudan was clearly defensible on grounds of existing links that would make some kind of constitutional or political bond necessary or desirable. "Physical contiguity, a common religion and racial affinities", he stated flatly, were not normally considered reasons for political association between two countries. Cairo might be the religious and cultural centre of Middle Eastern Islam, just as Rome was the centre of the Catholic world, but this was no more an argument for a special political association between Egypt and Sudan than it would be for a similar association between Egypt and any other Middle Eastern state or between Italy and any other Catholic state. Furthermore, at least one third of the Sudan's population was neither Arab nor Muslim and there was a 'strong admixture' of African blood in a large part of the rest of the population.

Howe cited statistics to prove that there were no special economic links between the two countries. The value of Sudan's trade with Egypt had fallen steadily in relation to its trade with the rest of the world. In 1920, the value of Sudan's imports from Egypt was 55 per cent of total imports, while the value of exports to Egypt was 46 per cent of the total exports; the corresponding figures for 1953 were 8 and 6 per cent respectively. The economies of the two countries were in no sense complementary – and when it came to exporting long-staple cotton, on which the finances and economy of Sudan largely depended, they were in fact competitors.

Howe singled out the Nile as the only really special link – but again, he stressed that its significance lay not in the fact of a single river running through both countries but rather in the fact that Egypt and Sudan were effectively rivals in the use of Nile water, with the requirement of both constantly increasing. Politically, therefore, the Nile was the opposite of a link: its most significant feature, from an Egyptian perspective, was precisely that it traversed Sudan before reaching Egypt – and it was this that made Cairo so anxious to secure a national water supply by finishing the High Aswan Dam, regardless of Sudan's own interests. Howe noted what had been said during recent discussions in Khartoum on this subject:

> The Egyptian irrigation experts have proposed that the Sudan's share in the Nile waters should be increased to 8 milliards [billions] of the natural river flow at Aswan Dam; the Sudan uses at the present 4 milliards to Egypt's 48 milliards. The total natural discharge of the Nile at Aswan is some 84 milliards, and Egypt is proposing that of the 32 milliards at present unutilized, 28 should be taken by Egypt and 4 by the Sudan. But Sudan irrigation experts consider that Sudan's ultimate share should be in the region of 25 milliards.

Howe observed that there was a steady growth of nationalist feeling among Sudanese of all kinds – and a corresponding weakening of any desire for a close link with Egypt. For all these reasons, Howe recommended that Britain should let the existing process take its natural course and continue to avoid any form of interference, particularly such as would hinder the achievement of independence. In these circumstances the British attitude toward the Egyptians regarding the Sudan should be along the following lines:

a) To continue to maintain our own strict neutrality, and we should take every opportunity to speak frankly to the Egyptians about their interference in Sudan;
b) Try to persuade the Egyptians that their policy of interference and of trying to impose a constitutional link between the two countries against the wishes of a large number of Sudanese and would produce the chaos and strife in the Sudan which they apparently fear so much;
c) Try to persuade the Egyptians that Britain is not working for an independent Sudan under British influence and at enmity to Egypt; but on the contrary we consider it most important to an independent Sudan to have close and friendly treaty relations with Egypt;
d) We should recognise Egypt's fear for its water supply and should persuade it to earn Sudanese goodwill by recognising Sudan's own right to a fair share in the waters of the Nile and by coming to an agreement now on what the ultimate share should be.

v. Britain rejects reconsideration of its Sudan policy

The Foreign Office in London rejected the arguments for reconsidering its Sudan policy, which aimed to reach an understanding with Egypt. Instead, most of the arguments expounded by Howe and by Philip Adams, the UK Trade Commissioner in Khartoum, were adopted.[10] These positions included:

a) An attempt to reach such an understanding with Egypt on her future constitutional relations with Sudan would be fatal to the position of the British administration there. Recognition by the British Government of Egyptian claims in any form would be considered by many in Sudan as a gross breach of faith and interference with the free choice of the Sudanese people in contravention to the 1953 Agreement.
b) As a new and a more satisfactory relationship with the present Sudanese Government and, to some extent, the Egyptians had been achieved, the British Government could go no further than it already gone in the direction of reaching an understanding with Egypt on Sudan without being exposed to the accusation of handing Sudan over to Egypt and therefore violating the Agreement. To do this would be to imperil Sudan's stability by driving the opposition to extreme courses; this would be incompatible with the assurances given to the British Parliament and to the Sudanese over a long period of years.
c) The present crisis in the Sudanese Government was the latest of many indications that the independence movement was gaining ground. It would be a mistake to interfere with that process by attempting to reach an understanding with Egypt on the future relations of the two countries simply to rescue the Egyptians from the consequences of their own policy of interference in Sudan.
d) The British Government desired close and friendly relations between Egypt and Sudan and had no intention of encouraging either the Government or opposition to pursue a policy of

---

[10] National Archives, Kew, FO 371/108381: Adams, Khartoum, to Eden, 12 November 1953.

hostility to Egypt. However, it could not authorize any departure from its established policy of assuring the Sudanese of their right to self-determination and uphold their choice of independence if that was indeed their preference.

e) The best advice to be given to the Egyptians was to maintain an attitude of impartiality and to allow the Sudanese to determine their own future without interference. Nothing was more likely to make the Sudanese hostile to Egypt than the policy of pressure and menace in which Cairo is so often inclined to indulge.[11]

---

[11] Ibid., Bromley, Foreign Office, to Murray, Cairo, 29 December 1954.

CHAPTER 7

Cabinet Crisis and the Beginning of the NUP's Disintegration: December 1954

i. Public announcement of the crisis

Ismāʿīl al-Azharī's Government had known no harmony or mutual understanding since its formation on 9 January 1954 and throughout its first year. This internal friction worsened after a reshuffle on 4 May 1954, which tightened the hold of al-Azharī's faction of the Ashiqqāʾ but triggered a crisis in the Cabinet.[1]

In the reshuffle, two Ashiqqāʾ members joined the Cabinet: Muḥammad Aḥmad al-Marḍī as holder of the new Local Government portfolio and Yaḥya al Faḍlī in another new department, the Ministry of Social Affairs. The latter comprised units that had previously been part of the Public Liaison Office, such as radio broadcasting, and the Department of Labour was also added to this Ministry. We shall later see how the al-Azharī Government, through the Labour Department under the direct supervision of Yaḥya al Faḍlī, planned and acted to eradicate any communist influence within the labour movement – and it solicited the advice and help of the British Government in this endeavour. Among others who joined the Cabinet on 4 May were Khidir Ḥamad of the Unionist Party and Aḥmad Jallī of the National Front, i.e. the Khatmīa sect, both as ministers without portfolio.[2]

The Cabinet crisis became public knowledge for the first time on 19 December 1954, when al-Azharī issued a statement in which he

---

[1] Yāsin, *Mudhakkirāt*, pp. 270-1.

[2] Summary of Intelligence Report No. 4 (April-May 1954), in Ṣāliḥ, *British Documents on the Sudan*, vol. 9/1, p. 124.

described how, on his return from Europe on 3 December, he had been informed by Mubārak Zarūq, who had been deputising for him during his absence, that one of the ministers had conveyed to him a message to the effect that the said minister and some of his colleagues were demanding the removal of three members of the Cabinet.[3] If the three were not removed, they and various members of the House of Representatives were in agreement with the Umma Party to bring the Government down and form a joint Cabinet headed by one of the three.

Mubārak Zarūq

al-Azharī made it clear that he took the matter extremely seriously but had put off dealing with it as he was focused on the completion of the Sudanisation process, which he hoped to announce before the end of the year. For this reason, he called an extraordinary Cabinet meeting, at which he stressed this priority, pointing out that 1 January 1955 was the start of a new era under the Compensation of Alien Employees Order. At that same meeting, al-Azharī continued, he had charged Mubārak Zarūq with chairing Cabinet during his absence in

[3] These ministers were understood to be ʿAlī ʿAbd-al-Raḥman, Yaḥya al Faḍlī and Muḥammad Nūr al-Dīn: *al-Ahrām*, 20 December 1954.

Darfur to attend a tribal meeting in Dār al-Rizeiqāt which would commence on 13 December 1954.

Prior to al-Azharī's departure to Darfur, a dispute arose as to who would preside over the Council of Ministers in his absence. al-Azharī named Mubārak Zarūq. Mīrghanī Ḥamza objected and informed al-Azharī by a written message that he would boycott the Cabinet during his absence. Khalafallah Khālid joined in. Both Ministers belong to the Khatmīa sect.

Mīrghanī Ḥamza claimed in his message that during al-Azharī's absence in Darfur the Cabinet meetings would not be conducted properly, for there would arise a situation which he could not reconcile with his dignity and self-respect.

On his part al-Azharī regretted the boycott of the two Ministers. He claimed that its effect was disruptive to the meetings of the Council of Ministers and obstructive to the extremely serious work of liberation of the country and its capacity for self-determination.

It is worth noting that the third Khatmi Minister in the Cabinet Aḥmad Jallī accompanied al-Azharī in his visit to Darfur.

ii. The three Ministers' reply to al-Azharī

The three Khatmi Ministers Ḥamza, Khālid and Jallī issued a joint statement in the newspaper *Ṣawt al-Sūdān* on 20 December 1954, in which they contended that, had al-Azharī been consistent and if the absence of a minister or two could bring such calamities down upon the country, the Prime Minister would not have permitted himself to cruise off to London on a courtesy visit, accompanied by two members of his Cabinet. Indeed, he had spent several weeks after that dawdling around Europe before returning to Sudan to find this apparently grievous state of affairs – only to head off once more to attend a tribal parade, accompanied by two Ministers, one of whom was accused of being implicated in a serious plot to topple the Government. [4]

The three Ministers' statement described the situation as more 'deep-rooted and serious' than the Prime Minister would like people to

---

[4] National Archives, Kew, FO 371/108326: Adams, UK Trade Commissioner, Khartoum, to Foreign Office, 20 December 1954. See also *al-Ahrām*, 20 December 1954.

believe. They added that work in the Cabinet was run on a two-tier system: an inner ring composed of the Prime Minister and four or five members of his clique who alone dealt with serious political assignments – and an outer circle comprised of the remaining members of the Cabinet who were left to handle the day-to-day administrative routine. That inner circle made decisions and undertook actions that had a far-reaching impact on Sudan's very existence, its future and its interests, in a climate of secrecy where hidden motives and covert external influences surrounded every such decision and action. These were implemented either under the authority of al-Azharī or any of his coterie, who rarely bothered to inform their Cabinet colleagues of the outcome, let alone solicit a collective decision. The statement cited numerous examples:

a) Secret meetings and discussions about Sudan's future relations with Egypt, as well as the status of talks over Nile waters. These issues were the root of the crisis, because the 'inner circle' had held meetings with Ṣalāḥ Sālim during his recent visit to Sudan – and the Egyptian officer had told Mīrghanī Ḥamza that it was al-Azharī who had categorically rejected the involvement of the remaining ministers in those discussions.
b) The visit to Britain had not been put before the Cabinet so that the appropriate minister could be chosen to accompany the Prime Minister. It was the inner circle that chose the delegation. No report on the trip was submitted to Cabinet – and, while the Prime Minister had claimed that the visit was merely a courtesy call, reports in the British press revealed that he and his delegation had discussed serious matters with far-reaching consequences for Sudan.
c) Two ministers had travelled to Mecca on the pretext of performing the ʿUmra; instead, they had a prearranged meeting with Ṣalāḥ Sālim and for two successive nights discussed with him Sudan's affairs and future. The outer circle was left in the dark over those discussions.[5]
d) The words and deeds of the Prime Minister and his cronies exhibited a clear partisan bias. Whenever al-Azharī deputised ʿAlī

[5] British documents revealed that the two were ʿAlī ʿAbd-al-Raḥman and Yaḥya al Faḍlī: ibid.

ʿAbd-al-Raḥman to speak on his behalf, his proxy used all his speeches to glorify the Ashiqqāʾ faction, attributing every patriotic measure to them. Even when the Prime Minister's attention was drawn to this contradiction in the Party's political line, ʿAbd-al-Raḥman continued to emphasise the patriotic acts of the Ashiqqāʾ in every speech he made – even prevented the crowds from slogans in praise of anyone but the Prime Minister, the saviour of the nation.

In the final paragraph of their statement, the three Ministers denied that they had colluded with the Umma Party to topple the Government – or that they had even communicated with the Umma over the crisis or on any other topic. All the aforementioned, they asserted, would not deter them from their nationalist duty of remaining clear and frank in specifying the relation between Egypt and Sudan, a relation which had always been and remained free from deceit or concealment, both before and since the elections. For them, the ideal relationship with Egypt would be one that maintained the fundamentals of Sudanese freedom, entity, policy and international identity. It would be based on complete freedom for both peoples to pursue their common interests without one country exerting influence or control over the other.[6]

al-Azharī refrained from replying directly to the specific points raised in the statement. But in an interview with the Editor-in-Chief of *al-Ayyām*, he said that the disagreement with the three Ministers had nothing to do with principles: it was all about personalities, questions about regulations and the conduct of affairs within the Cabinet. al-Azharī said that no disagreement could arise in Cabinet over goals, as goals and principles were purely partisan questions that had nothing to do with the Cabinet – nor were they part of the Government's remit. No minister had ever sought to discuss this matter in open Cabinet. The Prime Minister added that, generally speaking, the goal of the NUP was unity, although members differed over the type of union or the relationship between Egypt and Sudan. Some might want it to be a strong union while others might prefer it to take a different form.[7]

---

[6] *al-Ahrām*, 21 December 1954. See also National Archives, Kew, FO 371/113581: Governor-General's Office, Khartoum, to Foreign Office, 1 January 1955.
[7] *al- Ayyām*, 26 December 1954.

iii. Sacking the three Ministers

Three ministers – Amīn al-Sayyid, Ḥammād Ṭawfīq and Khidir Ḥamad – tried to mend the rift but, despite the great efforts they put in, their work was in vain.[8] William Luce wrote later that there was evidence that al-Azharī had telephoned Ṣalāḥ Sālim following the failure of mediation to ask him what to do and that the latter had advised him to do with Sayyid ʿAlī al-Mīrghanī what they had done with Muḥammad Nagīb: present him with a *fait accompli*, i.e. get rid of the Khatmīa ministers and appoint new ministers who were loyal to him.[9] It is worth mentioning that Sayyid ʿAlī was in Alexandria recuperating from illness. He returned to Sudan by sea on 27 December 1954 – 4 days after the announcement that the three ministers had been sacked – on board the Egyptian presidential yacht *al-Maḥrūsa*.[10] There to welcome him home in Port Sudan were al-Azharī himself, no fewer than eight of his ministers, as well were Mīrghanī Ḥamza, Khalafallah Khālid and Aḥmad Jallī.[11]

As a result of the sacking of the three ministers, a new team was required and a reshuffle was carried out: ʿAlī ʿAbd-al-Raḥman was given Education, Khidir Ḥamad took over Irrigation, while al-Azharī himself took on the Ministry of Defence in addition to the Interior portfolio. Two new departments were created: the Ministry of Supply, headed by Santino Deng Teng, and the Ministry of Mechanical Transport taken by Dak Dei.[12] Muddathir al-Būshī joined the Cabinet as Minister of Justice, Ḥassan ʿAwaḍallah Muṣtafa as Minister of Agriculture and Ibrahim Hasan al-Maḥalāwī as Minister of Mineral Resources.[13]

---

[8] National Archives, Kew, FO 371/108328: Adams to Foreign Office, 22 December 1954.

[9] Ibid., FO 371/113581: Luce to Lampen, Sudan Agent, London, 28 December 1954; also FO 371/108326: Governor-General's Office to FO, 27 December 1854.

[10] *al-Maḥrūsa* was commissioned by the Khedive Ismāʿīl in 1863 and remains in service today. She was renamed al-*Ḥurrīyya* from 1952-2000.

[11] National Archives, Kew, FO 371/108326: Howe, Khartoum, to FO, 22 December 1854; also FO 371/113581: Luce to Lampen, Sudan Agent, London, 28 December 1954.

[12] Daly, *Imperial Sudan*, p. 384.

[13] National Archives, Kew, FO 371/108326: Sudan Agent, London, to African Department, Foreign Office, 28 December 1954.

iv. British analysis of the crisis

According to Luce, despite the assertions of al-Azharī and Mubārak Zarūq that the cause of the crisis had been Mīrghanī Ḥamza's objection to Zarūq deputising for al-Azharī in his absence when he aspired to play that part himself, the real reasons went much deeper. Here Luce referred to the old rivalry between the Khatmīa and the Ashiqqā', which manifested itself in the animosity of Mīrghanī Ḥamza and Khalafallah Khālid towards Yaḥya al Faḍlī, who together with his two colleagues, 'Alī 'Abd-al-Raḥman and Muḥammad Aḥmad al-Marḍī, were enjoying a growing influence over al-Azharī. Furthermore, the two sides disagreed over the future of relations with Egypt, the escalation of Egyptian anger at Khatmīa leaders for their blunt call for independence and the firm stance of Mīrghanī Ḥamza in respect of Nile waters. But the straw that broke the camel's back, Luce believed, was al-Azharī's choice of companions on his visit to England.[14]

Luce was not, however, the only British official with a view on the subject. Philip Adams, the British Trade Commissioner in Khartoum, observed that – even though the crisis reflected the position of the different party factions and the view of the Khatmīa leadership over relations with Egypt – there were many aspects of the crisis that were personal. Adams quoted al-Azharī as putting it like this: Mīrghanī Ḥamza was a capable and respected figure in his late fifties, who resented not only being excluded from the inner circle of the Cabinet but also having to watch the preferment of the 33-year-old Mubārak Zarūq as Deputy Prime Minister.[15]

v. Consequences of the crisis

The immediate result of the crisis in Cabinet was that the three ex-ministers and several of their supporters left the NUP and formed the Independence Republican Party, under the leadership of Mīrghanī Ḥamza. The Party's aims and principles stipulated that it would cooperate and liaise with Egypt over joint issues such as the Nile waters, as well as

---

[14] Ibid., FO 371/113581: Luce to Lampen, Sudan Agent, London, 28 December 1954.

[15] Ibid., Adams to Eden, 31 December 1954.

economic and cultural matters, in a way that would secure total sovereignty for both countries.[16]

Sayyid ʿAlī al-Mīrghanī issued no expression of support, direct or implicit, for the new party. None of the bloc formerly known as Khatmīa MPs – who had demanded in writing that al-Azharī should declare his view on Sudan's self-determination and future relations with Egypt, following the ouster of President Nagīb and the crackdown on the Muslim Brotherhood – joined the new party.[17]

The second important outcome of the crisis was the creation by al-Azharī – who needed to secure the support of as many NUP deputies as possible and so shore up his own Government – of 17 new parliamentary under-secretary positions, each commanding an annual salary of 12,000 pounds and other perks.[18] With the exception of Senator Bashīr ʿAbd-al-Raḥīm, who was appointed Parliamentary Under-Secretary for the Ministry of Irrigation, all the new appointees were members of the House of Representatives.[19] The opposition criticized these appointments, describing them as 'bribery' and a despicable act on the part of the Government.[20] A memorandum sent to the Prime Minister and members of the Cabinet by the Front Against Colonialization stated that resolution of the crisis "would not be achieved by covering it up through winning MPs over by employing them in the executive, by spoiling them financially or by sacking ministers and appointing new ones."[21]

---

[16] Ibid., BBC Monitoring, 7 January 1955.

[17] Khidir Ḥamad, *Mudhakkirāt: al-Ḥaraka al-Waṭanīa al-Sūdānīa: al-Istiqlāl wa mā Baʿduhu* (*Memoirs: The Sudanese Nationalist Movement: Independence and Beyond*) (Khartoum: East and West Publishers, 1980), pp. 190-1. Muḥammad Nagīb was forced by Gamāl ʿAbd-al-Nāṣir to resign as President of Egypt on 14 November 1954.

[18] National Archives, Kew, FO 371/113581: Luce to Lampen, 29 December 1954, and Adams to Eden, 31 December 1954.

[19] Ibid., Extract from Sudanese Press Agency, December 1954. See Appendix 2 for a full list of the new appointees.

[20] Amīn al-Tūm, *Dhikrayāt wa Mawāqif 1914-1969* (*Memories and Situations 1914-1969*) (Khartoum: Sudanese House of Books, 2004), p. 140.

[21] Muḥammad Suleimān, *al-Yasār al-Sūdānī fī ʿAsharat Aʿwām 1954-1963* (*A Decade in the Sudanese Left 1954-1963*) (Wad Medani: al-Fajr Library, 1967), p. 124.

The third result of the crisis was that al-Azharī was forced to explain his own view on the principles of union with Egypt. This he did in a statement made to *al-Ayyām* newspaper on 25 December 1954, published the following day in a special supplement. This statement will be examined in greater detail in the next chapter.

CHAPTER 8

The NUP Renounces the Principle of Unity with Egypt

In Chapter 1, we discussed how the Constitution of the NUP provided for the foundation of a democratic Sudanese Government in union with Egypt – with the precise basis of that union to be decided after self-determination. At that point, the NUP formulated no precise vision of the form or nature of this union, with options ranging from total merger to a loose confederation. One faction of the NUP, in fact, considered the slogan of 'Union with Egypt' merely as a tool to get rid of British rule.

After Ismāʿīl al-Azharī took over as Prime Minister, he and his ministers were bombarded with questions about the nature of the bond with Egypt following self-determination. The press, particularly *al-Ayyām*, mounted a campaign to force al-Azharī's Government to declare its position. But al-Azharī declined to declare any precise interpretation of the principle of union with Egypt in case it triggered conflict among the various trends and factions within his Party. It is possible that he thought it was not yet time to turn his back on his Egyptian allies – because, as would be seen later, total independence was indeed al-Azharī's goal. He had confided as much to William Luce, adviser to the Governor-General, when they met on 16 February 1954.

So al-Azharī suffered immense embarrassment when, on 9 January 1954, the Egyptian newspaper *Akhbār al-Yūm* published a statement by him to the effect that Sudan would inevitably unite with Egypt and that he was not the type of person who would change his principles.[1] Pro-independence papers in Sudan re-published the statement in full. In an editorial, *al-Ayyām* commented that al-Azharī's statement was inconsistent with the Statute on self-determination that provided for a transitional 'liquidation period' – during which Sudan would be free from any foreign influence so that it would conduct the self-determination process in a climate of complete freedom and neutrality. *al-Ayyām* reiterated its call for al-Azharī to specify what he meant by union with Egypt.

It is interesting to note that al-Azharī justified his statement by inventing a distinction between his roles of NUP Chairman and Prime Minister. He said that, during an ordinary conversation with *Akhbār al-Yūm*, a rumour was mentioned in passing to the effect that the NUP had abandoned union with Egypt. He had, he said, denied the rumour in his capacity as NUP Chairman – because the Party's declared goal was a bond with Egypt in the form of a union – but not in his capacity as Prime Minister. Nor had he made any statement that his Government was inclined towards implementing the goals of the Party. al-Azharī further stated that the obligations of his Government were clearly defined in the 1953 Agreement as Sudanisation, evacuation and preparing the free neutral climate for the election of a Constituent Assembly for self-determination. As such, the policy of his Government would be a national policy of liberation, not of self-determination.[2]

al-Azharī took refuge in the same distinction in his reply to a question in Parliament from Buth Diu on 18 January 1954 about how he would reconcile his Party's call for unity with Egypt with his responsibility to prepare a free neutral climate. At first, the Prime Minister refused to reply, on the basis that posing the question in that manner was against parliamentary procedures and regulations. He insisted on his refusal to reply. After much argument, however, Speaker Bābikr ʿAwaḍallah ordered al-Azharī to answer the question. In response, al-Azharī repeated that he chaired the NUP, which worked towards effecting a form of union with Egypt, and at the same time headed the Government, which worked

[1] National Archives, Kew, FO 371/108320: Chancery of the Office of the UK Trade Commissioner to Foreign Office, 16 January 1954.

[2] Ibid., Chancery of the Office of the UK Trade Commissioner to Foreign Office, 23 January 1954.

on a national measure to implement the 1953 Agreement and had absolutely no relation with self-determination.[3]

i. al-Azharī informs Luce of his ambitions for independence

On 16 February 1954, al-Azharī met Luce and his assistant, John Kenrick.[4] The meeting covered many topics, including relations with Egypt. Luce said that it was the wish of every British official that the Sudanese should govern themselves – and any fears felt by the British were due solely to the feeling that, after their departure, Sudan might fall prey to Egyptian domination. When al-Azharī asked him to define domination in that context, Luce replied that he meant not physical possession but economic domination. While much had been said about ties of common religion, language and ethnicity, these factors would count for nothing when it came to economic competition between the two countries. Egypt was the stronger: if she were to dominate Sudan, Sudan's interests would be submerged.

al-Azharī welcomed the opportunity to tell Luce his feelings on these matters. No-one in his senses, he said, who had thrown off one master would put himself under a new one. Most people in the country, he added, had felt for some time that it would be easier and more practical to ally themselves temporarily with Egypt to get rid of the British – but that did not mean that they wished to subordinate themselves to the Egyptians. The old idea of unity, al-Azharī assured Luce, was dead as a political force. Every day that a Sudanese Government ran the country – particularly after the withdrawal of the British – would add to the certainty that Egyptian aims of domination were doomed. The Prime Minister asserted that his aims were simple: full independence for Sudan and a close friendship with Egypt. Then, after the withdrawal of the British, which he hoped would take place with dignity, leaving behind a

---

[3] Chancery of the Office of the UK Trade Commissioner to Foreign Office, Bimonthly Report No.21 (17-30 January 1954), 29 January 1954, in Ṣālih, *British Documents on the Sudan*, vol. 9/1, p. 35. See also *al-Ayyām*, 19 January 1954, and *al-Rāyī al-ʿAm*, 19 January 1954.

[4] John Kenrick had served in Sudan since 1936 in Equatoria and Kordofan. Before his appointment as Assistant Advisor on Constitutional and External Affairs to the Governor-General, he had been District Commissioner for Omdurman: Sudan Archive, University of Durham (John Wynn Kenrick Papers), SAD.815/4/1-22.

fund of goodwill with the Sudanese whom they had served so long, the time would come to enter into a friendly and useful relationship with Great Britain.[5]

Sayyid ʿAlī al-Mīrghanī

al-Azharī's views on the relationship between Egypt and Sudan were strikingly similar to those expressed by Sayyid ʿAlī al-Mīrghanī to Kenrick six months earlier. It had been one of the rare instances when Sayyid ʿAlī spoke directly about a political matter. He told Kenrick in August 1953 that the old slogans of unity and of 'one crown' were dead: the Sudanese nation desired independence and they would get it. When asked by Kenrick whether they favoured some form of federation with Egypt, Sayyid ʿAlī said all that was a thing of the past. Everyone wanted an independent Sudan and, once independence had been achieved,

[5] National Archives, Kew, FO 371/108344 (Minutes of conversations of various senior Sudanese Ministers with UK Trade Commissions, Khartoum and with Minister of State for Foreign Affairs, Selwyn Lloyd, during his visit to Khartoum): Record of Conversation with Azhari on 16 February 1954, 18 February 1954.

Sudan would enter into relations with other countries; doubtless those arranged with Egypt would be close.[6]

Following another meeting on 23 May 1954, Kenrick reported that Sayyid ʿAlī had told him repeatedly and in different ways that the British should have "no fear at all" that Sudan would forge a union with Egypt in any tangible way. There would be friendship and cooperation but on the basis of each country's independence. People might talk, Sayyid ʿAlī said, about federation, a merger of armed forces or a joint Foreign Ministry – but this was all nonsense, merely empty talk. Those who indulged in it were blind to see the essential truth that the Sudanese desired self-government in every aspect and they would reject any form of subjugation.[7]

ii. al-Azharī uses the word 'independence' in public for the first time: November 1954

During his visit to Britain in November 1954, al-Azharī held public meetings with Sudanese nationals who were studying in the UK. During these meetings, in London and Oxford, al-Azharī observed a sweeping enthusiasm for complete independence as an option for Sudan. At a reception held for him by the Federation of Sudanese Students in the UK at Sudan House on 15 November 1954, al-Azharī said that public opinion in Sudan was now more inclined towards independence than ever before. He added that the claim alleging that the call for independence was 'inauthentic' was a dying claim. The NUP had not yet decided its political programme – but it would not be able to ignore the prevailing sentiment in Sudanese public opinion and impose any form of unity or union that might deprive the Sudan people of their right to sovereignty and independence. Any type of independence decided by the NUP, he went on to say, had to come with firm guarantees for the maintenance of Sudan's independent identity, sovereignty and enhancement of its international status. As for union with Egypt, it should be a relationship

---

[6] Ibid., FO 371/102711 (The Mixed Electoral Commission and the General Elections in Sudan): Record of Conversation with Sayyid Ali, 3 August 1953.
[7] Ibid., FO 371/108328: Kenrick to Bromley, 25 May 1954.

akin to that between fellow Arab countries. For *al-Ayyām*, this was the first time al-Azharī had deliberately uttered the word 'independence'.[8]

iii. al-Azharī's personal view on relations with Egypt

On 25 December 1954, al-Azharī invited the Editor-in-Chief of *al-Ayyām*, Bashīr Muḥammad Sa'īd, to meet him at his home. During their conversation, the journalist asked al-Azharī for his personal opinion on union with Egypt. al-Azharī's reply was as follows:

a) Sudan had to be a republic, like Egypt, with its own president, cabinet and parliament;
b) Any future union between Egypt and Sudan should feature a Supreme Assembly composed of both cabinets, who would meet at least once a year to discuss matters of mutual interest, including defence, foreign policy and the Nile waters;
c) Any decision made by this Supreme Assembly would be put to Parliament for approval, veto or amendment.

al-Azharī added that he would present this personal viewpoint to his Party executive, who would discuss it, alongside other opinions, and approve, veto or amend accordingly. The decision of the executive would then be put before the Party's General Committee and the Parliamentary Party for approval.[9]

It was obviously no coincidence that this declaration of al-Azharī's personal opinion came two days after the sacking of the three National Front ministers, Mīrghanī Ḥamza, Aḥmad Jallī and Khalafallah Khālid. Indeed, Mubārak Zarūq told Luce that the Cabinet crisis had forced al-Azharī to make such a declaration about future relations with Egypt, when the Prime Minister realised that he had to make an announcement

---

[8] *al-Ayyām*, 16 November 1954.

[9] Ibid., 26 December 1954. See also National Archives, Kew, FO 371/108326: Khartoum to Foreign Office, 27 December 1954.

that would reassure Sudanese public opinion that he and the Ashiqqāʾ were not committed to forging a close bond with Egypt.[10]

Commenting on al-Azharī's personal opinion, Luce thought that the Prime Minister was trying as far as possible to satisfy both parties but without committing himself to anything. His choice of the Editor-in-Chief of *al-Ayyām* – as well as publication in a special supplement – was, for Luce, a clever move. Bashīr Muḥammad Saʿīd was one of the best journalists in the country, known for his vocal support for independence. Luce also noted that al-Azharī's actual actions were inconsistent with the general trend among Sudanese towards independence and distance from Egypt. While the opinion that he had just declared might temporarily allay the fears of the enlightened public, this effect will soon wear off if his Government followed a pro-Egyptian policy.

Luce noted that the Nile waters would be the important test. Would the Sudanese Government stand firm on the Sudan rights to a fair share or would they capitulate to the Egyptians? According to Luce, the latter would expose them to a violent attack by the Sudanese. While the former would displease their Egyptian friends.[11]

iv. Reactions to al-Azharī's personal view

The Umma Party decisively rejected al-Azharī's position because it was a unionist and not a pro-independence opinion. It deprived Sudan of all the fundamentals of absolute independence. As the Party said in a public statement: "The independence we know needs no terms and conditions. If our foreign affairs and our defence tools are the subject of consultations with foreign countries, what is left for us when we lose control over the army and lose our foreign entity and identity?"[12]

In a statement published on 26 January 1955, the University College Students' Union – then under the charge of a committee composed mostly of independent and Muslim Brotherhood students –

---

[10] National Archives, Kew, FO 371/108326: Governor-General's Office to Foreign Office, 28 December 1954.
[11] Ibid., FO 371/113581: Luce to Lampen, 29 December 1954, enclosed in Lampen to Foreign Office, 4 January 1955.
[12] *al-Rāyī al-ʿAm*, 27 December 1954.

also rejected al-Azharī's personal opinion.[13] The Union argued that the idea of a union with Egypt called for by the NUP leadership betrayed the desire of the Sudanese people for liberty and total independence. When voters had bestowed their trust on pro-union candidates in the general elections and since, they did so not out of a desire to be in a union with Egypt but because the advocates of this opinion represented the anti-British colonials and their allies. So how dare they claim that the NUP's electoral victory had been a victory for the idea of union with Egypt? Such a claim was a grave error.

Bashīr Muḥammad Sa'īd

The Union's statement dismissed al-Azharī's personal opinion as a distortion of the people's genuine desire for total independence, free from any bonds with Egypt which would undermine Sudanese sovereignty. The opinion had been forced by the sweeping pro-independence tide and as such it was no more than a glossy version of union with Egypt. The statement considered any linkage of Sudan's foreign, defence and trade policies with Egypt as exposing Sudanese

---

[13] The Secretary-General of the Union was Mūsa 'Awaḍ Bilāl. The Committee's membership included 'Uthmān Sid Aḥmad (Chairman), al-Ṭāhir Faḍl, 'Awaḍ Muḥammad 'Abdallah, 'Umar Muṣtafa al-Makkī, Mūsa al-Mubārak, 'Abd-al-Shakūr 'Umar 'Aṭiyya, 'Amir Ḥassan, 'Umar Muḥammad Sa'īd and al-Kheir Muṣtafa: *al-Rāyī al-'Am*, 16 November 1954.

sovereignty to certain extinction – especially if links were established with reactionary governments like the dictatorial regime currently governing Egypt. The generals, after all, had opted to side with the colonial powers by signing the Suez Canal Base Agreement[14] with the British and the Point Four Program with the Americans[15] – and were even now poised to conclude a new defence agreement that would cripple the Egyptian people and add to their chains.

In sum, the Students' Union called for Sudan's total independence – unarguably the nation's natural future – whatever the nature of Egypt's political regime. The Students' Union criticized NUP leaders for appeasing the military dictatorship in Cairo instead of having complete confidence in the Sudanese people and their call for independence. The Union stressed that it was time for a national charter, based on the following principles:

a) Total and unconditional independence;
b) Avoiding military pacts and alliances;
c) Refusing any external aid that undermines Sudanese sovereignty;
d) Securing fundamental public freedoms so that the people could decide freely on self-determination.[16]

We shall see in Chapter 9 that in January 1955, the Parties of Umma, the Republican, Anti-Colonial and Republican Socialists and the Front Against Colonialization met and on the basis of these principles formed the Independence Front.

---

[14] This 1954 agreement provided for the establishment of a series of British military installations and support facilities along the Suez Canal: C.B. Selak, 'The Suez Canal Base Agreement of 1954', *American Journal of International Law* 49/4 (1955), pp. 487-505.
[15] See Chapter 1, Note 55.
[16] *al-Ayyām*, 26 January 1955.

v. NUP Parliamentary Party aligned with independence

On 31 March 1955, the Secretary of the NUP Parliamentary Party issued an official statement which embodied decisions taken by the Group:

1. A unanimous decision that the main feature of the political future of the Sudan should be the independence and complete sovereignty.
2. That relations between the independent and fully sovereign Sudan and Egypt should be defined in a way which would neither prejudice nor cut through Sudan's sovereignty and identity.
3. That the relations should be defined immediately so that people might be aware when they exercised the right to self-determination of the relation which would take place between them and the others and so that the people might not be misled, deceived or taken by surprise before they gave their views.
4. A unanimous decision that the statement made by al-Azharī in his personal capacity would be a good basis for its decision because that statement called in essence for a fully sovereign republic with its own president, government and parliament, with all other makings of independence.

The Parliamentary Party then decided to appoint a select committee to consider the suggestions of al-Azharī regarding the relations between the Sudan and Egypt. The committee consisted of 5 NUP members of Parliament and 5 NUP Cabinet Ministers, hence the name Committee of the Ten.

The outcome of the work of the Committee of the Ten was eventually submitted to the Executive Committee of the NUP. The Parliamentary Party expected that the Executive Committee would give a special consideration for the decision of the Group because it was unanimous and represented an expression of the views of the various parts of the country.[17]

---

[17] Ibid., 1 April 1955. See also National Archives, Kew, FO 371/113609 (Political relations between UK, Egypt and Sudan): Enclosure in Adams to Foreign Office, 1 April 1955.

vi. The Independence Front welcomes the recommendations of the Committee of the Ten

Newspapers of 8 April 1955 carried a statement from the Independence Front welcoming the decision of NUP Parliamentary Group of setting up a completely independent and fully sovereign Sudanese republic. The Front noted that the gap between the two fronts had been narrowed and that the next step should be that the Sudanese political parties should agree to conclude a national charter to secure complete independence and full sovereignty for the Sudan.

The last part of the Front's statement called for avoidance of the self-determination process and to work through Parliament to eliminate self-determination and declare the Sudan completely independent. Evidently that meant to dispense with Articles 10, 11 and 12 of the 1953 Agreement.[18]

vii. NUP Executive Committee adopts interpretation for the principle of union with Egypt

The Executive Committee on 8 and 9 April 1955, and on the basis of the recommendations of the Committee of the Ten, issued the following decisions on the interpretation of the principle of union with Egypt:

> The setting up of an independent and fully sovereign Sudanese Republic and the co-ordination of common relations with Egypt as follows:
>
> a) Defence. An Advisory Council to be formed of an equal number of representatives of the two parties to exchange views on defence matters when circumstances so demand.
>
> b) Foreign Policy. Our policy aims, in the handling of foreign affairs, at understanding and cooperation with the Arab League countries, or any other country or organization with which we have links or particular interests, provided always that the Sudan's interest is sought and without any permanent

[18] National Archives, Kew, FO 371/113609, Khartoum to Foreign Office, see also: *al-Ayyām*, 8 April 1955.

commitments to a particular situation which may not accord with that interest.

c) Economic interests between the Sudan and Egypt have much in common and it is necessary that there should be understanding on these interests. But owing to their varying nature, we recommend that it be left to the new Government to lay down, through its experts, the plans for cooperation.

d) Culture. The committee recommends exclusion of this question at the present time, since cultural relations are not subject to definite rules, and leaving it to future Government to decide it according to Sudanese requirements.

e) Nile Waters. As the Nile is the main source of life for the two countries, connects Egypt with the Sudan and also runs through many countries, questions relating to the Nile Waters should be determined through co-ordination of relations and through official treaties between the two Governments."[19]

Thomas Bromley of the Foreign Office said that "the main feature of the statement is that Union with Egypt now means co-operation between equal partners on subjects of vital mutual interest with nothing more specific than an advisory council on defence and treaties on Nile waters." [20]

Philip Adams, the UK Trade Commissioner in Khartoum, conveyed the latest developments in the ranks of the NUP to the new Foreign Secretary in Eden's Government, Harold Macmillan, noting that it was evident during the second half of 1954 that the leaders of the NUP "could not ignore the tide of public opinion running ever more strongly in favour of independence and sovereignty for the Sudan. But it was difficult for them to turn their backs upon their Egyptian friends, who had given them moral and financial support for many years before they came to power."

Adams also noted that "As the British rule was withdrawn, the development of pro-independence sentiments grew within the NUP, and

---

[19] National Archives, Kew, FO 371/113609. See also *al-Ayyām*, 7 April 1955.

[20] National Archives, Kew,FO 371/113610 (Political relations between UK, Egypt and Sudan): Note on 'National Unionist Party Policy' by Bromley, 12 April 1955.

this growth was accelerated by Egypt's heavy-handed attempts to control Sudanese affairs."[21]

Meanwhile the NUP's decisions to change course towards full independence gave Major Ṣalāḥ Sālim, the Egyptian Minister for Sudanese Affairs, a severe shock. He had neither expected it nor made any preparations for it – so he did his best to undermine the position of Ismāʿīl al-Azharī and to boost instead the profile of his deputy, Muḥammad Nūr al-Dīn. To that end he used two tactics. The first was simple bribery, aimed at creating splits in the NUP, as well as inciting Southerners to foster separatist tendencies among them. His second weapon was propaganda: devoting Egyptian press coverage and radio broadcasts – especially Radio Cairo's Sudan Service which claimed that the reversion of al-Azharī to a pro-independence policy was British-inspired. He was called derogatory names of the kind customarily used by the Egyptian media to abuse anyone who advocated Sudan's independence.

viii. Some Southerners call for a constitutional link with Egypt

In the first week of April 1955, the NUP's Southern MPs, including Bullen Alier, Minister of Animal Resources, issued a statement wherein they expressed their disappointment in their government colleagues, for the following reasons:

a) Despite their strenuous efforts to bring pressure on the Government, not a single Southern civil servant had benefitted from Sudanisation;
b) The Prime Minister and his colleagues had deliberately given priority to economic development in the North, and refrained from economic development in the South, leaving it at the mercy of the owners of private agricultural schemes;
c) The political views of Southerners had deliberately not been taken into consideration and eventually were ignored altogether;

[21] Ibid., Adams to Macmillan, 15 April 1955.

d) Because of the above, the NUP's Southern parliamentarians were demanding federation between North and South and that this federation should be declared as future policy for Sudan;
e) Finally, a bond with Egypt was much better than the continuation of the *status quo*.[22]

In the second week of April 1955, eleven of the members of the Southern Liberal Party, who were also members of Parliament (MPs), submitted a letter to Ismāʿīl al-Azharī wherein they stated the following:

(a) The Northern Sudan had already received its share of economic, cultural and social development thanks to the Egyptian aid, which provided directly the larger part of it;
(b) We are prepared to support the Government if it devised a decisive economic and cultural programme;
(c) When the NUP set up plans for Sudan's future as an 'indivisible whole', such plans should include within the bonds that tie up the Sudan to Egypt, a stipulation that would guarantee the development of the three Southern Provinces;
(d) They would not rest assured that this stipulation existed unless it was provided for in a special instrument regarding the common interests of Egypt and the Sudan.

On the basis of the aforementioned, the members of the Liberal Party who signed the Letter declared that they did not accept the decisions of the Committee of the Ten on 6 April 1955, because they do not bind the two countries to ensure their interests. They expressed hope that the NUP would revise those decisions.

Among those who signed the Letter were Buth Diu (MP for Wadi al-Zaraf), Joshua Malwal (MP for Western Nuer), Elia Kuze(MP for Zandi East), Muḥammad Nigumi (MP for River Jur South), Lino Tombe Laco (MP for Juba) and Edward Adoc (MP for Shilluk).

We have mentioned in Chapter 5 that the Second Juba Conference held in October 1954 in which all Liberal Party members took

[22] Ibid., Khartoum to Foreign Office, 5 April 1955.

part, chose independence for the Sudan and no delegate voted for Union with Egypt. [23]

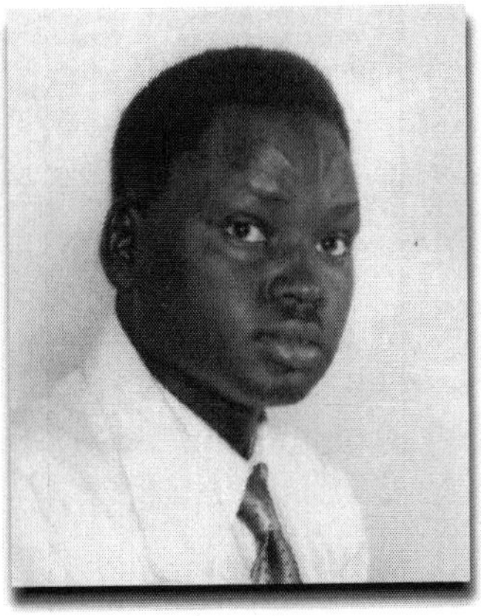

Bullen Alier

ix. Zulfiqār defines 'true independence' for the Sudanese

About a month after the NUP's decision to change course towards full independence, Ḥussein Ẓulfiqār Ṣabrī, Egypt's representative on the Governor-General's Commission, issued a statement wherein he defined three possible types of independence open to the Sudan in the world conditions of today:

a) 'Isolated independence', exposed to the ambitions of the various colonial powers;
b) 'Separatist independence', protected by foreign influence in the form of alliances or of economic or administrative controls;
c) 'True independence', safeguarded by a constitutional link with Egypt.[24]

---

[23] *al-Ahrām*, 14 April 1955.
[24] National Archives, Kew, UK Trade Commissioner, Khartoum, to Foreign Office, FO 371/113610, 31 May 1955.

al-Ayyām newspaper asked Ẓulfiqār what type of independence Egypt herself enjoyed, since she had no constitutional link with anybody. And where is the Egyptian Constitution which is to be linked to that of the Sudan? [25]

x. Britain strongly protests against Ẓulfiqār's statement

The Egyptian Ambassador in London was summoned on 6 June 1955 to the Foreign Office, where he was received by the Minister of State, Anthony Nutting. Minister Nutting told the Ambassador that Ẓulfiqār's statement could not be reconciled with the provision of the 1953 Agreement, which stipulated that the Sudanese should have a free choice between independence and a link with Egypt. But Ẓulfiqār's statement was clearly designed to influence Sudanese opinion towards choosing a link with Egypt. As such it was a breach of the 1953 Agreement which provided that the choice of the Sudanese must be made in a free and neutral atmosphere.

Nutting further told the Egyptian Ambassador that the British Government had observed the letter and spirit of the 1953 Agreement and it expected the Egyptian Government to do likewise. But instead of that the Egyptian Government persisted in a policy of interference and bribery.[26]

xi. Muḥammad Nūr al-Dīn and Bullen Alier lose their jobs

On 20 June 1955, al-Azharī issued a statement to the effect that, while he was abroad attending the Bandung Conference,[27] 'certain acts' had been perpetrated by his Minister of Works, Muḥammad Nūr al-Dīn, and Minister of Animal Resources, Bullen Alier, which al-Azharī considered to have been 'mistakes' in relation to their official ministerial duties. When the Prime Minister had spoken separately to both colleagues about their conduct, the statement continued, their replies

[25] National Archives, Kew, FO 371/113582: Khartoum to Foreign Office, 31 May 1955.

[26] National Archives, Kew, FO 371/113611, Minute by Nutting, 6 June 1955.

[27] A meeting of African and Asian nations, many of them either newly independent or expecting to become so in the near future, convened in Indonesia from 18-24 April 1955.

had not been satisfactory. As a result, he had asked the Governor-General to relieve them of their portfolios under Article 18/2 (d) of the Self-Government Statute.[28]

While al-Azharī may have justified his decision to fire his colleagues by blaming it on their shortcomings in terms of ministerial performance, both circumstances and timing support the view that the decision was taken for purely political reasons. Nūr al-Dīn, the Vice-President of the NUP, was the main tool of Egyptian activities in Sudan. Alier had incited the NUP's Southern parliamentarians to rebel against the Party's decisions in respect of the interpretation of the principle of 'union with Egypt'.

xii. Nūr al-Dīn supports a 'connective' independence

Muḥammad Nūr al-Dīn seemed to have been influenced by Ẓulfiqār's classification of the three types of independence. He devised a distinction between a 'connective independence' which he embraced and a 'separative independence' which he refused and accused al-Azharī of conspiring to adopt as NUP policy against the wishes of the majority of the General Assembly of the Party which support a link with Egypt.

Nūr al-Dīn challenged the validity of the pro-independence decisions adopted by the Parliamentary Group and the Executive Committee. The competent organ of the NUP to decide on such matters, he argued, was the General Assembly of the Party.[29]

---

[28] National Archives, Kew, FO 371/113582: News Telegrams Nos. 1301 and 1302 from Davies, Sudan Agent, to London, 20 June 1955. See also *al-Ahrām*, 20 June 1955.
[29] *al-Ahrām*, 5 and 11 July 1955.

Muḥammad Nūr al-Dīn

Luce wrote that Nūr al-Dīn believed that "with Egyptian assistance, he and his supporters are doing all they can to swing the branch committees of the party back to a link with Egypt, in the hope that when the General Assembly is called it would be possible to reverse the pro-independence movement in the NUP."[30] But that did not materialize.

xiii. Britain denounces Egyptian interference

In August, the British Prime Minister, Anthony Eden, expressed his concern about Egypt's conduct in Sudan, especially the press campaign being waged against al-Azharī. Accordingly, Eden directed the Foreign Office to send instructions to the British Ambassador to Cairo to discuss these concerns at his next meeting with the Egyptian Prime Minister, Gamāl ʿAbd-al-Nāṣir. These instructions were included in a telegram dated 13 August 1955, which noted that the Egyptians were doing their best to interfere in Sudan, undermine confidence in al-Azharī and ensure that Sudan would choose a future that suited Egypt.[31] Eden expressed his annoyance at the 'state of hysteria' afflicting the Egyptians:

---

[30] National Archives, Kew, FO 371/113610: Luce to Bromley, 22 April 1955, on Egyptian efforts to overturn NUP pro-independence policy.

[31] National Archives, Kew, FO 371/113614 (Political relations between UK, Egypt and Sudan): Foreign Office to Cairo, 13 August 1955.

> I would like you to speak about this to the Egyptian Prime Minister when you see him. ... You should say to him that I have noticed with disquiet the campaign being openly waged by Egypt publicly to bring pressure to bear upon the Sudanese. I perfectly understand the concern of the Egyptian Government that Egypt's vital interests should not be endangered as the result of self-determination in the Sudan but find it hard to reconcile present Egyptian behaviour with the Agreement on the Sudan which we have both signed.[32]

The next paragraph of the telegram included a subtle threat that the British Government might emulate Egyptian activity in Sudan to influence self-determination. The British Ambassador, Sir Ralph Stevenson, was instructed to ask Nāṣir whether Egypt was behaving in accordance with the letter and the spirit of the Anglo-Egyptian Agreement : "If he tries to claim that it is, you should ask him whether you can report to your Government that he would not object if they were to enter the lists, proclaim what the Sudanese should do and turn on the full force of their propaganda backed up by a lavish expenditure of money." [33]

In conclusion, the telegram instructed the Ambassador to confirm to Nāṣir that London intended to observe the spirit of the Agreement and expected Cairo to do the same thing – not to invoke the Agreement only when it suited them. The British Government, finally, was ready to discuss any matter relating to Sudan, although the manner in which the Egyptians had been behaving was a bad omen for the future of Sudanese-Egyptian relations and hardly encouraged trust in Cairo's intentions.

xiv. al-Azharī wins control of the NUP

The struggle between Ismāʿīl al-Azharī and Muḥammad Nūr al-Dīn for control of the Party ended conclusively with the victory of al-Azharī and his supporters. It triggered the departure of three of the NUP's

---

[32] Ibid.

[33] Ibid.

constituent components – the Ashiqqā᾿ (Nūr al-Dīn faction); the Liberal Unionists Party and the Nile Valley Unity Party – but without causing any demonstrable damage at grassroots level, among the ranks of the leadership, among the Parliamentary Group or within the Council of Ministers.

Nūr al-Dīn, it emerged, had few supporters. As for the Liberal Unionists and the Nile Valley Unity Party, the public knew nothing about them. Nūr al-Dīn's departure left no impact on the Cabinet. Only one minister showed solidarity with him. The Minister of Mineral Resources, Ibrāhīm Ḥassan al-Maḥalāwī, justified his resignation by stating that there was 'no harmony' between himself on one hand and the Prime Minister and his Cabinet on the other: they had forsaken the cause of the union with Egypt, in which he remained a believer, and they had compromised the 'free and neutral atmosphere' by touring all over the country making speeches promoting independence.[34] Just one junior official resigned: the Under-Secretary for Special Affairs, Uqeil Aḥmad Uqeil.[35]

Ṣalāḥ Sālim and his colleagues had gambled on Nūr al-Dīn – spending lavishly to attract supporters to the unionist path – and lost. In so doing, he damaged Egypt's reputation in Sudan grievously. This defeat caused him a second loss: that of his job in government. On 31 August 1955, Nāṣir's Revolutionary Command Council (RCC) formally accepted his resignation.[36] Reasons for the resignation were not given but it was clear from the circumstances that it was the total failure of his Sudan policy which caused his downfall.

When the RCC met on 25 August, at Ṣalāḥ Sālim's request, to discuss Egypt's position regarding union with Sudan, the RCC heard presentations by General Ṣāliḥ Ḥarb, a former Minister of War, Muḥammad Khalīl Ibrāhīm, Inspector-General of Egyptian Irrigation in Sudan, Ḥussein Ẓulfiqār Ṣabrī of the Governor-General's Commission, ʿAbd-al-Fatāḥ Ḥassan , Chief of Staff of the Egyptian Forces in Sudan and journalist Aḥmad Gasim Juda of *al-Jamhūrīa*, who had just returned from Sudan.

---

[34] National Archives, Kew, FO 371/113583: Khartoum to Foreign Office, 11 August 1955. See also *al-Rāyī al-ʿAm*, 10 August 1955.

[35] Ibid., Adams to Bromley, August 1955.

[36] ʿAbd-al-Raḥman al-Rāfaʿī. *Thawrat 23 Yūliyū 1952-59* (*The 23 July Revolution 1952-59*) (Cairo: Dār al-Maʿārif, 1989), p. 193.

They all agreed that there was no longer any hope of achieving a formal union. By bribing a large number of Sudanese, Egypt had damaged its reputation in Sudan and cast suspicion on any Sudanese who called for union with Egypt. Furthermore, Muḥammad Nūr al-Dīn – on whom Egypt had relied – was weak and his supporters were insignificant and few.[37]

After accepting Sālim's resignation, the RCC members agreed that Nāṣir himself should take over the Sudan file. Nāṣir requested a member of the RCC to help him. He selected the Interior Minister, Zakarīa Muhī al-Dīn, because in the General Intelligence Department of his Ministry there was a special Sudan Section.[38]

---

[37] ʿAbd-al-Laṭīf al-Baghdādī, *Mudhakkirāt* (*Memoirs*) (Cairo: al-Maktab al-Miṣrī al-Ḥadīth, 1977), pp. 273-6.
[38] Ibid., p. 293.

CHAPTER 9

The Independence Front and the National Charter Project: January 1955

A political gathering held on 23 January 1955 at the headquarters of the Front Against Colonialization was addressed by speakers from the Umma Party and the Republican Independence Party. At that meeting the Leader of the Opposition, Muḥammad Aḥmad Maḥjūb, called for the establishment of a National Front for Independence.[1] Maḥjūb's proposal was concurred to by the Umma, the Republican, the Republican Socialist and the Front Against Colonialization Parties, as well as some independent persons and Labour Union leaders.

The Front's first meeting on 26 January 1955 adopted the principles proposed by the University College Students' Union as a basis around which should rally all Sudanese who truly wish to liberate their country. The liberation that would preserve its pride and progress. Those principles were:

a) full independence;
b) maintenance of fundamental freedoms;
c) non-engagement in military alliances or affiliations; and
d) Non-acceptance of foreign aid that would compromise sovereignty.

The Front identified certain practical duties which should henceforth be undertaken:

---

[1] *al-Ayyām*, 24 January 1955.

a) Adoption of a decision in Parliament to fix a date for the withdrawal of the British and Egyptian forces; and
b) The choice laid down in Article 12 of the 1953 Agreement for a link with Egypt or independence should be made by plebiscite instead of by an elected Constituent Assembly.

The Front warned that self-determination should not rest on the hands of members of the Constituent Assembly and called to mind the 1953 elections which had been marred by Egyptian propaganda and bribery, and subsequently succumbing of Members of Parliament to bribery to change their political affiliation or revert to a link with Egypt. The Front argued that a handful of members of the Constituent Assembly could be bribed to vote for a link with Egypt, but it would be impossible to influence the electorate of a nation-wide plebiscite. [2]

Muḥammad Aḥmad Maḥjūb

[2] On this see also: FO 371/113610, Luce to Bromley, 22 April 1955: Egyptian Political Activity.

On the basis of the aforementioned principles and duties, the Front called for the following:

a) To issue a resolution in Parliament to amend the 1953 Self-Determination and Self-Government Agreement to change the method of self-determination to be by plebiscite instead of the Constituent Assembly provided for in Article 12 of the Agreement;
b) To amend the Press Ordinance and other important legislation in light of the memoranda of the General Organisation for the Defence of Freedoms; and
c) Party committees, their leaders and independent personalities should confirm the commitment not to engage in military alliances.[3]

i. Umma Party-Communists alliance queried

The alliance between the Umma Party and the Front Against Colonialization – a Communist Party front – provoked astonishment on the Sudanese left and among the British. According to the account of Kāmil Maḥjūb, co-operation with the Umma Party in the Independence Front was justified by the Secretary-General of the Communist Party, ʿAbd-al-Khāliq Maḥjūb, in a session of the Central Committee by the view that even the most reactionary factions could end up nationalist, after independence, as they had rid themselves of the influence and pressures of colonialism. Kāmil Maḥjūb added that he disagreed with that analysis.[4]

---

[3] *al-Hayyʿat al-ʿAma li al-Difāʿ ʿan al-Ḥurriyyāt*: *al-Ayyām,* 4 February 1955.
[4] Maḥjūb, *Tilk al-Ayyām*, p. 110.

'Abdallah Khalīl

As for ʿAbdallah Khalīl, Secretary-General of the Umma Party, he drew a demarcation line between his Party and the Communist Party. On 24 January 1955, he told William Luce that: "they are not afraid of co-operating with the communists for the purpose of obtaining independence, but there are no illusions on either side about their attitude towards each other on every other count; the communists know that if the Umma came to power after self-determination, they would do all they could to suppress communism."[5]

ii. The Muslim Brotherhood and the Independence Front

The Muslim Brotherhood did not join the Independence Front, either because they were then still just a small student movement or because of their reservations regarding some of the components of the Independence Front itself. The Brotherhood's position on self-determination was expressed in August 1955 in a statement issued by al-Rashīd al-Ṭāhir Bakr, who said that the call for union with Egypt had been based on 'wild sentiments' and had not fulfilled the requirements of political maturity or awareness.[6] He added that when his movement reached its final position on future relations with Egypt and other countries, it would do so by balancing the interests of the Islamic call and the interests of Sudan as an Islamic nation.

---

[5] National Archives, Kew, FO 371/113581: 'Record of conversation on 24 January 1955 with Abdulla Khalil', in Luce to Bromley, 29 January 1955.
[6] *al-Rāyī al-ʿAm*, 9 August 1955.

The interests of the Islamic movement, he continued, necessitated a persistent demand for independence, which alone would bring him and his fellow Brothers the protection and peace of mind that would enable their call to flourish. Independence, furthermore, would enable the *umma* – the wider community of Muslims – to help the miserable people of Egypt to get rid of the regime under whose yoke they were suffering. In other words, a so far captive Islam would be freed from behind its bars to liberate Egypt from despotism. Any tie with Egypt meant a tie with a military dictatorship that had declared its position in respect of international conflict by standing with the West when it accepted both the Suez Canal Base Agreement and the American Point Four Program, with all its associated American money. Through such a link, Anglo-American colonialism could penetrate Sudan in many ways.

iii. The Independence Front's proposal in Parliament for the evacuation of foreign troops

At a meeting held on 5 March 1955, the Independence Front voted to submit to Parliament a proposal to call for the immediate evacuation of Egyptian and British troops from Sudan, under Article 9 of the 1953 Agreement on Self-Government and Self-Determination. "The sooner evacuation was effected," the Front said in a formal statement, "the faster we can exercise our self-determination so as not to leave the door open for the conspiracies of our enemies and so that our country will no longer be attached to the coat-tails of foreign armies."[7]

On 15 March 1955, the Clerk of the House of Representatives received the formal proposal on evacuation from an Independence Front delegation made up of Muḥammad Aḥmad Maḥjūb (Leader of the Opposition), ʿAbdallah Khalīl (Umma Party), Yūsuf al-ʿAjab (Republican Socialist Party), Buth Diu (Liberal Party), Ḥassan al-Ṭāhir Zarūq (Front Against Colonialization) and Mīrghanī Ḥamza (Republican Independence Party but taking part in a personal capacity).[8]

This formal submission triggered legal arguments in respect of the interpretation of Article 9 of the Agreement, which stipulated that "Subject to the completion of the Sudanisation as outlined in Annex III to

---

[7] Suleimān, *al-Yasār al-Sūdānī*, p. 107.
[8] Ibid., p. 113.

this Agreement, the two contracting governments undertake to bring the transitional period to an end as soon as possible. In any case this period shall not exceed three years". It also stipulated that this period would be brought to an end when "The Sudanese Parliament shall pass a resolution expressing their desire that arrangements for Self-Determination shall be put in motion and the Governor-General shall notify the two contracting governments of this resolution". Whereas Article 11 provided that:

> Egyptian and British Military Forces shall withdraw from the Sudan immediately upon the Sudanese Parliament adopting a resolution expressing its desire that arrangements for Self-Determination be put in motion. The two contracting governments undertake to complete the withdrawal of their forces from the Sudan within a period not exceeding three months.[9]

These legal issues were discussed in a meeting convened on 17 March 1955 and attended by the Speaker of the House of Representatives, Bābikr ʿAwaḍallah, and his counterpart in the Senate, Aḥmad Muḥammad Yāsin; the Majority Leader in the House of Representatives, Mubārak Zarūq, and his counterpart in the Senate, Bashīr ʿAbd-al-Raḥīm Ḥāmid; the Government's Legal Adviser, Aḥmad Mutawallī al-ʿAtabānī, and the Clerk of the House of Representatives, Muḥammad ʿAmir Bashīr Fawrāwī. The Independence Front was represented by the Leader of the Opposition in the House of Representatives, Muḥammad Aḥmad Maḥjūb, his counterparts in the Senate, Stanislaus Paysama, and Ḥassan al-Ṭāhir Zarūq.[10]

The two Speakers, supported by the Government, were of the view that the completion of Sudanisation was a prerequisite for debating the evacuation proposal. The Independence Front, by contrast, argued that the phrase '[s]ubject to the completion of the Sudanisation' in Article 9 imposed an obligation upon the two contracting Governments not upon Parliament, which should be free to debate the proposal whenever it wished.[11] In view of the position of the two Speakers, Bābikr ʿAwaḍallah

---

[9] See Appendix 1.

[10] Suleimān, *al-Yasār al-Sūdānī*, p. 120.

[11] National Archives, Kew, FO 371/113783 (Self-determination for the Sudan: decision to hold plebiscite): Adams to Bromley, 18 March 1955.

referred the matter to the Sudanisation Commission, which stated that it could not testify that the Sudanisation had been completed. Consequently, it was decided that the evacuation proposal presented by the Independence Front was premature and irregular and as such could not be tabled for debate.[12]

At that 17 March 1955 meeting, the two Government's representatives Mubārak Zarūq and Bashīr ʿAbd-al-Raḥīm, proposed a compromise solution, accepted by the Independence Front, which stated that Sudanisation could be completed by 30 June 1955. Then it would be possible to schedule proceedings for a debate on evacuation and self-determination in July 1955.[13]

iv. A draft National Charter

In April 1955, the Independence Front prepared a draft of a new National Charter, which was circulated to the secretaries of all Sudan's political parties and organisations to abide and be guided by its provisions until the country was liberated from colonial rule and achieved total independence. The Charter read as follows:

> 1. Aims
>
> To achieve the complete and unconditional independence of Sudan by the creation of an independent republic with full sovereignty, as represented in its army, flag, currency, economy and foreign policy.
>
> 2. Means
>
> a) The Government and opposition, acting together, shall present in Parliament a proposal to the two Condominium Governments demanding that they evacuate their troops from the country next August, pursuant to Article 11 of the 1953 Agreement.
>
> b) The Government and opposition, acting together, shall present in Parliament a proposal to the two Condominium

[12] Ibid., Governor-General's Office to Foreign Office, 15 and 22 March 1955.

[13] Ibid., Adams to Bromley, 18 March 1955. See also Suleimān, *al-Yasār al-Sūdānī*, p. 120.

Governments demanding the amendment of Article 12 of the 1953 Agreement, whereby the section on self-determination is deleted, since all the Sudanese, as represented by their political parties and organisations, are unanimous on complete independence. If one or both Condominium states decline to accept this request, we all pledge to insist on a plebiscite to reflect the true will of the people.

3. Maintaining Sudan's independence and preservation of its unity

a) Non-participation in any military pact or bloc with any state, so that Sudan would not be compelled to participate in a war in which it has no interest.

b) Ensuring general freedoms, respecting minority rights and providing social justice.

c) Forming a cross-party committee to consider the interests of the South, so that the Government might work on realizing them as soon as possible, in order that national unity could be properly attained.

d) Maintaining the bonds of friendship and good neighbourliness with Egypt and strengthening ties with the Egyptian and other neighbouring peoples.[14]

The Independence Front intended the National Charter to be the basis for a non-partisan approach to self-determination. Therefore, the Front called for a national festival to be held on the evening of Friday 8 July 1955 at the Khalifa's Mosque in Omdurman. The Front hoped that the carnival would achieve a two-fold purpose: to be a national ceremony, through which the people would express their commitment to the Charter and an expression of the people's desire for political parties, organisations and individuals to stand together and establish a fully independent Republic of Sudan.[15] But the festival was promptly banned by the Governor of Khartoum. The National Unionist Party Secretary-General, Khidir Ḥamad, described the Charter as a 'plot against the

[14] *al-Nīl*, 4 May 1955, and *al-Ayyām*, 21 April 1955.
[15]*al-Nīl*, 15 June 1955.

country' and appealed to the people to boycott this 'separatists charter' and stand fast behind their own great Party with its glorious history.

v. The NUP rejects the Charter proposal

The NUP issued a statement in which it rejected the notion of a National Charter in toto, warned Party followers not to pay heed to its siren call and described it as "a conspiracy designed by dishonest people to drag the NUP into the abyss."[16]

The NUP's statement added warned about proposed changes to the 1953 Agreement in respect of self-determination: any amendment would be construed by the Condominium countries as a license to tamper with its provisions and eventually abolish it. The statement added that every separatist party – with the exception of the communists – had consented to the Agreement as it stood: why would they come back and seek to revoke it?

vi. Withdrawals from the Independence Front

In mid-June 1955, the Republican Party announced its withdrawal from the Independence Front because, it argued, the idea of independence had gripped in the minds of all Sudanese. A Party statement noted that key events had taken place since the formation of the Front, proving that all Sudanese – apart from a tiny minority acting in bad faith – believed in the full independence of a completely sovereign Sudan. The most important of these events were the moves of the NUP MPs that had resulted in the decision of the Committee of the Ten.[17]

Three months later, the Front Against Colonialization also withdrew from the Independence Front. Among the reasons given was a disagreement with the Umma Party over the concept of independence. The Umma, said the Front, had not shown any enthusiasm or taken any practical steps to implement the terms of the Charter – and its attitude towards other political parties was not serious. It opposed the participation of Sudan in the International Commission and approved the participation of Pakistan despite its blatant involvement in military pacts.

---

[16]*al-Ahrām*, 19 May 1955.
[17]*al-Nīl*, 18 June 1955, and *al-Ayyām*, 16 June 1955.

As we will see later, the International Commission was provided for in Article 10 of the 1953 Agreement to oversee the process of self-determination – and a supplementary agreement between the British and Egyptian governments would be concluded on 3 December 1955 to formulate provisions for the composition and functions of the Commission.[18]

On 6 September 1955, the Front Against Colonialization issued a statement stating that its participation in the Independence Front, which included what they regarded as 'reactionary' parties such as the Umma and the Socialist Republicans, was 'an unfamiliar act' for the Sudanese left which had led them to 'incorrect' positions. [19]

The Front Against Colonialization added that the Umma Party's stance on fundamental freedoms was similar to its position on pacts: despite agreement among Independence Front members to oppose any recess of Parliament until all ordinances that restricted freedom were revoked, the Umma Party had violated that agreement.[20]

vii. The Umma Party's response

The Umma Party retorted that the Front Against Colonialization had been for some time searching for a cause to withdraw from the Independence Front, presumably influenced by the writings of some of its deserters who were opposed to cooperation with the Umma Party. The Umma Party stated that the two reasons on which the Front Against Colonialization based its withdrawal from the Independence Front were not properly founded.[21] The Umma Party though aware that Sudan was not in a position to adopt a specific foreign policy and that the question of military alliances was premature, nonetheless it supported the Independence Front's proposals of rejecting military alliances, and their

---

[18] *Supplementary agreement between the government of the United Kingdom of Great Britain and Northern Ireland and the Egyptian Government for the establishment of an international commission to supervise the process of self-determination in the Sudan and exchange of notes modifying the Anglo-Egyptian agreement of the 12th of February, 1953 concerning self-government and self-determination for the Sudan* (London: HMSO, 1955).

[19] Suleimān, *al-Yasār al-Sūdānī*, p. 105.

[20] *al-Ahrām*, 6 September 1955.

[21]Umma Party statement, 6 September 1955.

inclusion in the National Charter. The Party strongly expressed its adherence to those proposals through Party publications, the Party's press, public meetings and statements by its leadership.

It is utterly erroneous to allege that it was the Umma Party which nominated Pakistan to the membership of the International Commission. In fact, it had been the Independence Front's parties and organisations which collectively took the decision that India and Pakistan should be included in the membership of the International Commission. As for the question of 'general freedoms' – cited by the Front Against Colonialization as another reason for its withdrawal – the Umma Party explained that it had not objected to tabling it for debate before recess: it was the Speaker of the House who saw fit to postpone tabling it to another session, this being his constitutional right.

It is worth mentioning, in concluding this Chapter, that the most important stipulation in the Independence Front's draft National Charter was the proposed amendment of Article 12 of the 1953 Agreement. It was intended to remove the part relating to self-determination – i.e. the choice of a link with Egypt in any form or complete independence – because the Sudanese people, as represented by their elected representatives, had unanimously chosen independence. If Britain and Egypt refused to adopt the proposed amendment, the draft stipulated that the Sudanese should then request an amendment of Article 12 in such a way as to achieve self-determination via plebiscite instead of the Constituent Assembly.

We saw earlier that the ruling NUP categorically rejected any amendment to the 1953 Agreement – but, as we shall see, the Condominium States agreed, through an exchange of letters on 3 December 1955, to amend Articles 10, 12 and 13 of the 1953 Agreement related to the self-determination process to include the notion of a plebiscite. On the same date, the Condominium Governments concluded a Supplementary Agreement containing the composition and terms of reference of the Commission that would supervise arrangements for the plebiscite. All this, however, was about to be cut short by a telegram – No. 388, dated 6 October 1955 – from the Foreign Secretary, Harold

Macmillan to Sir Alexander Knox Helm, Britain's last Governor-General in Khartoum.[22]

The telegram laid the ground for bypassing the whole self-determination process provided for in the Agreement and its various amendments. In it, Macmillan asked Knox Helm to inform Ismāʿīl al-Azharī that the British Government was prepared to recognise Sudanese independence forthwith if that was the desire of the Sudanese. Macmillan said: 'There seems no valid reason why the Sudanese should not be allowed to decide upon independence without going through these difficult and perhaps dangerous processes.'[23]

---

[22]Johnson, *British Documents*, Series B, vol. 5, Part II, p. 450.

[23] See Sudan Archive, University of Durham (Luce Papers): SAD.829/6/1-93 for more detail on this important period.

CHAPTER 10

al-Azharī's Government Seeks British Advice on Combatting Communism

i. Emergence of the Communist movement

British documents suggested that the greatest contribution to the introduction of the communist movement into Sudan was the Egyptian Government policy of offering scholarships at Egyptian universities to Sudanese students. This began with a visit paid to Sudan in 1946 by the Egyptian Minister of Education, ʿAbd-al-Razzāq al-Sanhūrī, who came to inaugurate the Fārūq Secondary School in Khartoum.[1] It was no surprise, then, that most of the founding members of the Sudanese Movement for National Liberation, HASATU,[2] were either candidates for a 'Sanhūrī scholarship' or among those who came to study in Egypt via a different route.[3]

The British Government indicated that some expatriates resident in Sudan believed in Marxism without seeking to diffuse it – although it was conceded in contemporary documents that assessing the

---

[1] National Archives, Kew, FO 371/73471 (Communism in the Sudan): Secretariat, Khartoum, to George Clutton, Head of Africa Department, Foreign Office, 1949.

[2] See Chapter 1, Note 37.

[3] National Archives, Kew, FO 371/80352 (Communism in the Sudan): 'Communism in the Anglo-Egyptian Sudan', Civil Secretary Office, 10 October 1949; Appendix 1, 'Communist Personalities', enclosed in Robertson to Foreign Office, 28 September 1950. Among those listed were ʿAbd-al-Khāliq Maḥjūb, ʿAwaḍ ʿAbd-al-Rāziq, Aḥmad Suleimān, al-Tijānī al-Ṭayyib Bābikr, al-Jineid ʿAlī ʿUmar, Aḥmad Khojalī Muḥammad Kheir, ʿAbd-al-Ghaffār ʿAbd-al-Raḥīm, ʿIzz al-Dīn ʿAlī Amir, ʿAbd-al-Raḥman ʿAbd-al-Raḥīm al-Wasīla, ʿAbd-al-Waḥāb Zein al-ʿAbdīn ʿAbd-al-Tām, ʿAbd-al-Majīd Abū-Ḥassabū and Muḥammad Amīn Ḥussein.

extent of their impact was difficult. Among the names mentioned were Harold Sandon, a lecturer at Gordon Memorial College, and his wife; Alfred Dickinson, an engineer with the Sudan Light and Power Co.; John Beckett, who worked for International Air Radio, formerly worked at the British Royal Air Force (RAF) and Walter Hans Haas, an Austrian national. The British administration in Khartoum did not exclude the possibility that there were communists serving in the British army or RAF in Sudan – but as contact with local inhabitants was limited, it was considered unlikely that they would have much opportunity to proselytise among the Sudanese.[4] It has also been claimed that Ḥassan al-Ṭāhir Zarūq and Aḥmad Zein al-ʿAbdīn were indoctrinated with Marxist beliefs by a British conscript called Herbert Storey.[5]

The first formal Sudanese communist organisation was started in Egypt in 1945 as a section of the Egyptian Movement for National Liberation. This group, founded by a naturalised Egyptian of Jewish origin named Henri Curiel, called for a joint struggle by the peoples of Sudan and Egypt. British documents reveal that ʿAbd-al-Waḥāb Zein al-ʿAbdīn was the link between the 'Sudan Section' in Cairo and Sudan itself. In March 1945, the Sudan Section began publishing a magazine called *Omdurman*, staffed by numerous cadres from the Movement's Sudan Section and Nubian Section. Among the magazine's writers were the licence holder, Muḥammad Amīn Ḥussein, the Editor-in-Chief ʿAbd-al-Laṭīf Ḍahab Ḥassanein, as well as Ḥāmid Ḥamdī, ʿAbd-al-Majīd Abū-Ḥassabū, ʿIzz al-Dīn ʿAlī Amir and Ṣāliḥ ʿUrābī. The leftist Egyptian historian Rifʿat al-Saʿīd described *Omdurman* as the 'joint struggle magazine' and the first to be produced and controlled by the Movement. Its core function was to serve as a counterbalance to another magazine, *al-Sūdān*, published in Cairo in 1944 by ʿAlī al-Bireir to promote the concept of Nile Valley unity.[6]

---

[4] Ibid., 'Communism in the Anglo-Egyptian Sudan'.

[5] Mohamed Nuri El-Amin, *The Emergence and Development of the Leftist Movement in the Sudan during the 1930's and 1940's* (Khartoum: KUP, 1984), pp. 96-109.

[6] Rifʿat al-Saʿīd, *Tārīkh al-Ḥaraka al-Shiyūʿīa al-Miṣriyya* (*A History of the Egyptian Communist Movement*) (3 vols.) (Cairo: Dār al-Amal li al-Ṭabāʿa wa al-Nashr, 1987), vol. 1 (1900-40), pp. 725-50, and vol. 3 (1940-50), pp. 227-41.

In the summer of 1947, the Egyptian Movement for National Liberation merged with another communist group, Iskra – also known as *al-Sharāra* or 'The Spark'[7] – to become the Democratic Movement for National Liberation, HADITU.[8] The Sudan Section took the opportunity, at that time or shortly afterwards, to change its own name to become the Sudanese Movement for National Liberation, HASATU.[9] British documents show how the dissemination of communist thought among students escalated rapidly in 1947 – with communist students taking over the Union of Sudanese Students in Egypt and involving themselves in Egyptian political activities. In 1948 and early 1949, the Egyptian security authorities used the provisions of martial law to carry out a wide-ranging campaign of searches and arrests among the student body, including Sudanese. Some were variously expelled from university, detained at a wartime airbase named Camp Huckstep, put in an Egyptian jail or deported to Sudan.[10]

In September 1947, HASATU attracted the attention of the Sudan Government by distributing a mass-produced circular, with the movement's signature, in Atbara, Sudan's national rail hub, inciting the workers to go on strike.[11] It is worth mentioning that some of HASATU's cadres had joined other unionist parties as leftist members, especially the Liberal Unionists Party, which Ḥassan al-Ṭāhir Zarūq and Ḥassan Salāma, had joined. Others joined the Unionist Party Youth faction. HASATU participated effectively, using pamphlets, in mobilising the masses to boycott the Legislative Assembly elections. The movement also participated in political gatherings and demonstrations mounted for that purpose, via a Youth Conference that it had set up in August 1948 as a public front.[12] Importantly, however, the movement did not reveal its true communist identity except in leaflets distributed in Khartoum

---

[7] Ibid., vol. 3, pp. 261-3. Iskra had been founded in 1942 by another Egyptian Jew, Hillel Schwartz.

[8] The Arabic acronym for *al-Ḥaraka al-Dīmuqrāṭīa li al-Taḥarur al-Waṭanī.*

[9] *al-Ḥaraka al-Sūdānīa li al-Taḥarur al-Waṭanī.*

[10] National Archives, Kew, FO 371/80352: 'Communism in the Anglo-Egyptian Sudan'.

[11] Ibid., FO 371/73471: 'The Sudanese Movement for National Liberation', 3 February 1949.

[12] The Secretary-General of the Youth Conference was 'Awaḍ 'Abd-al-Rāziq: ibid., FO 371/80352: 'Communism in the Anglo-Egyptian Sudan'.

Province on 11 January 1949.[13] HASATU also used the Gordon College Students' Union, where it won more than half the seats on the Executive at the 1949 annual meeting. It led a student strike the same year in protest against the Ministry of Education's refusal to allow secondary school students to join the Students' Conference. As a result of the strike, the college was closed and three HASATU leaders were expelled.[14]

Changes occurred in the leadership of the movement during the pre-independence period. In July 1947, ʿAbd-al-Waḥāb Zein al-ʿAbdīn ʿAbd-al-Tām was removed from his post as HASATU Secretary-General and replaced by ʿAwaḍ ʿAbd-al-Rāziq. ʿAbd-al-Waḥāb had been criticised for his lack of assertiveness in highlighting the movement's programme, the joint document signed with Egyptian communists calling for evacuation from Egypt and Sudan and the right of the Sudanese to self-determination, and for subscribing publicly to the slogan of Nile Valley unity under the Egyptian crown.[15] Lambasting the very concept of Nile Valley unity, ʿAbd-al-Khāliq Maḥjūb wrote that the slogan "expresses the political and economic impotence of the Sudanese middle classes more than it expresses the desire of the masses to liberate themselves from the oppression of British colonialism." To prove his point, ʿAbd-al-Khāliq stated that large sections of the Sudanese people saw in the Egyptian military and civilian personnel in Sudan a reflection of the force that had crushed the country's independence in the late 1890s, perpetrating disgraceful acts against the Sudanese. Before their very eyes, Sudanese were forced to witness the Egyptian *maʿmūr* carrying out the orders of his colonial masters in a severe and merciless manner. So a slogan advocating Nile Valley unity could never mobilise the masses in an anti-colonialism movement.[16]

The second change was more important due to the problems it triggered and the split which resulted from it. At an extraordinary conference of the movement, convened in January 1949, it was decided to dump ʿAwaḍ ʿAbd-al-Rāziq and appoint ʿAbd-al-Khāliq Maḥjūb as

---

[13] Ibid., FO 371/73471: 'The Sudanese Movement for National Liberation', 3 February 1949.

[14] The union President, Muṣtafa al-Saʿīd, Deputy President al-Ṭāhir ʿAbd-al-Bāṣit and the Secretary-General, Maḥjūb Muḥammad Ṣāliḥ.

[15] Maḥjūb, *Lamahāt min Tārīkh*, p. 44.

[16] Ibid., p. 18.

HASATU Secretary-General. ʿAbd-al-Khāliq later summed up the reasons for this dramatic action: under ʿAwaḍ ʿAbd-al-Rāziq's leadership, a trend towards opportunism, defeated in 1947, had resurfaced, leading the movement to "fall under the influence of national capitalism and restrict the Party 's independent activities. Nepotism was rife, Party regulations were ignored and stagnation prevailed over the study of Marxism: in short, the Party's inner life deteriorated and its Marxist-Leninist standards had dropped."[17]

ʿAbd-al-Khāliq Maḥjūb

By contrast, ʿAwaḍ ʿAbd-al-Rāziq's own account, handwritten during the period between July 1947 and October 1952, gave a different and detailed version of these controversial issues.[18] His report opened with a rejection of any political line that called for isolation, does not call for the independence of the movement's platform or calls for dissolving the movement in other political parties. For ʿAwaḍ ʿAbd-al-Rāziq, asserting HASATU's independent identity through its daily struggles was vital. He believed that it was premature to attempt to bypass a step-by-step development of the movement by adopting an extreme and over-

[17] Ibid., pp. 52-4.

[18] Author's personal copy, obtained thanks to Dr Fārūq Muḥammad Ibrāhīm.

hasty transformation of the Sudanese Movement for National Liberation into a Marxist-Leninist party based on workers, farmers and revolutionary intellectuals. ʿAwaḍ ʿAbd-al-Rāziq's justifications for this view were as follows:

a) The working class was still new and restricted to service sector workers in auxiliary roles such as the railways, postal services, seaports and river transport. The working class was still at a formative stage and could only complete its growth under the conditions of a national democratic revolution that would achieve a wide-ranging industrial structure. This in turn would make the working class a leading force, capable of building a strong vanguard to take it and wider society towards socialism.
b) Farmers had consciousness equivalent to the level of agricultural production in Sudan, i.e. still seasonal and at a subsistence level. Even in its highest form, e.g. the Gezira Scheme, farmers in such locations did not amount to a social class with concerns and consciousness that would qualify it to achieve the alliance between workers and farmers.
c) Marxism-Leninism was still an elitist ideology restricted to the circles of the *affandīa*, i.e. white-collar government employees who suffered greatly in their attempt to understand Marxism-Leninism as a philosophy, far removed from just the slogans. Establishing a Communist Party on these issues would be considered a superficial act supported only by revolutionary slogans that did not absorb or even fully appreciate national circumstances, and which highlighted a tradition based on rote learning. Simply aping the experiences of other peoples and nations without realising Sudan's particular circumstances was a dangerous and foolish game.

The issues raised in ʿAwaḍ ʿAbd-al-Rāziq's analysis remained bones of contention at successive conferences and were not settled decisively until 1952 – in favour of ʿAbd-al-Khāliq Maḥjūb and his supporters. This prompted many intellectuals to leave the movement.[19]

---

[19] For more details on the schism, see Maḥjūb, *Tilk al-Ayyām*, p. 100-102.

But despite the gravity of the schism – and the quality of those who left HASATU – the rival organisations they subsequently set up did not amount to any lasting or effective competition to the movement. British documents describe how some ex-HASATU members formed the Sudanese Democratic Movement, which later split into an underground organisation called the Communist Group and a public one named the Progressive Democratic Party.[20]

ii. Annulment of the Anti-subversive Activities Order

Under Article 3 of the Unlawful Associations Ordinance of 1924,[21] the Governor-General may by an Order published in the Gazette declare an association illegal if he deems that it interferes, or that its object is the interference in the establishment of law and order, or that it constitutes a danger to public peace. Under that ordinance, the Governor-General on 25 November 1950, declared illegal in the Sudan any association whatever may be its name, which preaches, promotes or practises the theories or the principles of international communism, or the apparatus known by the name of Cominform.[22] Under the same Ordinance he issued in May 1952 another order which makes it illegal for associations in the Sudan to have contacts with communist movements or associations in other countries.[23]

In 1953, the Governor-General issued the Anti-subversive Activities Provisional Order. That order makes it an offence for individuals to receive communist literature from abroad. The promulgation of the Order into Law was held up by the dissolution of the legislative Assembly. When submitted to Parliament on 30 March 1954 under Articles 57 and 58 of the Self-Government Statute, it was annulled by agreement of both Government and opposition.

---

[20] National Archives, Kew, FO 371/108323: 'Note on Communism in the Sudan' in Buxton, Office of the UK Trade Commissioner, Khartoum, to Morris, 27 May 1954.
[21] This regulation allowed the Governor-General to proscribe any organisation found to be interfering in the maintenance of peace and security: *Sudan Government Gazette* No. 445/1924.
[22] The Cominform was a short-lived (1950-56) alliance of European Marxist-Leninist Communist parties, whose activities were coordinated by the Soviet Union via its headquarters in Yugoslavia.
[23] Ibid., Buxton to Allen, 29 October 1950.

On 30 March 1954, the House of Representatives, by prior agreement between the Government and the opposition, voted against the confirmation of the Provisional Order. During the debate, the Majority Leader, Mubārak Zarūq, said that the Provisional Order had been issued before Ismā'īl al-Azharī's administration had come to power – and it had pledged to annul it as part of its commitment to the people's freedom. Zarūq described the Order as 'too elastic' – that is, it allowed room for the suppression of that freedom – and he expressed his hope that the Government would never be forced by future circumstances to promulgate such legislation again.[24]

In the same debate, Ḥassan al-Ṭāhir Zarūq of the Front Against Colonialization referred to the 'interpretative memorandum' of the Order, which stated that communism had spread and should be fought. He contended that, even if communism had spread, that diffusion had not been through criminal means, with communists carrying spears or swords to force people to follow certain views. It was common practice, he added, to describe any free man who fought to liberate his country as a communist. "If this is communism," he concluded, "we are all unapologetic communists."

iii. The Government prepares new legislation to combat communism

When al-Azharī's Government took office in January 1954, the communists controlled the central committees of both the Rail Workers' Union and the Sudanese Workers' Trade Union Federation (SWTUF). They also wielded influence, through officers who were Party members, over other unions including unions such as the Post and Telegraph Workers' Union and the River Transport Workers' Union. In the February 1954 elections for the General Union of Gezira Farmers, a member of the Communist Party, al-Amīn Muḥammad al-Amīn, was elected President, while Kāmil Maḥjūb, a Party functionary in Blue Nile Province, was also appointed as a union officer.[25]

As mentioned earlier, the Government and opposition agreed on 30 March 1954 not to promulgate into law the Provisional Order relating

---

[24] *al-Ayyām*, 31 March 1954.
[25] Maḥjūb, *Tilk al-Ayyām*, pp. 63-81.

to the suppression of subversive activities – but in September of the same year, the Government asked its Legal Adviser, Aḥmad Mutawallī al-ʿAtabānī, to draft a bill for the combatting of communism, with a view to tabling it before Parliament. By way of justification of the move, it was argued that some citizens had 'grievously exploited freedom of speech' in such a way as to destabilise the system. It was also alleged that communist activities had already permeated groups such as the General Union of Gezira Farmers.[26] The following month, ʿAlī ʿAbd-al-Raḥman, the Minister of Justice, announced that when Parliament convenes in November, the Government would submit a bill proscribing communism in Sudan because the communists exploited the absence of such legislation to carry out wide-ranging subversive activities. The Minister insisted that his Government did not want to restrict freedoms but desired instead to protect freedoms from the 'communist sabotage' that had infiltrated various institutions.[27]

This plan faced immediate opposition from many political parties, organisations and public figures – a position expressed in a document signed by the Umma Party, the Republican Party, the Front Against Colonialization, the SWTUF, the Union of Gezira Farmers, the Islamic Jamaʿa and the Society for Sudanese Thought. Muḥammad Aḥmad Maḥjūb and Ḥussein al-Hindī were amongst the public figures who also signed the document. One key paragraph of the document read as follows:

> "Promulgating a new law, under the pretext of combatting communism alone or under any other pretext, would be a restriction on the freedom of citizens, would obstruct the free neutral atmosphere and would be a weapon to put pressure on the Sudanese to concede their independence and national sovereignty."[28]

The Government's determination to draft anti-communism legislation coincided with intensive activity on the part of the National

---

[26] *al-Ayyām*, 2 September 1954, and *al-Rāyī al-ʿAm*, 7 October 1954.
[27] *al-Ayyām*, 19 October 1954.
[28] Suleimān, *al-Yasār al-Sūdānī*, p. 77.

Unionist Party rank-and file to remove communists from leading positions in the wider union movement. That activity was led and directed by the Minister of Social Affairs, Yaḥya al-Faḍlī, under whose jurisdiction the Department of Labour fell. As a result, in the election of 25 October 1954, pro-government activists took over the leadership of the Rail Workers' Union for the 1953-4 session – leaving its Committee devoid of any elements known to be pro-communist.[29] Commenting on that election, the Minister said that it proved beyond doubt that most workers were politically aware in a way that immunised them against the propaganda of saboteurs – and that they could distinguish between those who truly worked for them those who worked towards subversive principles.[30]

Trade union elections were also the subject of an exchange between Yaḥya al-Faḍlī and the British Trade Commissioner in Khartoum, Philip Adams, in the first week of November 1954 – a few days before the Minister left for Britain as part of the delegation accompanying Prime Minister Ismāʿīl al-Azharī. The Minister expressed satisfaction at the way trade union elections were going – apparently referring to the recent Rail Workers' Union election – as a number of communists had been defeated. al-Faḍlī expressed his hope that non-communist elements would soon seize control of the larger Sudanese Workers' Trade Union Federation.[31] But when the SWTUF's Third Conference convened in Khartoum on 12 December – and despite the campaign waged by the Rail Workers' Union against the Federation's leftist leadership – all three top union officers were re-elected the following week.[32]

Meanwhile there seems to have been some obstacles which prevent legislation combatting communism. Yaḥya al-Faḍlī told Adams in the first week of December 1954 that the Cabinet had once again discussed presenting anti-communism legislation during the current

---

[29] ʿAlī Muḥammad Bashīr Mūsa, *Tārīkh Niqābat al-Sikka al-Ḥadīdīa* (*A History of the Rail Union*) (Khartoum: ʿAzza Publishers and Distributors, 2007), pp. 157-8. Also *al-Sūdān al-Jadīd*, 26 October 1954.

[30] *al-Ayyām*, 10 November 1954.

[31] National Archives, Kew, FO 371/108348 (Communism in Sudan): Minutes by Adams, 4 November 1954.

[32] They were Muḥammad al-Sayyid Sallām (President), al-Shāfī Aḥmad al-Sheikh (Secretary-General) and Jāffar ʿAbbās (Treasurer): *al-Rāyī al-ʿAm*, 16 December 1954.

parliamentary session – but now it was not only the opposition that was objecting: even Cabinet colleagues were against it as well. The Minister went on to say that, despite the considerable steps that had been taken to rid trade unions of communist influence, the process was costly and the NUP's own Party agencies did not have additional financial resources. So, without a blush, Yaḥya al-Faḍlī was turning to the British for advice. The response from Adams was curt: the Minister should not expect the British Government to supply any funds for such activities.[33]

iv. British advice on the proposed legislation

While in Britain as part of the delegation accompanying al-Azharī in November 1954, Yaḥya al-Faḍlī contacted a number of personalities about communism. The Foreign Office observed that he received conflicting advice because he asked about two different aspects of the problem: "on some occasions he was talking specifically about anti-communist legislation and on others mainly about combatting communism in the trade unions."[34] Alongside ʿAlī ʿAbd-al-Raḥman, the Minister of Justice, al-Faḍlī met Walter Monckton, the Minister of Labour, to seek advice on how best to combat communists in the unions. al-Faḍlī noted that currently all trade union leaders in Sudan were communists and the Government was considering promulgating anti-communist legislation. Monckton explained to his two guests that the situation in Britain was different: most trade union leaders were not communists – indeed they could be relied on to take the necessary steps to resist communist activities. For that reason, British methods might not be effective under Sudanese conditions. Monckton also discussed with ʿAlī ʿAbd-al-Raḥman, in his capacity as Minister of Justice, the problem of arriving at a satisfactory legal definition of communism.

At another meeting, the General Secretary of the Trades Union Congress (TUC), Vincent Tewson, advised Yaḥya al-Faḍlī that legislation was not a satisfactory route: it was far better for the unions themselves to act against the communists, though it might take longer. Expulsion by the Government would leave non-communists open to the charge of

---

[33] National Archives, Kew, FO 371/108348: Minutes by Adams, 8 December 1954.

[34] Ibid., Minutes by Barnes, 2 December 1954.

being the Government stooges and therefore not representatives of the workers. The advice of the TUC, therefore, was to adopt a proactive policy aimed at strengthening non-communist elements in the unions. A social policy was called for that would diminish the appeal of communist propaganda, making it possible for non-communist union figures to show their members that improvements in their standard of living could be secured via the processes of democratic trade unionism. TUC delegates at the meeting recommended that their guests promote active contacts, if possible, between Sudanese trade unions and similar more highly developed trade union movements, either directly via national bodies such as the TUC itself or the International Confederation of Free Trade Unions (ICFTU).

After considering the advice sought by Yaḥya al-Faḍlī, the Foreign Office decided not to give the Sudanese Minister any specific advice on anti-communist legislation. Bromley of the Foreign Office wrote to Adams, Trade Commissioner in Khartoum, on 3 February 1955:

> The fact that Fadli is a very tricky customer make [sic] it undesirable that you should give Fadli specific advice about legislation, since we do not want to get into a position in which Fadli might produce legislation against communism and be tempted to quote advice from you in justification if it arouses political opposition in the Sudan.

In taking this position, the Foreign Office considered a number of factors, including the possibility that al-Faḍlī had over-estimated the importance of communism in his country and that communists in Sudan were already working covertly and would only be driven further underground by legislation. Furthermore, the appeal of communism was to some extent bound up with anti-colonialism – a factor of decreasing importance in Sudan – and that the political situation in Sudan at the time was very fluid.

For all these reasons, Foreign Office advice to al-Faḍlī concluded that the best method for confronting communism was not legislation but "a healthy social, political and economic system which provided outlets for the energies and ambitions of the of the effendi class, which would otherwise form the communist cadres, and also removing the grievances of the masses who may otherwise turn to the communists for leadership."[35] As for the unions, the Foreign Office believed that the best approach was to encourage moderate elements to wage the anti-communist battle themselves. For this purpose, it might be possible for them to establish contacts with European unions and with the ICFTU.

By the end of March 1955, it became evident that Ismāʿīl al-Azharī's Government had dropped, at least for the time being, any idea of introducing anti-communist legislation – although al-Faḍlī told Philip Adams, the Trade Commissioner in Khartoum, that he would recommend setting up a special section in the Interior Ministry, staffed by both police and civilian personnel – to speed up anti-communist activities. Adams privately expressed doubt that such a recommendation would secure the approval of al-Faḍlī's Cabinet colleagues.[36] It is worth remembering that – as we saw in Chapter 9 – while the Government was still thinking about anti-communist legislation, the Umma Party, as the largest opposition party, was cooperating with the Front Against Colonialization in the context of the Independence Front. This, perhaps, was what compelled Adams to say, in the same report to London, that the Umma leadership 'remained annoyingly like an ostrich, as far as communism was concerned.'

---

[35] Ibid., FO 371/113589 (Communism in the Sudan): Bromley, Foreign Office, to Adams, 3 February 1955.
[36] Ibid., Adams to Bromley, 24 March 1955.

CHAPTER 11

Completion of Sudanisation and Passing the Self-Determination Resolution

i. The Sudanisation Commission: Terms of Reference

To provide the free and neutral atmosphere for self-determination, Article 8 of the 1953 Agreement provided for the establishment of a Sudanisation Committee[1] consisting of:

1) An Egyptian and a British member to be nominated by their respective Governments and appointed by the Governor-General.
2) Three Sudanese members to be selected by the Governor-General from a list of five names submitted to him by the Prime Minister.
3) One or more members from the Public Service Commission in an advisory capacity without the right to vote. Article 8 of the Self-Government Statute provides that the chairman and members of the commission shall be appointed by the Governor-General in consultation with the Prime minister.

Annex III of the Agreement provides for the terms of reference of the Sudanisation Committee. Primarily the committee has been charged with the duty to complete the Sudanisation of administration, the police and the Sudan Defence Force and any other Government post that may affect the freedom of the Sudanese at the time of Self-

[1] See Appendix 1.

Determination. Clause 4 of Annex III provides that the Committee completes its duties within a period not exceeding three years. This Clause also provides that the Committee shall render periodical reports to the Governor-General to consider in conjunction with his Commission. The reports with any comments thereon shall be transmitted to the Government.

Clause 3 of Annex III provides that the Committee shall take its decisions by majority vote. Its decisions shall be submitted to the Council of Ministers. This clause also provided for rules to deal with the cases when the Governor-General does not agree with any decision of the Committee or with the views of the Council Ministers or in the event of disagreement with his Commission.

According to Article 8 of the Agreement, Cairo appointed ʿAbd-al-Ḥamīd Dāūd, the Inspector-General of Egyptian Irrigation in Sudan, to represent Egypt on the Committee.[2] London appointed Robert Burnett as its representative.[3] The Sudanese Prime Minister, Ismāʿīl al-Azharī, submitted a list of five names from which the Governor-General would select three for membership of the Committee: Muḥammad Amīn Ḥussein, Zakaria Jambo, ʿUthmān Yūsuf Abū-Bakr, Ibrāhīm Yūsuf Suleimān and Maḥmūd al-Faḍlī.[4] The Governor-General, Robert Howe, was not pleased with these nominees – whom he described as being "of very poor calibre with no qualifications" and "strong NUP supporters and rabid anti-British" – but he felt that he had "no escape from the indignity of having to select three of this disreputable bunch to preside over the liquidation of the best of the Sudan Civil Service."[5]

On 20 February 1954, Howe confirmed the appointments of the British and Egyptian nominees as members of the Sudanisation Committee. Of al-Azharī's nominees, he selected Ibrāhīm Yūsuf Suleimān,

---

[2] After his transfer to Egypt, he was succeeded by Muḥammad Khalīl Ibrāhīm in both positions.

[3] National Archives, Kew, FO 371/108377 (Instructions issued by the FO for the British member of the Sudanisation Committee in Khartoum): Selwyn Lloyd to Burnett, 6 April 1954.

[4] *al-Ahrām*, 1 February 1954.

[5] National Archives, Kew, FO 371/108330 (Nominations for membership of the Sudanisation Committee): Howe to Foreign Office, 3 February 1954.

ʿUthmān Yūsuf Abū-Bakr and Maḥmūd al-Faḍlī.[6] In addition, the Governor-General appointed several non-voting Committee members: the Chairman of the Civil Service Commission, ʿAbd-al-Majīd Aḥmad, and two members of the Public Service Commission, Aḥmad Mutawallī al-ʿAtabānī and Arthur Hankin.[7]

Howe nominated Muḥammad Aḥmad Abū-Rannāt for membership of the Public Service Commission but the Council of Ministers preferred Aḥmad Mutawallī al-ʿAtabānī. The Council did approve – albeit without much enthusiasm – the Governor-General's nomination of ʿAbd-al-Majīd Aḥmad as the Commission's chairman, and that of Nāṣr al-Ḥajj ʿAlī, the Deputy Director of Education, as a Commission member.[8]

al-Azharī defended his shortlist of Sudanisation Committee nominees when he met Howe on 22 November 1954. When the Governor-General complained that individuals of higher calibre could have been nominated, and that it was inappropriate for other Committee members to be landed with colleagues of inferior qualifications, al-Azharī replied that the nominations had been the result of a vote in the Council of Ministers. He did concede, however, that the vote had been conducted on partisan lines. al-Azharī pointed out that Sudanisation was a Party political issue. It would be contrary to the goals of his own Party to nominate anyone who disagreed with the Party's position – so his nominees would support the completion of Sudanisation as soon as possible.[9]

---

[6] Ibid., FO 371/108341 (Activities of the Sudanisation Committee): Osman Yousif Abu Akar to Howe, 1 April 1954.

[7] Hankin was a veteran of Sudan colonial service, having been an Assistant District Commissioner in the eastern Bija District in the mid-1930s and Private Secretary to Sir Stewart Symes. He had more recently been working in the Ministry of Finance in Khartoum. See Sudan Archive, University of Durham (JW Robertson Papers), SAD.519/10/1-7, for Hankin's own views on the Sudanisation process.

[8] National Archives, Kew, FO 371/108343 (Appointment of a Public Service Commission under the Sudan Self-Government Statute): Luce to Basil Boothby, Head of Africa Department, Foreign Office, 11 February 1954.

[9] Ibid., FO 371/108321: Luce to Boothby, 24 February 1954.

ii. Sudanisation of the police, Sudan Defence Force and the administration

On 7 March 1954, the Sudanisation Committee held its first official meeting, at which it approved its rules of business. The first rule established was that members of the Committee would assume the chairmanship on a monthly rotation. At their second meeting the following day, the Committee considered the Sudanisation of the police force. The Committee heard testimony from two senior Sudanese police officers and decided unanimously that Sudanisation could be achieved immediately, without detriment to the efficiency of the force.

At their third and fourth meetings, held on 9 and 10 March, the Committee discussed the Sudanisation of the SDF. At their fifth meeting, on 13 March 1954, the Committee welcomed the SDF's commanding officer, Major-General Reginald Scoones, and six senior Sudanese officers, headed by *Miralai* (Brigadier-General)[10] Ibrāhīm ʿAbbūd. Having heard their views, the Committee decided by a majority vote at its sixth meeting on 14 March 1954 on the immediate Sudanisation of all positions in the SDF currently held by British Officers, Warrant Officers and Non-Commissioned Officers (NCOs) within two months. Just two positions – radio mechanics in the Signal Training Centre, currently occupied by British NCOs – were to be Sudanised as soon as suitable Sudanese replacements were available.[11] Robert Burnett, the British member of the Committee, presented a formal Note of Dissent which contained a phased programme of Sudanisation over a period of 18 months rather than two – without, he argued, detriment to the efficiency of the force or the plan to raise its numbers from 5,000 to 8,000.[12]

The Committee began discussing the Sudanisation of the civil administration at a series of meetings beginning on 17 March 1954. Representatives of the Sudanese Administrative Officers' Association expressed their views on the future strength of the civil service and on ways of filling the posts vacated by British colleagues. The Committee also heard representatives of the administration's clerical staff. At the tenth

---

[10] Hill, *Biographical Dictionary*, p. xii, explains the Ottoman-era roots of Sudan's military rankings.

[11] National Archives, Kew, FO 371/108341: Abu Akar to Howe, 1 April 1954.

[12] See Burnett's Note of Dissent in Salih, *British Documents*, vol. 10, Part II, p. 60.

and eleventh meetings, on 23 and 24 March, the Permanent Undersecretary of the Ministry of Interior, Mr A.C. Beaton, and his senior officials conveyed their views about the Sudanisation of the administration to the Committee.[13] Beaton proposed that the Sudanisation of the administration should start from the bottom up: that way the more experienced administrators would remain to the very end, offering advice and aid to Sudanese colleagues in their new posts.[14]

The Sudanisation Committee chose not to heed Mr Beaton's advice. Instead, the Committee unanimously decided to recommend the following:

1) to select as soon as possible 19 Sudanese who are to become Governors and Deputy Governors and send them to their provinces with the least possible delay;
2) to begin immediately to select and post to districts the Administrators required to replace British staff; and
3) priority should be given to the selection and posting of 30 Sudanese Administrators required for the Southern Provinces.

To fill shortages in the administrative cadre, the Committee called to consider re-employment of pensioners from the Ministry of Interior, transfer to the administration of police officers and to appoint senior clerks to administrative posts.[15]

iii. Sudanisation of the Judiciary

At its 22nd meeting on 21 April 1954, the Committee considered the question of its competence to sudanise the Judiciary. It was agreed to invite Aḥmad Mutawallī al-ʿAtabānī to attend as advisory member of the Public Service Commission. It was also agreed to invite Bābikr ʿAwaḍallah,

---

[13] National Archives, Kew, FO 371/108341: Abu Akar to Howe, 1 April 1954. Beaton had spent many years as a provincial official in Equatoria Province: Daly, *Imperial Sudan*, p. 372.
[14] Ibid., FO 371/108340 (Activities of the Sudanisation Committee): Burnett to Bromley, 26 March 1954.
[15] Abu Akar to Council of Ministers, 7 April 1954, in Salih, *British Documents*, vol. 10, Part II, p. 73.

Speaker of the House of Representatives, to give his views as ex-member of the Judiciary. The British member proposed the invitation of the Chief Justice and Justice Abū-Rannāt to attend.

al-ʿAtabānī advised that posts in the Judiciary were posts which were likely to affect the freedom of the Sudanese at the time of self-determination, because their holders were in positions of authority, particularly in the Provinces. To support his argument al-ʿAtabānī referred to the *Travaux Préparatoires* of the 1953 Agreement. He said that after reading the record of the Agreement, one would find that it was the intention of the two Governments that the Judiciary should come within the terms of reference of the Sudanisation Committee. The Committee decided by majority vote, the British member dissenting, that it has the power to sudanise the Judiciary.

The British member announced that pending the receipt of his Government's instructions he would not take part in the discussions regarding the Sudanisation of posts in the Judiciary and he would not consider himself bound by a decision on the matter taken by the Committee in his absence.

On 22 April 1954, the Committee received a letter from the Chief Registrar of the Judiciary that the Chief Justice and Justice Abū-Rannāt would not appear before the Committee on that day because they had been instructed by the Governor-General not to attend until the question of the competence of the Judiciary had been settled. The Committee addressed the Governor-General pointing out that he should have obtained the prior approval of his Commission before issuing an instruction to the Chief Justice. Moreover, in declining to permit the Chief Justice to appear before the Committee, the Governor-General did not comply with the last sentence of Clause 4 of annex III. This sentence provides that the two Governments shall give every possible assistance for the completion of the Committee's task.

At its meeting on 28 April 1954, the Committee having considered the views of al-ʿAtabānī and ʿAwaḍallah, as ex-members of the Judiciary decided that all posts in the Judiciary held by expatriates, including the posts of Official Administrator, the Commissioner of Local Courts and the Chief Registrar of the Judiciary, should be sudanised immediately by suitably qualified Sudanese. This decision was subsequently submitted to the Council of Ministers.[16]

On his part the Governor-General informed the Foreign Office that the Council of Ministers would likely accept the decision of the Sudanisation Committee and ask for his assent. He proposed to the Foreign Office that he would refer the matter to the two Governments and would not take action on the Council of Ministers' submission until receipt of joint instructions from the two Governments that the matter was within the competence of the Sudanisation Committee.

The Governor-General advised the British Government to maintain that the sudanisation of the Judiciary was outside the competence of the Sudanisation Committee, because the holders of posts in the Judiciary were protected by Article 85 of the Self-Government Statute which provided for the removal and retirement of judges.[17]

Contrary to what had been contemplated, no controversy arose between the Governor-General and the Sudanisation Committee nor between the two Governments. The British judges unanimously decided to submit their resignations to the Governor-General in an attempt to keep the Judiciary out of politics for the future.[18]

On 2 August 1955, at its 115th meeting, the Sudanisation Committee decided that the Sudanisation process was completed. It submitted its final report to the Cabinet and forwarded it to the Speaker of the House of Representatives.

iv. The Self-Determination Resolution

The declaration that the Sudanisation Committee had completed its work was conveyed formally to the House of Representatives by the Speaker when it convened on 16 August 1955. Prime Minister al-Azharī then submitted a proposal, under Article 9 of the 1953 Agreement,[19] that the House would send a letter to the Governor-General as follows:

---

[16] National Archives, Kew, FO 371/108341: Abu Akar to Howe, 1 May 1954.

[17] Ibid., FO 371/108340: Howe to Foreign Office, 3 May 1954.

[18] Hawley, *Sandtracks in the Sudan*, p. 118.

[19] Article 9 stipulates that, subject to the completion of Sudanisation, the transitional period would be brought to end when the Sudanese Parliament

> We, members of the House of Representatives of the Sudanese Parliament, express our desire to initiate the arrangements for self-determination immediately. We request Your Excellency to transmit this to the two contracting governments forthwith under Article 9 of the Agreement.[20]

Several MPs took part in the debate on the Prime Minister's proposal, making noteworthy contributions. Muḥammad Aḥmad Maḥjūb, the Leader of the Opposition, said that the Sudanese always stood together as one bloc and became serious whenever difficulties arose. That was because they put the interests of their country before their personal interests and because they put national interest before party interests. The country, he concluded was in safe hands as long as it could come together over the most important matters. Buth Diu expressed his hope that future national governments would be based on democratic principles and that they would be governments of the people by the people for the people. He expressed his hope that the people of the South would find a wholly positive response to their legitimate demands.

Ḥassan al-Ṭāhir Zarūq of the Front Against Colonialization drew attention to the fact that there were in the South tribal communities that had been oppressed by colonialism and left in a primitive and unjustly backward situation. He called for the liberation of the people of the South from backwardness and oppression, and for granting them their right of designing their own local systems within a united country. Muḥammad Nūr al-Dīn focused on future guarantees of public freedoms and the abolition of laws that suppress freedoms. He demanded that equal opportunities be granted to the expression of the two viewpoints provided for in the Agreement and over which the Sudanese people would have a plebiscite: unity with Egypt, connective independence or separative independence.

---

passed a resolution expressing its desire that arrangements for self-determination were put in motion, at which point the Governor-General would notify London and Cairo of this resolution.

[20] National Archives, Kew, FO 371/113783: Minutes of the House of Representatives (3rd Session, Sitting No. 32), dated 16 August 1955.

Finally, winding up the debate for the Government, Mubārak Zarūq said:

> We are now living at a time when history is being made. If we wish to respond positively to this history and write with our own hands some of its chapters, then we have to be worthy of that in all our conduct, by freeing our minds from narrow thinking, our hearts from hate and our ranks from splitting. We have to fight our whims and lust and bury our greed.[21]

The motion proposed by the Prime Minister under Article 9 was passed unanimously. As a result, Article 11 of the Agreement – providing for the withdrawal of British and Egyptian troops from Sudan as soon as Parliament expressed its wish to put in motion arrangements for self-determination – came into force and both London and Cairo pledged to withdraw their forces within no more than three months.[22]

In the following chapter, we shall see how, just two days after that decision on self-determination was reached, i.e. on 18 August 1955, two companies of the Equatorial Corps mutinied at Torit. We shall also see how Ṣalāḥ Sālim persistently lobbied the British Government, through its Ambassador to Cairo, Sir Humphrey Trevelyan, to approve a joint British-Egyptian military intervention to restore law and order to the South of the Sudan.

---

[21] Muḥammad ʿAmir Bashīr, *al-Jalā' wa al-Istiqlāl* (*Evacuation and Independence*) (Khartoum: Dār al-Sūdānīa li al-Kutub, 1975), pp. 8-20.

[22] National Archives, Kew, FO 371/113783: Office of UK Trade Commissioner to Foreign Office, 16 August 1955.

CHAPTER 12

Mutiny of the Southern Troops at Torit: 18 August 1955[1]

On 18 August 1955, Governor-General Sir Alexander Knox Helm was on holiday in Scotland when he received a telegram via the Foreign Office from William Luce, his Adviser on Constitutional and External Affairs:

> The immediate situation is very grave and we must also clearly expect most serious repercussions from the Southerners, generally and from Egypt. In these circumstances I feel bound, with great regret, to ask you to return to Khartoum as urgently as possible. As you know I can assume power of acting Governor-General in your absence, and I shall do so if circumstances demand it before your arrival. But I am most anxious to avoid doing this if possible as it will only make matters worse with the Egyptians.[2]

Luce reported how he had been informed by Prime Minister Ismāʿīl al-Azharī that two companies of the Equatorial Corps stationed at Torit had mutinied that very morning; they had attacked their officers,

---

[1] The people of South Sudan still celebrate the anniversary of the 18 August 1955 mutiny as a national holiday. Addressing the first such celebration, in Juba on 18 August 2008, the then First Vice-President, Salva Kiir Mayardit, said that the mutiny had been 'the starting point of the real political movement in Southern Sudan': James Gatdet Dak, 'South Sudan celebrates Torit "revolution" day of 1955', *Sudan Tribune*, 19 August 2008 (https://sudantribune.com/article28280/).

[2] National Archives, Kew, FO 371/113697 (Mutiny in South Sudan): Luce to Foreign Office, 18 August 1955.

killing one and wounding two. Seven officers were still missing. Communications with Torit had been cut since the morning, so the situation there was still unknown. The lives of Northern Sudanese officials and merchants were certainly in danger, Luce added, and the contingent at Kapoeta should also be expected to mutiny. At al-Azharī's request, Luce had formally proclaimed a state of emergency in the three Southern Provinces. He noted that he had not proclaimed a state of constitutional emergency – as provided for in Article 102 (2) of the Self-Government Statute – as this would have required referring to the Governor-General's Commission.[3]

For details of the mutiny and the resulting disturbances, this account will rely to a great extent on the Report of the Commission formed by the Government on 8 September 1955 – pursuant to the 1954 Commissions of Inquiry Ordinance – to investigate the disturbances that occurred in Southern Sudan and report on their underlying causes.[4] The following individuals were appointed to the Commission: Taufik Cotran, a senior District Judge, as Chairman, with Khalīfa Maḥjūb, General Manager of Equatoria Projects Board, and Lolik Lado, Paramount Chief of the Lokoya people in Equatoria Province, as members. After performing its task, the Commission submitted its Report to the Interior Minister, ʿAlī ʿAbd-al-Raḥman, on 18 February 1956, for publication in Arabic and English.[5]

i. Disturbances in the three Southern Provinces

According to the Report, "the most serious disturbances took place in Equatoria Province. All towns and villages in the Province were affected. Complete disorder and chaos prevailed for two weeks during

---

[3] Ibid., Luce to Foreign Office and Luce to Helm, both on 19 August 1955.

[4] *Report of the Commission of Enquiry into the Disturbances in Southern Sudan during August 1955* (Khartoum, McCorquodale, 1956). Another useful source is Øystein H. Rolandsen, 'A False Start: Between War and Peace in the Southern Sudan, 1956-62', *Journal of African History* 52/1 (2011), pp. 105-23.

[5] In a preface to the report, the Minister wrote that 'the duty of the Commission was confined to an administrative inquiry into causes and factors which led to the disturbances. Political, social and other aspects are not discussed in this booklet though there is a close connection between them and the facts revealed in this Report.'

which the forces of disorder had the upper hand. As a result, communications were cut, public services came to a stop. All government offices were closed. Northern Sudanese lives and property were attacked; murder, arson and looting were committed. Southern soldiers, policemen, warders and civilians took part in these acts.[6] The Commission found that no killing occurred in Wau, the capital of Baḥr al-Ghazāl Province. The news of the mutiny of the Southern Division did not spread in Wau before the morning of 19 August. On 21 August, soldiers, policemen and prison guards broke open weapons and ammunition depots, with some individuals firing wildly into the air. The Commission attributed this act to a fear that Northern forces had been summoned to Wau and that they would need to defend themselves."

The Report added, however, that "the greatest amount of goodwill could never, in those days, convince Southerners in Bahr El Ghazal that the Northern troops were only coming to preserve law and order." Given the gravity of the situation, the Provincial Governor, Dāūd ʿAbd-al-Laṭīf, and his Deputy, Muḥammad Aḥmad Urwa, along with several other senior officials who had gathered at the Governor's residence, decided that the best thing to do was to leave. So that same evening, they embarked on the Government steamer, the *Dāl*,[7] and sailed towards Malakal. On this abrupt departure, the Commission commented:

> What would have happened had the Governor and other high-ranking Northern Government officials stayed in their posts will always remain a matter of conjecture. ... But this remains to be said, viz., that law and order, which is the fountain of all government, had disappeared and neither the Governor nor his colleagues were able to discharge their duties. ... It is also certain that, after their sudden departure there was a cooling down effect on the situation that was fraught with danger.[8]

---

[6] *Report of the Commission of Enquiry*, p. 32.

[7] The *Dāl* was a veteran of Sudan Government service, having been commissioned in 1885 and subsequently rebuilt or modified on several occasions: Richard Hill, 'A Register of Named Power-Driven River and Marine Harbour Craft Commissioned in the Sudan 1856-1964', *Sudan Notes and Records* 51 (1970), p. 136.

[8] *Report of the Commission of Enquiry*, pp. 75-6.

In Upper Nile Province, meanwhile, the Commandant of No. 4 Company (Southern Division), stationed at Malakal, was able to leave, as ordered, by boat to Khartoum in the evening of 18 rather than 19 August. The Report praised the authorities in Upper Nile for handling the situation with 'ability and foresight'. District Commissioners were quickly on the spot, reassuring local Chiefs and inhabitants. The Report added that, "apart from Malakal, the police, especially the Nilotics, were generally loyal."[9]

The Commissioners identified 336 Northerners as having been killed by firearms and spears or by burning: these included army officers, NCOs, other ranks, administrators, teachers, roads and forests supervisors, farm inspectors, technicians, traders, workers, as well as women and children. The Report noted that mutinying soldiers, policemen and prison warders hand-picked their victims – with foreigners and their property remaining untouched, except in two exceptional cases. In all instances, Copts, Syrians, Egyptians and British nationals were carefully separated, set apart and consequently set free. 75 Southerners were reported to have been killed, 55 of them after drowning in the Kinyeti River.[10]

ii. Causes of the disturbances

The Commission indicated that without focusing on the following points, the causes of the disturbances could never be understood. First, there was very little in common between Northern and Southern Sudanese – and, for historical reasons, Southerners regarded Northerners as their traditional enemies. Secondly, British administrative policy had always been to let the Southern Sudanese "progress on African and Negroid lines". As a result, for financial, economic, political and geographical reasons, Northern Sudan had progressed rapidly in every field, while Southern Sudan lagged far behind. This difference in development created a feeling of being cheated, exploited and dominated.

These factors contributed to a general lack of fellow citizenship among Southerners with respect to Northerners – and a lack of

---

[9] Ibid., pp. 66-7 and 71.
[10] Ibid., pp. 78-80.

nationalism or patriotism to Sudan as a whole. An individual's loyalty was only to his own tribe. When political awareness was born among Southern Sudanese, it was bound to be initially regional and not national. More specifically, the Commission cited the following as triggers for the disturbances:

a. A forged telegram attributed to Ismāʿīl al-Azharī

In July 1955, a fake telegram was widely distributed in the South. It was typed on official paper and, in Equatoria Province, reached Torit, Yambio, Maridi, Nzara and Yei. It read:

> To my administrators in the three Southern Provinces: I have just signed a document for self-determination. Do not listen to the childish complaints of the Southerners. Persecute them, oppress them, ill-treat them according to my earlier orders.
>
> Any administrator who fails to comply with my orders will be liable for prosecution. In three months' time, all of you will come round and enjoy the work you have done.[11]

Copies of the bogus telegram were sent to various politically minded clerks, as well as to Southern police officers and men. One copy reached a Deputy Company Quartermaster Sergeant[12] in the Southern Corps at Torit named Saturlino Oboyo. Saturlino changed the phrase "to my administrators in the three Southern Provinces" to "my Northern Officers in the Southern Corps". He then called a meeting attended by 2nd Lieutenant Emilio Taffeng Lodongi and several NCOs. Although the fake telegram was widely circulated, it does not seem to have reached the attention of the police authorities until 7 August. No effort was made to discover its source– and it was noted later that, while some in the administration had heard of the telegram, others did not hear about it until after the disturbances. The Commission's Report found that no

---

[11] Ibid., p. 82.

[12] The rank given in the report is *Wakīl Bulūk Amīn*: see Hill, *Biographical Dictionary*, p. x.

active steps were taken to deny its contents, nor to allay the fears and misconceptions it created in the minds of Southerners.[13]

b. Loss of confidence due to interference of Equatoria's administrators in politics

We have seen in Chapter 5 that the Liberal Party sponsored the call for the 3rd Juba Conference of July 1955. As invitations were sent to the NUP members of Parliament, the Government attempted to frustrate the Conference. For this purpose, a hint was sent from a Government source to some politically-minded administrators in Equatoria to arrange for telegrams to be sent to Khartoum deprecating the aims of the Conference and supporting the Government.

The District Commissioner (DC) of Yambio and his Assistant therefore toured their District to obtain signatures from tribal chiefs in support of the Government. All forms of pressure were used to obtain their consent, trickery not excluded.

The Assistant District Commissioner (ADC) sent to Khartoum in his name a telegram on behalf of the thirteen Chiefs who signed.[14] The telegram was given wide publicity by Radio Omdurman. The object of this was to show that all was well in the South and that the people were solidly behind the Government. It was also intended to demonstrate to the NUP's Southern members of Parliament whose loyalty began to waver that Liberal Party MPs represented nobody but themselves.

The Commission considered the interference of the Assistant District Commissioner in politics in such a way deplorable in a moral sense and in administrative sense and asserted that it was "manifestly wrong for an administrator to allow his party loyalty to carry him beyond his duty to his people and to the public service. It certainly led to his public losing confidence in his impartiality."

---

13 *Report of the Commission of Enquiry*, p. 83.

14 Raphael Koba Badal, 'British Administration in Southern Sudan' (PhD, University of London, 1977), p. 285: https://eprints.soas.ac.uk/29707/1/10752679.pdf.

The Commission believed that the Governor and the Deputy Governor in Equatoria were well aware of the activities of their subordinates.[15]

c. The trial of Elia Kuze: 25 July 1955

Elia Kuze was a Member of the House of Representatives whose constituency was in Zande District. When the Assistant District Commissioner of Yambio sent the declaration of support, subsequently to be broadcast by Radio Omdurman, this act so stirred Kuze up that he retaliated against administrative officers in his own region, denouncing the chiefs who had agreed to sign the declaration supporting the Government. Kuze organised a meeting on 7 July 1955, attended by a crowd estimated to be between 300-500 people. They resolved that Kuze was the only person competent to speak on their behalf and that he should have been consulted prior to the telegram being sent. They also resolved that they did not want to be ruled by Northerners. They considered the conduct of the Assistant District Commissioner interference in politics contrary to Government regulations and demanded the removal from office of all the Chiefs who had signed the declaration.

This demand offended the Chiefs, who lodged a formal complaint against Elia Kuze. His trial, and that of his aides, opened on 25 July 1955 before the Chiefs' Court. Under Article 441 of the Sudan Penal Code, the Court sentenced Elia and his aides to 20 years' imprisonment each. The sentence was later reduced to two years, after the District Commissioner explained to the Court that two years was the maximum sentence under the law for such an offence. The Commission's Report described the trial as "a farce and a usurpation of the machinery of justice", for the following reasons:

1) The District Commissioner's motive for the trial was simply the restoration of his prestige and the prestige of some of his Chiefs.

[15] *Report of the Commission of Enquiry*, pp. 84-91.

2) Some of the members of the Court were themselves the complainants in the action. They were in fact sitting as judges in their own cause.
3) The trial is contrary to the spirit and intention of the Chiefs' Court Ordinance, a legislation principally passed for the trial of ordinary offenders according to native law and customs. It was never intended to be used for the trial of political offenders.

The Commission blamed the Governor and Deputy Governor of the Province for non-intervention in the trial of Elia Kuze for "both are magistrates of the first class and well conversant with law and procedure, were aware of the trial but had nevertheless allowed to continue."[16]

The Commission also noted the failure of the administration to "assess public feeling, and by attempting to assert authority and prestige, had contributed so much to what, in a little while later, gave birth to complete loss of authority and prestige."

d. Events in Nzara: 26 July 1955

On 26 July 1955, the management of the Equatorial Projects Board sacked some 300 workers *en masse*. The Commission considered that act a major blunder, because the dismissals came as the numbers of technical staff from Northern Sudan were increasing because of Sudanisation. The dismissal failed to take into consideration the potential repercussions on the prevailing political situation. Southerners interpreted it as a deliberate attempt by Northern management to deprive them of their livelihoods and import Northerners instead.

---

[16] *Report of the Commission of Enquiry*, pp. 91-7. The Acting Chief Justice of Sudan, Muḥammad Aḥmad Abū-Rannāt, quashed Kuze's conviction and ordered a retrial. In Criminal Court Circular No. 41, dated 20 August 1955, he directed that no MP charged with committing an offence or offences under the Code of Criminal Procedure should be tried before full information showing the nature of the offence with which he is charged was made available and the approximate date of the trial was sent either to the Speaker of the House of Representatives or the Speaker of the Senate.

The same day, workers in the weaving and spinning mills demanded higher wages, warning that they would go on strike, starting on 1 August, if management refused the demand. On the same day, workers took to the streets in a rally ending at the Nzara market. They were joined by locals armed with spears, bows and arrows. There were only three policemen in Nzara: they were unable to enforce law and order in the face of crowds estimated to number between 700 and 1000 demonstrators. In an effort to control the situation, the Yambio Assistant District Commissioner arrived in Nzara with an officer from the Sudan Defence Force.

The Commission commented in its Report that 11 SDF soldiers and five policemen were not enough to restore order by peaceful means. Both ADC and SDF officers were young and inexperienced: they were overwhelmed when they saw such a large and violent crowd and they promptly resorted to means that were not licensed by law. Tear gas and firearms were used, with the result that six Zande men were killed and others sustained injuries. The Commission concluded that, whether or not the situation was well handled, the incident itself had a detrimental effect on the minds of Southerners and was regarded by them as the beginning of war. If there had been any confidence left in the administration, it had then disappeared completely.

In spite of known communist activity in Nzara, the Commission found that the disturbances of 26 July 1955 were not communist inspired.[17] They were industrial unrest due to mass dismissals and the prevailing political atmosphere. The people of the South, the Commission noted, did not understand or care about the theories of Marx or Lenin, nor did the Southern intelligentsia care much about abstract communist theories – although their attention had been caught by extracts about the power of collective strike action when demanding higher wages and of slogans calling for equal pay for equal work or local rule for the South within a united Sudan.[18]

---

[17] In January and February 1955, some prominent members of the Front Against Colonialization had visited parts of Equatoria Province and propagated their ideas to many Southerners: *Report of the Commission of Enquiry*, pp. 97-9.
[18] Ibid., pp. 97-102.

e. Failure to take necessary action on discovery of the plot

At a meeting held in Khartoum on 23 July 1955 for Corps Commanders, it was decided to form a Khartoum District Garrison following the evacuation of British and Egyptian troops. It was also decided that the garrison would be drawn from the five existing companies of the SDF, with the addition of No. 2 Company (Southern Division).[19]

On 6 August 1955, Sergeant Saturlino fired an arrow at a Northern Assistant Postmaster but missed him and hit another Southern soldier instead. Saturlino confessed that he had been aiming at the Deputy Commander of the Southern Division. A search of his home led to the seizure of documents that revealed a plot, involving most senior NCOs, to stage a mutiny in the Southern Division.[20]

The Commission's Report stated that the authorities showed 'considerable weakness' as it did not immediately arrest any SDF personnel, instead detaining two Juba civilians and charging them with involvement in the mutiny plot. As a result, crowds demonstrated outside the government building in Juba, demanding the release of the accused. They attempted to attack the DC but were dispersed with the use of tear gas.[21]

On 17 August 1955, a meeting of military and civilian authorities in Equatoria Province decided that No. 2 Company (Equatoria Corps) must, for the prestige and dignity of the army, proceed to Khartoum. A week later, verbal orders for this movement – ostensibly to take part in a military parade to celebrate the evacuation of foreign troops – were received. On 16 August, written orders followed, issued by the Commander of the Equatoria Corps.[22] NCOs and other ranks were hostile to these orders – and did not conceal their displeasure. The Commission's Report noted that officers were fully aware of the fact that Southerners were extremely attached to their families and previous experiences with the Southern Corps showed their dislike of work outside their regions.[23] The only sensible thing to have been done, according to the Report, was

---

[19] Ibid., p. 102-103.
[20] Ibid., pp. 25-31.
[21] Ibid., pp. 31.
[22] Ibid., p. 105-109.
[23] Ibid., pp. 106-107.

to cancel the movement order forthwith. The Commission criticised the arguments of senior officers in the second Company about prestige and dignity when it was well known – not just to them but to everyone in Equatoria – that the men would refuse to obey the order and would mutiny. The only force that might have been relied upon to keep law and order and protect lives and property was a company composed of 200 soldiers from the Camel Corps – but they lacked the equipment, means of communication and firepower required in a province the size of Italy.[24]

f. Disappointment at the outcome of Sudanisation and fear of northern domination

The Commission found that Southerners – lacking seniority, experience and qualifications – were not much affected by Sudanisation. Only a handful were promoted to senior jobs in the civil service, with the highest post in the administration being ADC. The Sudanisation Commission stated that, as far as filling vacant jobs was concerned, it had been bound by regulations to award vacant posts to senior officials that came next on a list. Only through Government interference it would have been possible to bypass this process and promote Southerners solely on political grounds – and this would be a precedent that would go a long way to undermine and destroy the civil service, whose independence was essential for the maintenance of good government.

The Commission concluded that the most irreparable damage done to North-South relations was through the rash and irresponsible promises made by NUP politicians during their election campaigns in Southern Sudan. It subsequently became evident that the promises made to Southerners could not be kept – and this made the new Northern administration the principal target of Southerners' wrath. The average Southerner would not see any difference between government and administration. The Southerner's perspective, as noted by the Commission, was regional not national: a DC that one might see in person interested him more than a hypothetical representative in some Parliament or Government far away in Khartoum.[25]

---

[24] Ibid., pp. 110 and 22.

[25] Ibid., pp. 111-2.

g. The circulation of false rumours

The Commissioners' Report noted the absence of effective government propaganda in the South, with the result that false rumours spread quickly without any means to rebut them and allay misunderstandings. The Report added that, when a lie was repeated many times, that simple repetition would lead people in underdeveloped communities to believe it. The Commission noted that the national broadcasting service "seems to be exclusively for the benefit of the North. In the South itself, nobody in the Administration seems to have thought of mass education by use of mobile cinema, radio programmes or publication of news of local interest."[26]

iii. The Commission's Report addresses other matters

The Commission included in its Report some matters that it did not consider to be direct causes of the disturbances. It felt, however, that it was part of its duty to pay attention to them because they had created ill-feeling among Southerners and caused a loss of confidence in the Khartoum administration. The first of these was the conduct of some Northern Sudanese known as the Jallāba,[27] who had wrecked their relationship with the people of the South. The Commission cited instances of their misconduct:

a) Many of the Northern Sudanese, especially the uneducated, regarded Southerners as of an inferior race and the Jallāba were no exception as the majority of them were uneducated. It was a widespread practice across the South for Northern traders to refer to Southerners as *ʿabīd*, or slaves. This contemptuous term – a constant reminder of the region's experience during the years of the slave trade, a period they wanted to forget – had created widespread ill-feeling among Southerners.
b) The Jallāba interfered in provincial administration, especially in Equatoria. The actual administrators, because they either feared

[26] Ibid., p. 122.

[27] The Jallāba were primarily merchants from northern Sudan who were often recruited to help the understaffed British run extremely large provinces: Daly, Imperial Sudan, pp. 38-9.

or sympathised with them, gave them more protection than they afforded to other citizens. They also trusted the Jallāba as informants more than other citizens. [28]

The Commission also noted evidence that had been submitted that, in one district, the inhabitants rarely saw their DC, who was often seen playing cards in a shop. The Report observed that, in places where a DC was looked upon almost as a demi-god, his personal conduct was as much of his job as the work he did in his office – and had to be exemplary in every respect. [29] In the final paragraph of the Report, it was stated that:

> Another thing that the Commission felt had undermined confidence in the South was the attempt of some Northern Sudanese to change historically engrained cultural habits, such as nakedness. What the majority of the human race consider as a shameful practice, the majority of Southerners on the contrary, think that it is the essence of their manhood.[30]

iv. Ṣalāḥ Sālim demands Anglo-Egyptian intervention in the South

At 10 o'clock on the night of 22 August 1955, the British Ambassador to Cairo, Sir Humphrey Trevelyan, received Major Ṣalāḥ Sālim, Egypt's Minister of National Guidance and Sudanese Affairs.[31] Sālim told his host that he had just consulted the Prime Minister, Gamāl ʿAbd-al-Nāṣir. In view of the deteriorating situation in the South and the constant clashes between Northerners and Southerners, he continued, Cairo considered that the Condominium Governments should take joint measures to prevent further bloodshed and restore order. Sir Humphrey replied that, on the contrary, according to information received by the British the position had eased during the course of the day. Ṣalāḥ Sālim insisted that the Government of Egypt should make a formal declaration, that same night, of its desire to take joint action to restore the situation

---

[28] Ibid., pp. 123-4.

[29] Ibid., pp. 125-6.

[30] Ibid., p. 126.

[31] National Archives, Kew, FO 371/113697: Trevelyan to Foreign Office, 22 August 1955.

in collaboration with the British Government. Nor could the matter wait, according to Sālim, as the Egyptians were being accused in Khartoum of having started the trouble in the South with the intention of undermining the entire self-determination process. Sālim added that Egyptian inaction was being contrasted with the positive assistance being given by the British. The atmosphere was becoming heated and the lives of Egyptians in Khartoum were in danger.

Sir Humphrey suggested to Ṣalāḥ Sālim that the Egyptian Government might instead limit itself to a statement to the effect that, in conjunction with the British Government, it was ready to render such assistance as the Sudanese Government might require in restoring the situation in the Southern Provinces. Sālim was dissatisfied with the reference to the Sudanese Government: it would, he said, be interpreted as meaning that Egypt was prepared to assist the North against the South. After a good deal of argument, he accepted Trevelyan's proposed formula, substituting the Governor-General for the Sudanese Government.

The Major then suggested that the two governments should station British and Egyptian troops between Northern troops and Southern mutineers to prevent clashes and stop bloodshed. Sir Humphrey responded by advising the Egyptian to say as little as possible for now about military intervention, adding that Khartoum could manage without foreign assistance. If the Sudanese Government wanted direct military assistance from the Co-Domini – and he was certain that the situation would best be restored without it – it could request it via the Governor-General: Cairo and London had to wait for an initiative from him.

Ṣalāḥ Sālim, it seemed, believed that the situation required a declaration of constitutional emergency. Before leaving the Ambassador's residence, he referred to Article 102 of the 1953 Self-Government Statute, which gave the Governor-General the power to declare a constitutional emergency for 30 days "without prior or subsequent approval of his Commission". But, as we have mentioned above, the Governor-General had declared a 'normal' emergency in the three Southern Provinces, under the Sudan Defence Ordinance of 1939. In Chapter 6, we mentioned how Ṣalāḥ Sālim had warned Anthony Nutting, the British Minister of State for Foreign Affairs, in the presence of Gamāl ʿAbd-al-Nāṣir, that he expected chaos and bloodshed in Sudan after six or seven months.[32] One wonders whether the mutiny and the resulting disturbances were what he was expecting. One final point is worth noting in respect of the Report compiled by Taufik Cotran and his fellow Commissioners: one of the causes of the disturbances in Southern Sudan enumerated in the Report was deleted. A Deputy Undersecretary at the Sudanese Interior Ministry explained to the British Embassy in Khartoum that the deleted material was merely opinions and comments that might affect Sudan's relations with the Condominium Governments.[33]

---

[32] Ibid., FO 371/108380: Nutting to Eden, 28 October 1954.

[33] Ibid., FO 371/119604 (Internal political situation in Sudan, about to become an independent sovereign state): Edwin Chapman-Andrews [a future British Ambassador to Sudan, 1956-61], Khartoum, to Selwyn Lloyd, 30 October 1955.

CHAPTER 13

The International Commission and the Plebiscite

i. The International Commission

As mentioned in Chapter 11, Article 9 of the 1953 Agreement on Self-Government and Self-Determination provided that the transitional period would be terminated subsequent to the adoption of the Sudanese Parliament of a resolution expressing its desire put in motion the arrangements for Self-Determination.[1] This occurred on 16 August 1955. When according to Article 10 Britain and Egypt were duly informed of the resolution, the current Government should draw up a draft law for the election of a Constituent Assembly and submit it to Parliament for approval. The draft law would require the consent of the Governor-General with the agreement of his Commission.

Article 10 further provided that the detailed preparations for the process of self-determination, including safeguards to secure impartiality of the elections and any other arrangements designed to ensure a free and neutral atmosphere, shall be subject to international supervision. Britain and Egypt pledged to accept the recommendations of any International body set up to this end.

Article 11 of the 1953 Agreement provided that the Egyptian and British forces should be withdrawn from the Sudan immediately upon the adoption by the Sudanese Parliament of the resolution expressing the desire to put in motion arrangements for self-determination. The two Governments undertook to complete this within a period not exceeding three months.

---

[1] See Appendix 1.

Under Article 11 of the Self-Government Statute, the supreme military command would remain vested in the Governor-General, who would also be the Supreme Commander of the Sudan Defence Force (SDF). Annexed to the 1953 Agreement were memoranda exchanged between Nagīb and Ambassador Stevenson to confirm an understanding between them that amongst matters to be considered by the International Commission would be the question of the supreme command of the Sudanese Armed Forces as from and after the completion of the withdrawal of Egyptian and British armed forces from the Sudan.

The composition of the International Commission was a bone of contention between Egyptian and British Governments. Egypt proposed that the membership of the Commission should include Sudanese, Egyptian and British representation. Britain argued that this could not be reconciled with the spirit of neutrality called for by the 1953 Agreement.

That matter was referred by the British and Egyptian Governments to the Sudanese House of Representatives, [2] which resolved on 22 August 1955 against representation of Egypt and Britain in the International Commission. Majority leader Mubārak Zarūq argued that logic dictated that the British and Egyptian Governments should not be represented in the Commission which would supervise all arrangements necessary to secure a free and neutral atmosphere for self-determination. He said that the presence of Britain and Egypt in the most important Commission known to the Sudan would be nothing but a source of discord and conflict. He asserted that the Commission should be neutral and free from any element which would make its task difficult, and that the requisites of integrity, coherence and success should be made available to it.[3]

On the same date of 22 August 1955, the House of Representatives passed a resolution that Britain and Egypt should not be represented in the International Commission and that the Commission shall be composed of members from Sweden, Norway, India, Pakistan, Switzerland, Yugoslavia and Czechoslovakia.

---

[2] National Archives, Kew, FO 371/113583: Foreign Office note by Bromley, 25 August 1955. Also *al-Ahrām*, 16 August 1955.

[3] Minutes of the House of Representatives, Session No. 33, 22 August 1955.

ii. The plebiscite

The idea that the choice laid down in Article 12 of the 1953 Agreement should be effected by a plebiscite to avoid the perils of self-determination through a Constituent Assembly, emanated from within the ranks of the Independence Front. That was crystal clear in the statement issued by the Front in February 1955. The idea received support from all sections of the Sudanese press. They wrote that the plebiscite would obviate the need for holding elections for a Constituent Assembly and the risks which they would entail Egyptian interference.[4]

al-Ittiḥād newspaper, the mouthpiece of the NUP, advocated a plebiscite because "many Sudanese are apt to be confused by the changing political views of those who contest the elections. Judging by the past experiences, elected members are liable to change their colour and thereby misrepresent the real wish of their voters."

al-Ayyām, an independent newspaper, suggested a method whereby the elections for a Constituent Assembly and the plebiscite could take place simultaneously, to avert the possible defection of the members of the Constituent Assembly. Each voter would be given two ballot papers: one for independence or a link with Egypt and the other for voting to a candidate to the Constituent Assembly. The task of the assembly would thus be confined to drawing up a constitution for the Sudan compatible with the decision of the electorates.[5]

The demand that the Choice laid down in Article 12 of the 1953 Agreement be made by a plebiscite received the blessing and strong support of Sayyid ʿAlī al-Mīrghanī. He told Luce on 16 July 1955 that it was not reasonable to put the fate of 10 million Sudanese in the hands of a small body of men when it had been shown over the past two years how easily individuals in this country can be influenced.[6]

Sayyid ʿAlī reinforced his stance by a statement he issued on 15 August 1955. He advised the Sudanese people to adopt a direct public plebiscite in a free and neutral atmosphere to determine the status they wished for their country instead of by an elected Constituent Assembly

---

[4] *al-Ayyām*, 4 February 1955.

[5] Newspaper reports summarised in National Archives, Kew, FO 371/113783: UK Trade Commissioner, Khartoum, to Foreign Office, 9 July 1955.

[6] Ibid., Record of Conversation with Sayed Ali, 20 July 1955.

provided for in the 1953 Agreement. To this end he called on the Co-Domini to amend the agreement.[7]

Prime Minister al-Azharī and his Minister for Foreign Affairs Zarūq did their utmost to convince Sayyid ʿAlī to drop the idea of a plebiscite because of the danger of seeking any change in the 1953 Agreement. On their failure to convince him, they left it to Sayyid ʿAlī to convey his personal views direct to the Co-Domini but without expecting any initiative from the Sudanese Government.[8]

Sayyid ʿAlī therefore took the unprecedented step of directly making his views known to the Co-Domini. He asked the two senior Egyptian officials resident in Khartoum to convey his views to their Government. Those were the Economic Expert and the Inspector-General of Egyptian irrigation. Likewise he told Luce when he met him on 15 August 1955 to inform Her Majesty's Government. [9]

The NUP responded positively on 26 August 1955 to the advice of Sayyid ʿAlī on holding a plebiscite.[10] al-Azharī and Zarūq eventually accepted the idea and hoped that the Co-Domini would consider it favourably. But subsequently al-Azharī told Luce that the Sudanese Government as such would not take any initiative unless it was certain that the Egyptians were favourably disposed towards the idea.[11]

In an interview on 17 August 1955, with the Arab News Agency of Reuters, Sayyid ʿAbd-al-Raḥman al-Mahdī said that his support for the principle of plebiscite is not a new matter. He had explained it to the whole people on many occasions. But as the Sudanese people were now all unanimous in calling for independence, the plebiscite would be pointless. The correct step, he argued, would be the declaration by Egypt and Britain of the independence of the Sudan and the plebiscite would thereby be avoided.[12]

---

[7] *al-Rāyī al-ʿAm*, 15 August 1955.

[8] National Archives, Kew, FO 371/113583: Governor-General's Office, Khartoum to Foreign Office, 16 August 1955.

[9] Ibid.

[10] *al-Rāyī al-ʿAm*, 27 August 1955.

[11] National Archives, Kew, FO 371/113583: Governor-General's Office to Foreign Office, 16 August 1955, loc. cit.

[12] al-Ṣādiq al Mahdī (ed.), *Jihād fī Sabīl al-Istiqlāl* (*Jihad in the Cause of Independence*) (Khartoum: Government Press, 1965), p. 158.

iii. The respective positions of Egypt and Britain regarding the plebiscite

It seemed from correspondence exchanged between the Foreign Office and its Cairo Embassy prior to the adoption by the Sudanese Parliament of a resolution on the plebiscite, that the British Government accepted in principle the idea of holding a plebiscite though that was not officially announced.[13] But before the Sudanese Parliament passed its resolution on the plebiscite, the News Department of the Foreign Office told press correspondents that Britain would not oppose an appeal from the Sudan Government to amend the 1953 Agreement and would be willing to discuss with Egypt any cut in the self-determination process sponsored by the Sudan. Subsequent to the adoption of the plebiscite resolution, the News Department told correspondents that if the Sudanese wanted a plebiscite, and if Egypt supported it, Britain would not stand in the way.[14]

British officials – be they in London or Khartoum – did not hide their concern over the technical difficulties that would be raised by a plebiscite. To accept would mean that Britain would have to start from the very beginning: making preparations for conducting, as well as renegotiating with Egypt parts of the 1953 Agreement.[15] Nonetheless Britain was keen not to allow Egypt to take the initiative and unilaterally accept the plebiscite. Ambassador Trevelyan was therefore instructed to discuss the matter with the Egyptian Government, with a view to coordinating a joint reply to the Sudanese appeal for a plebiscite. Trevelyan duly met Ṣalāḥ Sālim on 21 August 1955 – about a week before the Revolutionary Command Council accepted the Major's resignation and Gamāl ʿAbd-al-Nāṣir assumed personal control over the Sudan portfolio, as mentioned in Chapter 8. Trevelyan reached an agreement with Sālim that, if the Sudanese Parliament proposed a plebiscite, the Co-Domini would send their consent to the proposal in a joint reply – although Ṣalāḥ Sālim went further when he hinted that Egypt was

---

[13] National Archives, Kew, FO 371/113784 (Self-determination for the Sudan: decision to hold plebiscite): Cairo to Foreign Office, 18 August 1955, Foreign Office to Cairo, 19 August 1955 and Foreign Office to Cairo, 19 September 1955.

[14] Ibid. Neither statement was to be attributed to the Foreign Office.

[15] Ibid., Foreign Office to Cairo, 18 August 1955.

prepared to give its consent to an ordinary resolution of the current Sudanese Parliament concerning the future of Sudan.[16]

On 29 August 1955, the Sudanese House of Representatives passed a resolution on the plebiscite, expressing its view that a direct popular vote was the most effective means to verify the real wishes of the Sudanese. It urged the Sudan Government to take 'all measures' to convey that resolution to the Governments of Egypt and the UK.[17]

On 13 September 1955, Knox Helm presented to the Foreign Office arguments for the immediate recognition of Sudan's independence. He suggested that the British Government must immediately propose to Nāṣir that the Co-Domini should recognise Sudanese independence forthwith and that they would agree to entrust to the current Parliament the preparation of the new Constitution and the electoral law. Of the reasons he gave for his suggestion were the following:

a) To terminate the present unsatisfactory transitional period. If it had to continue for another 18 months it would be more unsatisfactory;
b) The upset in a troubled country which would be caused by conducting a plebiscite, election of a Constituent Assembly and a final election – all within 15 months; and
c) The wide acceptance by the Sudanese of independence.[18]

On the same day, 13 September 1955, the Egyptian Foreign Minister issued a statement to the effect that Egypt would reject the plebiscite and wished to hold fast to the Agreement.[19] His British counterpart, Harold Macmillan, instructed Trevelyan to tell Nāṣir when he saw him that, "since both Britain and Egypt have publicly let it be known that we accepted the idea of a plebiscite on the independence question, there is no going back on this either for him or for us." As this long and laborious process was not in Sudan's interest, however, it must

---

[16] Ibid., Cairo to Foreign Office, 21 August 1955.
[17] Minutes of the House of Representatives, Session No. 34, 29 August 1955.
[18] National Archives, Kew, FO 371/113615: Knox Helm to Foreign Office, 13 September 1955.
[19] Ibid., FO 371/113784: Cairo to Foreign Office, 13 September 1955.

be speeded up. What was more, the disturbances in Southern Sudan increased the difficulties of conducting an effective plebiscite. Macmillan asked Trevelyan to propose to Nāṣir the acceptance of the principle of an independent Sudan and to allow the current Parliament in Khartoum to set about the job of constitution making. When this was satisfactorily done, a day would be appointed on which the new state of Sudan would formally come into being.[20]

Trevelyan met Nāṣir on 20 September 1955 and put to him the issues of the plebiscite and Sudanese independence as instructed by Macmillan. But Nāṣir said that he could not give the Ambassador an immediate answer: he had not previously had personal experience with Sudan and so he would rather postpone his formal response to a later meeting, to be arranged within a few days.[21] When Trevelyan met Nāṣir again on 1 October 1955, Nāṣir agreed to the question of the plebiscite but said he could not agree to a declaration of Sudanese independence for two reasons. First, although the prospects of unity with Egypt were over and Sudan would certainly vote for independence, he could not take the initiative in declaring independence since this would mean the public abandonment of those Sudanese who were still in favour of a link with Egypt. Secondly, the abandonment of what had been an important aim of the Egyptian revolution would make his internal position very difficult if he was seen to be taking the initiative. When Trevelyan asked Nāṣir whether he would agree to the Co-Domini inviting the Sudanese Parliament to declare on the issue, Nāṣir said that this would not help him to get over his difficulties, since everyone knew that the current Parliament was in favour of independence.[22]

It shall be mentioned in the next chapter, that notwithstanding the fact that the decisions of Parliament on the composition of the International Commission and the plebiscite were issued in August 1955, their approval by the Condominium Governments was not communicated to Parliament until November 1955. Moreover, the agreement regarding the amendments of the 1953 Agreement to incorporate the plebiscite idea, and the terms of reference of the

---

[20] Ibid., Foreign Office to Cairo, 16 September 1955.

[21] Ibid., Cairo to Foreign Office, 20 September 1955.

[22] Ibid., FO 371/113616 (Political relations between UK, Egypt and Sudan): Cairo to Foreign Office, 2 October 1955.

International Commission was not concluded until 3 December 1955. Consequent upon the conclusion by Egypt of the arms deal with Czechoslovakia on 27 September 1955,[23] Britain decided to proceed alone in speeding up the Sudan's independence: not through the procedure provided for by the 1953 Agreement, or the direct plebiscite, but via a third way.

[23] On this date, Egypt turned away from the US, UK and Western powers by signing an arms deal with Czechoslovakia that channeled 30 million Egyptian pounds ($83 million) worth of Soviet weaponry to Egypt. Gamāl ʿAbd-al-Nāṣir reminded the Egyptian people that building a strong national army had been one of the key pledges of the coup d'etat that overthrew King Fārūq.

CHAPTER 14

Britain Proposes to al-Azharī a Short Cut to Independence: October 1955

A reader of this book would not fail to observe that proposals to short cut or speed up the self-determination process had been mooted at different times and in different contexts. Briefly enumerated these are:

1. In the aftermath of Muḥammad Nagīb's resignation from the headship of the Egyptian Revolutionary Command Council in February 1954, the President of the Umma Party called for the Sudanese to cut short the self-determination and declare independence from within the existing Parliament.
2. Following on the disturbances of 1 March 1954, Sayyid ʿAbd-al-Raḥman al-Mahdī called on Britain to unilaterally declare Sudan's independence because of Egypt's violations of the 1953 Agreement.
3. The National Charter proposed by the Independence Front in April 1955, called for amendment of Article 12 of the 1953 Agreement to delete the provisions dealing with self-determination.
4. In a press interview in August 1955, Sayyid ʿAbd-al-Raḥman al-Mahdī declared that as the Sudanese were unanimously calling for independence, the correct step for the Co-Domini would be to declare the independence of the Sudan, and that holding a plebiscite would be pointless.
5. Prompted by a proposal tendered by Governor-General Knox Helm, Britain sought the approval of Gamāl ʿAbd-al-Nāṣir to recognition by the Co-Domini together of the independence of

the Sudan and entrusting to the current Parliament the task of drawing up a new constitution.

6. In a draft note dated 4 October 1955 to the Foreign Office, Helm advised that the best way out would be "for the Sudanese to take things into their own hands and face the Co-Domini with a *fait accompli*."[1]

i. Egypt outmanoeuvred by Britain:[2] Telegram No. 388

In the meanwhile, Egypt took a daring step which provoked fury in London. On 27 September 1955, it was announced that Egypt had concluded a substantial arms deal with Czechoslovakia.[3] In Cairo, Sir Humphrey Trevelyan spoke to Gamāl ʿAbd-al-Nāṣir on 6 October 1955 about the impact of the deal on Egypt's relations with the West. A long discussion developed over Israeli armament, in the course of which Nāṣir said all that he wanted was security. He had devoted all Egypt's resources to development – until the Israeli raid against Gaza on 28 February 1955.[4] Nāṣir added that he had not planned to spend so much on weapons but the raid on Gaza had compelled him to do so.[5]

The British Cabinet decided that the best response to Nāṣir's move should be made in Sudan. Harold Macmillan sent the following momentous telegram to Knox Helm in Khartoum:

---

[1] National Archives, Kew, FO 371/113619 (Political relations between UK, Egypt and Sudan): Enclosure in Knox Helm to Evelyn Shuckburgh [Under-Secretary in charge of Middle East affairs at the Foreign Office], 6 October 1955.

[2] Anthony Adamthwaite, 'Overstretched and Overstrung: Eden, the Foreign Office and the Making of Policy, 1951-5', *International Affairs* 64/2 (1988), pp. 241-59, is an interesting overview of what was going on behind the scenes in London.

[3] al-Rāfaʿī. *Thawrat 23 Yūliyū*, pp. 196 ff.

[4] The Gaza Strip was at the time under Egyptian control and 38 Egyptian soldiers were killed during what Israel called Operation Black Arrow. The incursion was unanimously condemned by the UN Security Council in Resolution 106 on 29 March 1955.

[5] National Archives, Kew, FO 371/113616: Trevelyan, Cairo, to Foreign Office, 7 October 1955. Also al-Rāfaʿī. *Thawrat 23 Yūliyū*, p. 167.

In view of Egyptian action in concluding an armament deal with Czechoslovakia, we need no longer feel obliged to consult Egyptian susceptibilities so carefully as hitherto over the Sudan. There is a strong case on merit for speeding up the process of the Sudanese towards independence. The original plan under the Anglo-Egyptian Agreement would have required election for a constituent assembly before self-determination. The next plan (advocated by the Sudan Parliament) was for a plebiscite. Both these arrangements would involve international supervision. There seems no valid reason why the Sudanese should not be allowed to decide upon independence without going through these difficult and perhaps dangerous processes. I have also been impressed by the difficulty of your position in the interim period, with responsibility but no power, and by your strong desire to see the whole process speeded up.

Subject, therefore, to your views, I propose that you should inform the Sudanese Prime Minister at an early date that Her Majesty's Government are ready to recognize the immediate independence of the Sudan if the Sudanese so desire and that an announcement to this effect will shortly be made. Proposal would be to make the public announcement not more than twenty four hours after Azhari had been informed. Thus he would have an opportunity to protest if he really objected, but leakage to the Egyptian would be avoided. The action would not (repeat not) be presented as a "tit for tat" against Nasser, but rather as something which Her Majesty's Government believe to be right and in the best interest of the Sudan. Nasser would be told immediately before publication.

I shall be glad to have your comments urgently and your advise [sic] upon methods and timing. In principle, we would like to take this action as soon as possible unless you think it necessary to wait for the departure of the main body of British and Egyptian troops.[6]

---

[6] Ibid., Macmillan to Knox Helm, 6 October 1955. Also Johnson, *British Documents*, vol. 5, Part II, p. 480.

Knox Helm welcomed Macmillan's proposal warmly.[7] Sir Humphrey Trevelyan in Cairo, by contrast, warned that, however the proposal was presented, it would be seen as nothing less than the abrogation of the 1953 Anglo-Egyptian Agreement on Sudan as a reprisal for the Czech arms deal. Trevelyan added that, were Macmillan's proposal to be adopted, London should be prepared for Egyptian retaliatory action against the 1954 Suez Canal Base Agreement[8] by actual abrogation or administrative obstruction.[9] As Macmillan considered the question, he noted that Trevelyan strongly insisted with Nāṣir that the Egyptian practice of forcing the British hand by press releases to take positions that Britain did not desire should cease, and since then Nāṣir had complied with this, thus it would be a mistake for London to revert to such a method.

Acting on Trevelyan's advice, Macmillan instructed the Governor-General that the best way to cut short the process of self-determination – while observing procedures agreed with Nāṣir – would be to arrange for the initiative to be taken by the Sudanese Government. Knox Helm was to put to Ismāʿīl al-Azharī the arguments in favour of the Sudanese Parliament itself choosing Sudan's future status – and then to urge the Prime Minister to request the Condominium Governments to agree to that proposal. The Governor-General, Macmillan added, should tell al-Azharī in confidence that, were he to make this request, Her Majesty's Government would be prepared to urge Nāṣir to accept. If Nāṣir agreed, then Eden's Government would have achieved its main objective; if he objected, then the British would be free to make their views public. Macmillan went on to stress that if al-Azharī declined to make the request, the whole matter would have to be reconsidered, with the conclusion that Britain could not necessarily rely on him to support any unilateral action which might be taken by the British Government to achieve a short cut to independence.[10]

It seems that the British proposal to cut short the process of self-determination was initially met with approval by al-Azharī's Government

---

[7] Ibid., Knox Helm to Foreign Office, 6 October 1955.

[8] See Chapter 8, Note 14.

[9] National Archives, Kew, FO 371/113616: Trevelyan, Cairo, to Foreign Office, 6 October 1955.

[10] Ibid., Macmillan to Knox Helm, 11 October 1955.

and most opposition parties. On 13 October 1955, Knox Helm informed the Foreign Office that conversations conducted with the Government and opposition representatives had shown a consensus in favour of achieving the goal by introducing a motion in Parliament authorising it to carry out the duties of the Constituent Assembly, as provided for in Article 12 of the Anglo-Egyptian Agreement. Alternatively Parliament might request the Condominium Governments to recognise Sudan as an independent country and give itself the power to draw up a new constitution.[11]

Meanwhile, William Luce had been talking to al-Azharī and Yaḥya al-Faḍlī, as well as Ṣiddīq al-Mahdī and his Umma Party colleague Muḥammad al-Khalīfa Sharīf. These conversations left Luce in do doubt as to their desire to cut short the self-determination process – and to avoid any plebiscite or elections. He gathered that they were all in agreement that carrying out elections or a plebiscite in the South of Sudan, especially in Equatoria Province, would not be practical in the near future.[12] As we shall see later, this consensus did not last long.

ii. Nāṣir demands an explanation for a statement attributed to Luce

On 13 October 1955, the Party newspaper *al-Umma* published a statement that it attributed to William Luce. The statement described British policy as "respect for the wishes of the Sudanese, maintenance of their friendship and consideration for their feelings as far as possible". "We will not in the future stop before any obstacle in the way of development, objective or national aspiration the Sudanese may wish." Luce added: "If the Sudanese Parliament decided itself to proclaim independence, Britain would recognise its decision." Luce concluded his statement by saying that "this policy could be expressed officially in writing if the Sudanese so wished."[13]

---

[11] Ibid., Knox Helm to Foreign Office, 13 October 1955.
[12] Ibid., FO 371/113618 (Political relations between UK, Egypt and Sudan): Luce to Lampen, 16 October 1955.
[13] *al-Umma*, 13 October 1955, and *al-Jamhūrīa* [an Egyptian newspaper, where Nāṣir presumably read it], 24 October 1955. The English text is in National Archives, Kew, FO 371/113617 (Political relations between UK, Egypt and

The statement provoked a storm of criticism in Egypt. It was considered a *prima facie* abrogation of the 1953 Agreement – and Britain was accused of pursuing its own interests in Sudan.[14] Gamāl ʿAbd-al-Nāṣir sent a signed letter to Knox Helm, asking for an explanation:

> "Mr Luce, who made this statement, is Your Excellency's political advisor, appointed under Article 103 of the Statute of Self-Government to assist Your Excellency in carrying out your responsibilities in governing the Sudan. If he made this declaration in that capacity, there can be no doubt that he did so on instructions about which Your Excellency did not inform the Egyptian Government in writing. Nor did you invite their opinion thereon, so that the declaration might express the views of the two governments that Your Excellency represent. The statement contradicts the provisions of the Agreement currently in force between our two governments, which should be respected.
>
> If, however, Mr Luce made this declaration as a spokesman for the British Government, then apart from the breach of Article 103 of the Self-Government Statute, the Egyptian Government would like to know whether this view expresses the official viewpoint of the British Government. The statement contradicts the text of the Anglo-Egyptian Agreement, the provisions of which the two Governments undertook to respect."[15]

William Luce promptly issued a denial to the Arab News Agency that he had made the statement attributed to him by *al-Umma*.[16] In his reply to Nāṣir, Governor-General Knox Helm also denied the statement's

---

Sudan): Trevelyan, Cairo, to Foreign Office, 19 October 1955. It is not clear whether this is Luce's original statement or a translation of the version in *al-Jamhūrīa*. Luce's own papers for this period are in Sudan Archive, University of Durham, SAD.829/5/1-40 and 6/1-93.

[14] *al-Ahrām*, 24 October 1955.

[15] National Archives, Kew, FO 371/113618: Gamal Abdel Nasser to Governor-General, Khartoum, 17 October 1955.

[16] *al-Ahrām*, 24 October 1955.

authorship.[17] Still, despite the denials, the attributed statement clearly meshed with the British plan to cut short the process of self-determination, so it is possible that the remarks carried by *al-Umma* had been leaked by one of the Umma Party leaders whom Luce had met.

iii. al-Azharī's statement to the Arab News Agency

On 17 October 1955, Ismāʿīl al-Azharī reiterated to Knox Helm that the prevailing sentiment among Sudanese was to pursue independence without resorting to either plebiscite or assembly elections. The task of drawing up a constitution and an electoral law were to be entrusted to parliamentary committees, in which all political parties would be represented, while the Government would remain responsible for the routine work of administration. al-Azharī made it clear to the Governor-General that he was in no hurry: new legislation could be introduced as late as March 1956; meanwhile, preparatory work on the new constitution would be in progress.

For Knox Helm, al-Azharī's remarks revealed "a degree of confused thinking", so he deemed it necessary "to impress with some force the realities of the situation". The Governor-General reminded the Prime Minister that, just the previous August, Parliament had requested the Co-Domini to endorse a plebiscite – and had even nominated the countries that would make up an International Commission. For the Co-Domini, those two resolutions represented the settled intent of the Sudanese – and actual measures to achieve them could not be postponed endlessly. London and Cairo might confirm at any moment that they would take the necessary steps to form the International Commission and carry out the plebiscite. After that, any request for further alteration in the process of self-determination would be more difficult to obtain. If the Sudanese wished further alteration, they should institute a motion in Parliament as soon as possible.[18]

It seems that the Governor-General's bracing comments had the desired effect: the following day, 18 October, al-Azharī gave the following statement to the Arab News Agency:

---

[17] National Archives, Kew, FO 371/113618: Governor-General, Khartoum, to Gamal Abdel Nasser, 19 October 1955.

[18] Ibid., FO 371/113617: Knox Helm to Foreign Office, 19 October 1955.

"No reply has yet been received from the British and Egyptian governments to the Sudanese request for a direct plebiscite. It appears that the public feeling is that the present Parliament should carry out the functions of the Constituent Assembly, as provided for by Article 12 of the Sudan Agreement, and that this Parliament, which represents all the parties, should decide the future of the Sudan by adopting one of the two alternatives laid down in the Agreement, and should draw up Sudan's Constitution and electoral law. If this feeling crystalises, the Parliament will pass a resolution requesting the amendment of the Agreement to enable the Parliament to exercise the functions of the Constituent Assembly."[19]

British officials both in London and Khartoum responded to this statement with great satisfaction, with Knox Helm considering it proof of Sudanese intentions. The Foreign Office took it as a pretext to suspend the process of self-determination provided for in the Agreement, especially given that the Parliament in Khartoum would not reconvene for its next session until 3 November 1955. The statement was also useful as proof for the argument that Sudan's request for a plebiscite had not necessarily been the last word. Based on al-Azharī's statement, London advised Cairo to wait and give the Sudanese Parliament 'sufficient opportunity' to express its view once more – and for the Co-Domini to consider a joint resolution in response.[20]

Britain went further in exploiting al-Azharī's statement. In a memorandum dated 26 October, the UK recommended to Egypt that the Co-Domini send the following message, via the Governor-General, to the Sudanese Government:

"In view of their joint wish to give complete consideration for Sudanese opinion, the two contracting countries shall agree to the Sudan's Parliament's proposal of 29 August if Sudan's Parliament still desires to have a plebiscite. However, we have

---

[19] *al-Nīl*, 29 October 1955.

[20] National Archives, Kew, FO 371/113617: Minute by Bromley (Foreign Office), 20 October 1955.

noted the statement made by the Sudanese Prime Minister on 18 October 1955, which indicates that the plebiscite option no more represents the view of the Sudanese Parliament. As such they request that the Sudanese Government call Parliament, when in session, to give its view on the best means to complete the process of Self-Determination, especially whether it desires for the future status of the Sudan to be decided by plebiscite or by other means." [21]

The Egyptian Government flatly rejected the proposed text: al-Azharī's statement did not justify suspending the obligations and responsibilities of the contracting countries under the 1953 Agreement on grounds that may or may not arise. The only wish expressed by the Sudanese Parliament on 29 August 1955 was for a direct popular plebiscite. The two Governments were informed of that wish, which was still in effect and enjoyed wide support.[22] Instead, as we shall see next, Egypt set out to frustrate the British plan to cut short the self-determination process in a way other than that provided for by the 1953 Agreement.

iv. Egypt attempts to foil the British plan

To foil the British plan of cutting short the process of self-determination, the Egyptian Government acting unilaterally and without seeking British agreement, urged the seven countries concerned to immediately nominate their representatives in the International Commission. Egypt fixed the last week of October 1955 [23] for holding the first meeting of the Commission. Egypt justified the haste on the ground that pursuant to memoranda annexed to the 1953 Agreement, the Commission had to decide on the matter of the supreme command of the Sudanese Armed Forces on the completion of the withdrawal from the Sudan the of the Co-Domini forces scheduled for 13 November 1955.

---

[21] Ibid., FO 371/113618: Trevelyan to Zakaria Mohiddein, Egyptian Interior Minister, 26 October 1955.

[22] Ibid., FO 371/113619: Zakaria Mohiddein to Trevelyan, 30 October 1955.

[23] Czechoslovakia, India, Norway, Pakistan, Sweden, Switzerland and Yugoslavia.

al-Ahrām considered the step taken in this respect as a triumph of the Egyptian diplomacy over the British scheme to endow al-Azharī with competence to transform the current Sudanese Parliament into a Constituent Assembly to perform self-determination.[24]

Egypt informed the British Government by a note of 19 October 1955 of the invitations issued to the representatives in Cairo of the seven States nominated for membership in the International Commission.[25]

In a British Note dated 22 October 1955, delivered in person by Ambassador Trevelyan to Zakarīa Muhī al-Dīn, Egypt's Interior Minister and Minister of State for Sudanese Affairs, the British Government stated that invitations have been issued on the basis of draft terms of reference the discussion of which has not been completed between the two Governments. Importantly the Supplementary Agreement providing for the establishment of the Commission has not yet been completed.

The British Government noted further that neither of these uncompleted documents takes account of the subsequent resolution of the Sudanese Parliament on 29 August 1955 requesting a plebiscite which would require their amendment.

The British Note referred to the public statement made by the Sudanese Prime Minister on 18 October 1955 that the Sudanese Parliament may wish shortly to make further proposals on the procedure to be adopted in carrying out the self-determination process. Such a resolution may be found to affect the nature of the work which the Commission is called upon to perform.

During the same meeting of 22 October 1955, the Egyptian Minister handed to Trevelyan a Note from the Egyptian Government wherein it declared her formal acceptance of the plebiscite in response to the desire expressed on 29 August 1955 by the Sudanese Parliament and to hold a concurrent election for a Constituent Assembly.[26]

To counter the Egyptian unilateral action, the British Government informed the countries nominated by the Sudanese Parliament to compose the International Commission that the invitations

---

[24] *al-Ahrām*, 23 October 1955.

[25] Minutes of the House of Representatives, Session No. 36, 10 November 1955.

[26] National Archives, Kew, FO 371/113617: Trevelyan to Foreign Office, 22 October 1955.

sent to them by the Egyptian Government to nominate their representatives had been issued against the wishes of the British Government. And that the British Government believed that the Egyptians took that action in order to argue that the self-determination process is firmly in the hands of the Commission and that it would not be legally open for the Co-Domini to vary the procedure laid down in the 1953 Agreement.

They were also informed that Sudanese opinion was increasingly in favour of obtaining independence without recourse to a plebiscite or Constituent Assembly. They were further informed that a resolution along the lines indicated by the Sudanese Prime Minister in his statement of 18 October 1955 cannot be introduced before 3 November 1955. The date when the Sudan Parliament assembles. It might ask the Co-Domini to amend the 1953 Agreement and empower the current Sudan Parliament to carry out the powers of the Constituent Assembly provided for in Article 12 of the Agreement, or might ask the Co-Domini to recognise outright the complete independence of the Sudan and empower the existing Parliament to draw up the Constitution. In which case there would be no need for the International Commission.

The British Government saw no necessity for the International Commission to assemble before 13 November 1955, because the supreme military command in the Sudan will automatically remain vested in the Governor-General under Article 11 of the Self-Government Statute until that Statute is amended by recommendation of the Commission after its establishment.[27] Even if the Commission is not required, the Governor-General would remain the supreme commander of the armed forces until the winding up of the Condominium or the Condominium Governments agree on another arrangement.

Czechoslovakia accepted Egypt's invitation.[28] All the other countries made their attendance subject to receiving an invitation from both Cairo and London, which did not happen.

---

[27] Ibid., Foreign Office to Oslo, Stockholm, Berne, Prague and Belgrade, 22 October 1955; also Commonwealth Relations Office to High Commissioners in India and Pakistan, 22 October 1955.
[28] Ibid., Prague to Foreign Office, 27 October 1955.

v. Failure of the first attempt to declare self-determination from within Parliament

We referred earlier to British confidence that their plan had the approval of both the Sudanese Government and the opposition. During an all-party meeting on 26 October 1955, however, differences rapidly emerged, leading to the loss of the opportunity to submit a proposal for self-determination from within Parliament, as proposed, on 3 November 1955.[29]

The proposal was rejected outright by Muḥammad Nūr al-Dīn, representing the Unionist Front, as the current Parliament no longer contained adequate representation of the still considerable pro-union element in the Sudan. Yūsuf al-ʿAjab, representing the Republican Socialist Party, and Benjamin Lwoki, the Liberal Party leader, both preferred the plebiscite option. Mīrghanī Ḥamza, President of the Republican Independence Party, and Ḥassan al-Ṭāhir Zarūq, representing the Front Against Colonialization, cast doubt on Britain's motives in supporting a curtailment of the self-determination process and expressed their fear that putting such a proposal before Parliament would trigger interminable arguments between the Co-Domini. The representative of the Independence Front seemed to accept the British-backed shortcut in principle, talking in terms of a declaration of independence by Parliament and stipulating the formation of a subsequent government of national unity. The Umma Party agreed: Parliament should declare independence and then a national government should be formed. Pushed on the legality of that option, the Umma leadership stated that presenting London and Cairo with a *fait accompli* would avert inevitable disputes between the Co-Domini if asked to recognize that the Sudan had become independent.[30]

It fell to Prime Minister Ismāʿīl al-Azharī to announce the failure to agree on a decision. He immediately informed Knox Helm and on 29 October 1955, issued the following statement:

---

[29] Ibid., FO 371/113618: Knox Helm to Foreign Office, 27 October 1955.

[30] *al-Rāyī al-ʿAm*, 27 October 1955, and *al-Ahrām* 30 October 1955. See also Helm to Lampen, 29 October 1955, in Sudan Archive, University of Durham (Luce Papers): SAD.829/5/35-40.

> "It may be some time before the possibility of a decision by the present Parliament is fully explored by the political parties, and until it is accepted or rejected, the Government will continue on the presumption that the future will be decided by a plebiscite or along the lines laid down in the 1953 Agreement. There are 14 months left for the transitional period and there is no hurry: in a few months an election should be possible throughout the country. For the present it is important that a reply is received about the Sudan's Parliament wish for a plebiscite and the International Commission is formed."[31]

Parliament difficulties regarding self-determination increased consequent upon two telegrams sent by Benjamin Lwoki on 31 October 1955 to the Co-Domini Governments, the Governor-General, the Prime Minister and the Speakers of the House of Representatives and the Senate. In the first telegram, Lwoki wrote: "In view of the present state of affairs in the Southern Provinces, the Liberal Party is not prepared to discuss the future of Sudan in Parliament." In the second, he wrote: "In view of the recent troubles in the Southern Sudan and the present persecution, oppression and duress on Southern people by Northerners, the South finally feels that the North should proceed to self-determination and for the South to remain under an international body supervised by the United Nations, as a self-governing state. This request resulted on Northerners' reluctance to accept the Southern demand for federation and England and Egypt having closed their ears to our appeals."[32]

The Foreign Office in London commented as follows: "If the Southern Liberal Party refuses to discuss the future of Sudan, it is going to be difficult for us to justify any attempts we might make to persuade the Egyptians to agree to shorten self-determination if asked by the

---

[31] National Archives, Kew, FO 371/113619: Knox Helm to Foreign Office, 2 November 1955. Contrary to what was stated in al-Azharī's statement, Sudan was at the time in the stage of self-determination. The transitional period ended after the Parliament's decision in August 1955 to start taking measures of self-determination.

[32] Ibid., Telegrams by Benjamin Lwoki, 31 October 1955.

Sudanese Parliament. We would seem to be acting contrary to the will of the South."[33]

Gamāl ʿAbd-al-Nāṣir

vi. Nāṣir's displeasure about the situation in Sudan

Trefor Evans, the Oriental Counsellor at the British Embassy in Cairo, had an informal meeting on 29 October 1955 with Gamāl ʿAbd-al-Nāṣir, at which the Egyptian Prime Minister expressed his displeasure with the way things were going in Sudan. He accused the British Government of working with the Sudanese to corner the Egyptians. According to reliable reports that he had received from Khartoum, Nāṣir complained, William Luce had urged Ismāʿīl al-Azharī to have Parliament declare independence, a declaration that Britain would recognise. Nāṣir said that he was particularly disappointed that this should have happened after Sir Humphrey Trevelyan had personally assured him, at the time of Ṣalāḥ Sālim's resignation, that it was British policy that the two Governments work together on Sudanese affairs.

[33] Ibid., Foreign Office Minute, 4 November 1955.

Nāṣir added that he was convinced that British policy was aimed at keeping the Governor-General in office after a declaration of independence by the Sudanese Parliament and during the process of constitution making. As evidence, Nāṣir cited the British attitude to the question of the supreme military command in Sudan after the withdrawal of British and Egyptian troops. Nāṣir also feared that, were the Sudanese Parliament to be entrusted with the process of self-determination, al-Azharī would remain in office and the Sudanese Parliament would remain as constituted indefinitely. The Egyptian Prime Minister concluded by saying that, if the British policy were indeed to corner the Egyptians, he would have to do the same to Britain. If the Sudanese Parliament unilaterally declared independence, therefore, without regard to Egypt's views, and if Britain recognised such a declaration, the Egyptian Government would announce that it was no longer bound by the 1953 Agreement.[34]

vii. Back to square one: The plebiscite and the International Commission

On 2 November 1955, the Governor-General in Khartoum advised the Foreign Office that it had become increasingly apparent during the past week that "there are no hopes of any agreement among the Sudanese on a motion to be put to Parliament". Sayyid ʿAlī al-Mīrghanī was definitely against a shortcut and was bound to influence the Government. The opposition distrusted al-Azharī, as well as the motives of the Co-Domini, and while the opposition would still favour a shortcut, they were demanding so many safeguards as to make agreement with the Government impracticable. Consequently, the best available option was a return to the plan for the plebiscite, Constituent Assembly and International Commission.[35]

The Foreign Office responded to this advice by instructing Trevelyan in Cairo that he should proceed on the assumption that there would be a plebiscite and that the International Commission would be required after all – but London would still like to keep open the possibility that, were the Sudanese Parliament to express fresh views on self-

[34] Ibid., Trevelyan, Cairo, to Foreign Office, 31 October 1955.
[35] Ibid., Knox Helm to Foreign Office, 2 November 1955.

determination at a later date, they would be considered by the Co-Domini. In view of the Sudanese Prime Minister's statement of 29 October 1955, taken with other indicators that the Sudanese were not yet ready to commit to any alternative, Trevelyan was also asked to inform Prime Minister Nāṣir that London would inform Governor-General Knox Helm of its acceptance of the plebiscite proposal. The British Government would also issue invitations to the governments participating in the International Commission and would ask the Governor-General to inform the Sudanese Government and Parliament accordingly. Sir Humphrey was asked to raise the following questions with Nāṣir:

a) If the Sudanese, at a later date, were to express a preference for some quicker method of self-determination, both Co-Domini would consider such proposals sympathetically.
b) The British Government would like to discuss with the Egyptians the terms of reference for the International Commission, which would require modification to take account of the plebiscite.[36]
c) Gamāl ʿAbd-al-Nāṣir had clearly misunderstood the British position in respect of the Governor-General: London had no desire to extend his period of office, nor was it seeking to retain supreme military command in his hands for any nefarious purpose. The Governor-General was already in a position in which his responsibilities were beyond his powers. Such authority as he was able to command was derived from his position as Commander-in-Chief of the SDF. It was only because he held this position that he was able to play so effective a part in ending the troubles in the South. It was not in the interests of either London or Cairo that Knox Helm's position should be made even more anomalous than it was already. London was ready to see the Condominium brought to an end as soon as possible; and the settlement of the question of the supreme command with new arrangements.

[36] Ibid., Foreign Office to Cairo, 3 November 1955.

The Sudanese Parliament was informed on 10 November 1955 that the British Government had expressed its agreement to the resolutions passed by Parliament on 22 August 1955, regarding the composition of the International Commission, and on 29 August 1955, whereby the choice provided for in Article 12 of the Agreement, i.e. between complete independence or a link to Egypt, was to be decided by direct plebiscite. Parliament was also informed that London, in its wish to speed up the remaining stages of self-determination, had sent invitations to the seven countries chosen by Parliament to be represented on the International Commission. MPs were also notified that the British Government was negotiating with its Egyptian counterparts with a view to concluding a Supplementary Agreement and Terms of Reference of the International Commission, as well as the necessary amendments to the 1953 Anglo-Egyptian Agreement.[37]

This was followed up on 10 November 1955 by the Egyptians, formally lodging with Parliament a number of documents, dated 15, 16 and 19 October 1955, to the effect that the Egyptian Government wished to resume negotiations with London on the terms of reference of the International Commission. These documents also conveyed Cairo's approval for Parliament's resolution on a plebiscite and a confirmation that it would negotiate with London to amend the Anglo-Egyptian Agreement.[38]

Despite all this rapid activity, the British Government did not lose hope that self-determination could yet be achieved via the shortcut. It instructed Knox Helm to tell al-Azharī in confidence that London had made it clear to the Egyptians that the Co-Domini should give 'sympathetic consideration' to any further proposals that the Sudanese Parliament might wish to make about the way in which self-determination was actually put into effect.[39] But, as we shall see shortly, the shortcut was achieved in an unexpected manner. On 12 December 1955, it was announced that the Sir Alexander Knox Helm had expressed his wish to resign as Governor-General for personal reasons and that the British Government did not intend to nominate another British national

[37] Ibid., Foreign Office to Khartoum, 5 November 1955.
[38] Minutes of the House of Representatives, Session No. 36, 10 November 1955.
[39] National Archives, Kew, FO 371/113619: Foreign Office to Khartoum, 5 November 1955.

to take his place. In fact, Knox Helm had not resigned: the British Government decided to vacate the office of the Governor-General.

CHAPTER 15

Disagreement over the Formation of a National Government

When Sudan entered the period of self-determination in August 1955, the opposition, supported by some independent newspapers, called for the formation of a national government to take the country towards independence by the shortest and safest route. The ruling National Unionist Party rejected this call, using pretexts including the claim that coalition governments were 'inconsistent with democratic systems' and that a national unity government would engage in 'side issues and partisan gains', consequently independence would not be realised at the appointed time.[1] The Khatmīa leadership, however, supported the formation of a national government to carry out the responsibilities of self-determination. The divergence of opinion on this matter between the NUP and the Khatmīa led to the fall of al-Azharī's administration and its removal from office – albeit for just a few days.

i. The fall and rise of al-Azharī's Government

On 10 November 1955, the same day that the House of Representatives was informed by the Co-Domini of their joint acceptance of their two resolutions regarding the plebiscite and the International Commission, al-Azharī's Government was defeated on the second reading of the budget.[2] Prompted by Sayyid ʿAlī al-Mīrghanī, spiritual leader of the Khatmīa, four parliamentary undersecretaries voted against

[1] Ḥamad, *Mudhakkirāt*, p. 227.

[2] Minutes of the House of Representatives, Session No. 36, 10 November 1955.

the Government.[3] Two MPs from Eastern Sudan joined them.[4] They explained their vote against the Government as a token of support for the formation of a national government. In total, 49 deputies voted against the Government while 43 voted for it.[5] Even as the vote took place, SDF Commanding Officer Reginald Scoones and other senior Britons were leaving Sudan for the last time via Khartoum airport.[6]

The five days between the fall of the Government and its return to power on 15 November 1955 were highly eventful. On 11 November 1955, the NUP Parliamentary Group decided not to participate in any national or coalition government as that was inconsistent with democratic and constitutional systems. If a group won the support and confidence of Parliament, it alone should have the right to govern – nor was it beneficial to be without an opposition. The following evening, a Saturday, Prime Minister Ismāʿīl al-Azharī received a four-member delegation from Sayyid ʿAlī al-Mīrghanī, conveying a message that he believed that a national government was in the best interests of the country in the coming era.[7] For that reason, Sayyid ʿAlī asked for the matter to be reviewed and for work to be undertaken to make it happen.[8]

On Monday 14 November 1955, *Ṣawt al-Sūdān*, mouthpiece of the Khatmīa, released a statement by Sayyid ʿAlī al-Mīrghanī wherein he defined the tasks which lie ahead in the Sudan: self-determination, plebiscite drawing up the permanent constitution for the Sudan, the electoral law for the new Parliament. To fulfil those tasks al-Mīrghanī urged all the Sudanese citizens irrespective of their political affiliations to unite and to commit themselves to the aims and high ideals of the country. Thus avoiding the slide of the country into wrangles and upheavals.

---

[3] They were Muḥammad Jubāra al-ʿAwaḍ, Ḥassan Muḥammad Zakī, Yūsuf ʿAbd-al-Qādir and ʿAbd-al-Nabī ʿAbd-al-Qādir.

[4] They were Abū-Fāṭima Bākāsh and Muḥammad Maḥmūd.

[5] Ḥamad, *Mudhakkirāt*, p. 227. See also Yāsin, *Mudhakkirāt*, pp. 294-5.

[6] National Archives, Kew, FO 371/113584 (Political developments in the Sudan during 1955): Adams, Trade Commissioner, Khartoum, to Macmillan, 18 November 1955.

[7] The four envoys were Idrīs al-Idrīsī, ʿUthmān Muṣtafa Urtatāshī, Muḥammad Ḥamad Abū-Sinn (MP for Qaḍārif North) and Muḥammad Aḥmad Abū-Sinn (MP for al-Rufāʿ).

[8] Ḥamad, *Mudhakkirāt*, pp. 228-9.

The central message in al-Mīrghanī's statement was his advice to all political parties and organisations to adopt a national policy to undertake those momentous tasks. As well as the administration of the country during this critical period in a way that enables it to realise its goals peacefully and in an atmosphere of security, stability and tranquillity.[9]

That same morning, Sayyid ʿAbd-al-Raḥman al-Mahdī received Prime Minister Ismāʿīl al-Azharī to discuss the current situation. According to *al-Rāyī al-ʿAm*, Sayyid ʿAbd-al-Raḥman's view was explicitly in favour of forming a national government. After a lengthy conversation, al-Azharī and his colleagues expressed their regret that they could not accept this outcome for a number of reasons, including the fact that they were bound by a collective Party decision to reject the idea.[10] After leaving Sayyid ʿAbd-al-Raḥman's residence, al-Azharī and his colleagues headed to Ḥillat Khojalī, the residence of Sayyid ʿAlī al-Mīrghanī. He spoke to them about his recent statement and whether it had been intended to result in 'national governance' or a national, i.e. national government. *al-Rāyī al-ʿAm* reported that, again, al-Azharī and his delegation explained to the Sayyid that it was impossible for them to support a national government.[11] Khiḍr Ḥamad, who attended the meeting, described in his memoirs how Sayyid ʿAlī explained clearly that he had not asked for the formation of a national government, as that was none of his business: all he wanted was for governance to be national, i.e. that all people should be equal before the government and that the government should view them as such.[12]

The House of Representatives convened on 15 November to elect a new Prime Minister. Mubārak Zarūq nominated Ismāʿīl al-Azharī and was seconded by Ḥassan ʿAbd-al-Qādir, an MP from al-ʿUbeiḍ. ʿAbdallah Khalīl nominated Mīrghanī Ḥamza and was seconded by Muḥammad Aḥmad Maḥjūb. al-Azharī won 48 votes to Ḥamza's 46. Following instructions from Sayyid ʿAlī al-Mīrghanī, three out of the four

---

[9] *Ṣawt al-Sūdān*, 14 November 1955.

[10] *al-Rāyī al-ʿAm* and *al-Sūdān al-Jadīd*, 15 November 1955.

[11] The Sayyid was accompanied by his son Ṣiddīq, ʿAbdallah Khalīl, ʿAbd-al-Raḥman ʿAlī Ṭaha and ʿAlī Badrī. The PM's delegation included Mubārak Zarūq, Muḥammad Aḥmad al-Marḍī and Yaḥya al-Faḍlī.

[12] Ḥamad, *Mudhakkirāt*, p. 229.

parliamentary undersecretaries voted for al-Azharī. Ḥassan al-Ṭāhir Zarūq of the Front Against Colonialization abstained.[13]

The victorious al-Azharī made no changes to his Cabinet, with the exception that Buth Diu, former Secretary-General of the Liberal Party, joined the Government as Minister of Animal Resources.[14] The Governor-General considered the addition to be "a useful Southern reinforcement" for the Government but added that al-Azharī had "lost a great opportunity when he won his vote by not immediately announcing his readiness to broaden his administration by bringing in representatives of the principal opposition parties for the remainder of the Self-Determination period. Then I should have viewed the political future with more confidence"[15]

The fall and return of al-Azharī's Government attracted wide press coverage. *al-ʿAlam*, the mouthpiece of the NUP, wrote that: "one of the lessons to be learned from the latest developments is that it is the people alone who can send representatives to Parliament or bring a party to power. The implication is that the electorates have freed themselves from sectarian influences." Whereas *Ṣawt al-Sūdān*, the mouthpiece of the Khatmīa believed that al-Azharī's victory meant that parliamentary rule was unstable in the Sudan and suggested that the Prime Minister should dissolve Parliament and confront the people direct.

al-Rāyī al-ʿAm, a non-party newspaper, said that al-Azharī had become a real political force, not only inside Parliament but outside too, and described him as a symbol of an extraordinary new political consciousness in the educated classes. While *al-Ayyām*, a non-party newspaper, condemned the methods of bribery and sectorial influence used in recent parliamentary struggles and appealed to al-Azharī to form a national government in accordance with the wishes of the people.[16] *al-*

---

[13] National Archives, Kew, FO 371/113584: Adams to Macmillan, 18 November 1955.

[14] On 13 September, the Liberal Party had asked Buth Diu to resign as Secretary-General following a disagreement over the party's stance regarding the Torit mutiny: *al-Ahrām*, 17 September 1955.

[15] National Archives, Kew, FO 371/113585 (Political developments in the Sudan during 1955): Knox Helm to Shuckburgh, 17 November 1955.

[16] National Archives, Kew, FO 371/113584: Khartoum to Foreign Office, 16 November 1955.

Mīdān, the mouthpiece of the Front Against Colonialization, favoured the formation of a national government, provided it adopted the National Charter proposed by the Front.[17]

ii. The British view on al-Azharī's return

Both Knox Helm and his adviser William Luce saw al-Azharī's return to office as an important development, noting that the politician had "scored over the two sayyids". "This is a new step on the Sudan's way to political maturity" wrote Knox Helm, "and as such it is to be welcomed. But the road is still long and it will be years before the victory of politicians is complete ... and even though his instructions decided the issue, Sayyid Ali Mirghani by his vacillations has permitted a dent to be made and the effect will not be lost."[18] Below is how Luce reported events to London:

> "Azhari, the politician, has scored a success over Sayyid Ali Mirghani, the sectarian leader, and many Sudanese feel that this marks an important and welcome development in the political life of the country, as educated Sudanese generally are becoming increasingly fed up with the sectarian influence on politics. But while recent events have most probably shaken Sayyid Ali's position to some extent with his more sophisticated followers, in assessing the true significance of this development, one has to make a clear distinction between politicians and the mass of the electorate. It may well be that Sayyid Ali will find himself increasingly less able to control the votes of the Khatmia Members of Parliament and the same may apply in a lesser degree to Sayyed Abdel Rahman. But this will not in my view materially affect the strength of their positions in the country constituencies, at least in the near future. A Khatmia MP who has defied Sayyed Ali is likely to find the full force of the latter's influence working against him when he stands for re-election, if indeed he could ever get himself nominated against Sayyed Ali's wishes. Even if Sayyed Ali got a new set of docile Khatmia into Parliament, they might well go through the same process of a

---

[17] Ibid., Khartoum to Foreign Office, 12 November 1955.
[18] Ibid., Helm to Shuckburgh, 17 November 1955.

shift from sectarian to political allegiance but this would take time. So while we may be witnessing the beginning of the breaking away of Sudanese politics from sectarian control the process will certainly be long and slow and is likely to resemble a game of snakes and ladders."[19]

iii. The two Sayyids: al-Mīrghanī and al-Mahdī support the immediate formation of a national government

Ever since mid-September 1955, there had been rumours in political circles about an imminent meeting between the two Sayyids. The communist newspaper, *al-Mīdān*, asked Sayyid ʿAbd-al-Raḥman al-Mahdī on 29 October 1955 about those rumours. In response, he said: "I hope agreement is reached between Sayyid ʿAlī al-Mīrghanī and myself. In fact, there is no antipathy between us. But personal agreement between us has no value in itself – although an agreement would be useful if its builds on national values that are beneficial to the country and if all political parties are bound by it." Answering a similar question, al-Mīrghanī replied: "There is no antagonism with the Mahdi's family: we both hope for the best outcome from the current attempts at concord."[20]

Pressure mounted on al-Azharī to form a national government when the two Sayyids met on 3 December 1955 and issued a statement which contained the following paragraph:

> "We hope this will prepare the suitable atmosphere for cooperation among our followers and supporters. And we also hope this will make possible agreement between all political parties on the immediate formation of a national government

---

[19] Luce to Lampen, 19 November 1955, in Sudan Archive, University of Durham (Luce Papers), SAD.829/6/38-44.

[20] *al-Ahrām*, 30 October 1955, has the original Arabic text of the interviews, as well as the draft of the National Charter proposed by the Front Against Colonialization. Translations are in National Archives, Kew, FO 371/113619: Enclosures in Khartoum to Foreign Office, 1 November 1955.

> which should be the safety valve and protect the country against any possible danger."[21]

On 6 December 1955 al-Mīrghanī issued a press statement wherein he said:

> "When Premier Azhari conferred with me this week, I told him that the statement which was issued between me and Sayed Abdel Rahman Al-Mahdi demanded the immediate formation of a national government. I told him the details were to be discussed by the political parties. We should endorse any decisions taken by the parties."[22]

al-Ayyām gave a cautious welcome to the meeting of the two sayyids. But it expressed concern lest its purpose was to control the political situation and the democratic organisations in the country. The paper wrote further that the rapprochement between the two sayyids should not extend to the political arena, and that they should content themselves with guidance and instruction to the extent permitted by their spiritual status alone.[23]

On perusal of the statements exchanged between the ruling NUP and opposition parties [24] during the last week of November and the first week of December 1955 one would no doubt observe the disparities on a number of key matters. The most important of which were: the object behind the formation of a national government, its functions, the ratio of representation in the government and the date of its inception. The ruling NUP set as a condition for the formation of a national government the agreement of the two Condominium Governments to amend the 1953 Agreement so that self-determination and attainment of

---

[21] *al-Nīl*, 4 December 1955. See also National Archives, Kew, FO 371/113585: Khartoum to Foreign Office, 4 December 1955.

[22] *Ṣawt al-Sūdān*, 6 December 1955. See also National Archives, Kew, FO 371/113585: Statement by Sayed Ali Mirghani, 6 December 1955.

[23] Quoted in Bashīr Muḥammad Saʿīd, *al-Zaʿīm al-Azharī wa 'Uṣruhu* (*al-Azharī the Leader and His Era*) (Cairo: Modern Printers, 1990), p. 288.

[24] The coalition parties comprised the Umma Party, the Republican Independence Party and the Socialist Republican Party.

independence would be secured through the shortest route, which is the current Parliament.

The coalition parties called for the prompt formation of the national government and argued that the agreement of the Condominium States is not the shortest or securest route for the attainment of independence in the light of the existing circumstances and constitutional conditions. For the parties this route should be decided upon by the national government whether it is through Parliament, a plebiscite or the Constituent Assembly.

There were also other points of difference. The NUP saw that the existing Parliament should be endowed with the competence to draw up the Constitution and the electoral law, whereas the coalition parties saw that those tasks should be entrusted to an all-party committee to be constituted by the national government. The ruling party posed a condition that the representation of the coalition parties in the national government should be proportional to the number of their MPs in Parliament. The coalition parties retorted that its concern is the formation of a real national government where no party would assume a numerical majority or a greater share of power, but rather solidarity and sincerity would dominate, qualities without which the objective of the national government could not be realised.

The ruling NUP set up yet another condition: the preservation of the rights and competencies provided for in the Constitution. The coalition parties interpreted this is as a ploy to maintain the extraordinary powers of the Governor-General in the Self-Government Statute, including the commandship of the armed forces and the power of the Prime Minister to dismiss his ministers as this would contradict the object of establishing the national government and threatens its continuity. The reason being that the national government is in essence the holding in abeyance of many provisions of the Constitution because of the unusual circumstances the country is passing through.[25]

Eventually pressure on the Government yielded fruit. On 6 December 1955, the Cabinet decided to invite the coalition parties to

---

[25] *al-Rāyī al-ʿAm*, 29 November and 4 December 1955. See also National Archives, Kew, FO 371/113585: Communique of the Joint Meeting of the Executive Committee and the Parliamentary Group of the National Unionist Party on 4 December; also Statement issued by the Opposition Parties.

negotiations for the formation of a national government, based on the statements issued by the two parties. The opposition accepted this invitation – a development applauded by *al-Rāyī al-'Am*. "A wave of celebration and optimism prevailed," it wrote, "among those who are enthusiastic about the future of this country when they learned that the Government had decided to negotiate with the coalition parties about the formation of a national government. Their happiness has been boosted with the announcement that followed, that the coalition parties have accepted."[26] These negotiations and their outcome will be the subject of the following Chapter.

---

[26] *al-Rāyī al-'Am*, 7 December 1955.

CHAPTER 16

Success of the Second Attempt to Declare Self-Determination from Within Parliament: 19 December 1955

i. Amendment of the 1953 Agreement and signature of a Supplementary Agreement

While controversy was flaring between the Government and the opposition regarding the formation of a national government, the Co-Domini without consulting the Sudanese Government or the opposition parties, signed three documents. Maḥmūd Fawzī, the Minister for Foreign Affairs signed on behalf of Egypt. The British Ambassador in Cairo, Sir Humphrey Trevelyan, signed on behalf of his country.

By an Exchange of Notes on 3 December 1955, Articles 10, 12 and 13 of the 1953 Agreement were amended to allow for the future of the Sudan to be decided by a plebiscite in accordance with the wish of the Sudanese House of Representatives, as expressed in the Resolution of 29 August 1955.

A Supplementary Agreement was also signed on 3 December 1955 concerning the establishment of an International Commission to supervise the process of self-determination. The terms of reference of the Commission were set out in a document annexed to the Agreement and regarded as an integral part thereto. Clause 1 (c) of this annex provided that:"If the Commission decided that conditions exist which make impossible the free expression of opinion by the electorate or the impartiality of the plebiscite or the elections, to postpone the whole process of self-determination.", and "it shall report its reasons to the Governor-General, who shall refer the report to the two contracting governments."

On 3 December 1955, the two Governments exchanged further notes wherein they agreed that as soon as the results of the plebiscite and of the elections for the Constituent Assembly were announced, the two Governments would consult together and with the representatives of the Sudanese Parliament on the steps to be taken to bring the process of self-determination and the Condominium to an end.[1]

Paragraph 1 (c), on the Commission's Terms of Reference, and the Exchange of Notes on the winding up of both the self-determination process and the Condominium itself stirred up a storm of criticism from the opposition and the press in Sudan. The Leader of the Opposition, Muḥammad Aḥmad Maḥjūb, said that granting the International Commission unlimited power to indefinitely postpone the process contradicted Article 9 of the 1953 Agreement. Maḥjūb expressed his astonishment at the consultation between the Co-Domini states and parliamentary representatives on steps to 'end the Condominium', when such steps have been decided and embodied in the 1953 Agreement.[2] Under the title 'A New Threat to Sudan's Independence', *al-Rāyī al-ʿAm* wrote:

> "One of the most serious powers which the Condominium states agreed to grant this Commission is the power to postpone the whole process of self-determination if it sees that circumstances are not suitable. Thus it has become clear to us that we are facing a new threat, before which all the threats we have been expecting pale into insignificance. The Co-Domini Governments have not planted this provision in the terms of reference of the Commission for no reason: they aim, no doubt, to obstruct our freedom and our independence, when they exploit it – either jointly or unilaterally – to fabricate some plot or riot as a pretext. ... We were, until yesterday, listing the strong reasons motivating us to support a declaration of independence by the current

[1] National Archives, Kew, FO 93/32/102 (Agreement and Exchanges of Notes. Self-determination for the Sudan). A full Arabic translation appeared in *al-Jamhūrīa*, 4 December 1955.

[2] National Archives, Kew, FO 371/113624 (Political relations between UK, Egypt and Sudan): UK Trade Commissioner, Khartoum, to Foreign Office, 10 December 1955.

Parliament. Today, we need no other reason than this. Indeed, it is reason enough for all parties to meet and agree on that goal, precisely to block the pretexts of the Condominium Governments."[3]

ii. Meetings of the ruling party and coalition parties on a national government

As we mentioned in Chapter 15, the Cabinet decided on 6 December 1955 to invite members of the opposition coalition to discuss a new national government, with statements issued by both sides to form a basis for the negotiations. The first meeting was convened two days later. The NUP was represented by Mubārak Zarūq, ʿAlī ʿAbd-al-Raḥman, Muḥammad Amīn al-Sayyid, Ibrāhīm al-Muftī and Khiḍr Ḥamad. The other representatives present were ʿAbdallah Khalīl (Umma Party), Mīrghanī Ḥamza (Republican Independence Party), Benjamin Lwoki (Liberal Party), Muḥammad Nūr al-Dīn (Unionist Front), Yūsuf al-ʿAjab (Republican Socialist Party) and Ḥassan al-Ṭāhir Zarūq (Front Against Colonialization). It was agreed that Muḥammad ʿAmir Bashīr Fawrāwī would register the minutes of the meetings and the resolutions.[4]

At the first and second meetings, on 8 and 10 December, the attendees agreed on the following:

a) Establishment of a national government, the basis of which is to be determined;
b) The aim of this national government shall be the arrival at the complete independence of Sudan via the shortest and securest route, whether by plebiscite or by Parliament declaring independence or by any other route;
c) Independence will be unconditional and not restricted by any pacts, treaties or by the favoured status of another country;

---

[3] *al-Rāyī al-ʿAm*, 8 December 1955. See also National Archives, Kew, FO 371/113624: UK Trade Commissioner, Khartoum, to Foreign Office, 8 December 1955.

[4] For a detailed account of the separate meetings, see Bashīr, *al-Jalāʾ wa'l-Istiqlāl*, pp. 31-54.

d) Without prejudice to paragraph (e) the process of plebiscite shall be put in motion without delay, to be realised as soon as possible;
e) Upon the establishment of the national government, the following shall be demanded of the Condominium States:
    1. the Sudanese Parliament should declare the independence of the Sudan; and
    2. subsequently the task of the Governor-General would lapse. His replacement would be a Sudanese body the members of which would be nominated by the national government pending the election of a head of state pursuant to the permanent constitution.

A notable absentee of the second meeting was Benjamin Lwoki, the representative of the Liberal Party. But ʿAbdallah Khalīl informed the meeting that the southerners authorised him to communicate to the meeting that they do not agree to the declaration of independence from within the Parliament because they were absent from their constituencies for a long time, and they were not certain that their electorates would accept the proposed measure.

Lwoki attended the third meeting held on 12 December 1955. As deliberations progressed, Lwoki said that the Liberal Party supported the formation of a national government but there were two problems: one concerning the whole country, the other the South. He hailed the usefulness of the ongoing discussions as they might help to restore confidence in that part of the country. But then he submitted what appeared to be a precondition for their acceptance of the declaration of independence from within the current Parliament. He said:" If the meeting wished that independence should be declared by the Parliament, then there should be an agreement for the establishment of a federal union between North and South within the existing boundaries of a unified Sudan."

The question of the federal union was discussed at length in the third and fourth meetings. But a number of the attendees believed that this topic should be deliberated when the new constitution was drawn after independence. In the fourth meeting Lwoki seemed to have modified his earlier views on the concept of federation. He explained that he did not mean the concept in the strict sense but rather proposing the formation of a committee of Northerners and Southerners to discuss the topic of coordinating the relations between North and South. This proposal was accepted unanimously, and it was also agreed that it should be submitted as a recommendation to the national government.

Prior to the fifth meeting scheduled for 13 December 1955,[5] the British Government announced on 12 December 1955 that the Governor-General had resigned and that it did not wish to nominate another British to replace him. This development prompted Mubārak Zarūq to comment in the fifth meeting that the time had come for the Parliament to declare independence forthwith and to communicate to the Co-Domini its views on the entity which would act as head of state. He then added that the road had become paved for the Egyptian Government because it had previously stated that it would agree to the declaration of independence if the Sudanese were unanimous on it and Britain did not object.

At the start of the fifth meeting, convened on 14 December, Zarūq proposed a three-item agenda.[6] The most important of which was the declaration of independence by Parliament, on the basis of which a national commission would be established to exercise sovereign powers. There was, he added, no reason to fear that Egypt or Britain or both would object to the declaration of independence. Indeed, an official Egyptian spokesman had confirmed that Cairo would pose no objection, while Britain would approve anything decided by Parliament. He added that the instrument that would make it a reality would be the new national government, which should be established promptly. He proposed that any of the three items could be discussed first as they were interlinked.

It was agreed at the sixth meeting, convened on 16 December, that the national commission would be the head of state which shall be composed of three members: one representing the Government, a second representing the opposition and a third member to be agreed upon by the Southerners in the Liberal Party and the NUP.

It seemed clear from the exchanges during the fifth and sixth meetings that the real obstacle was the post of Prime Minister in the national government. The view of the NUP delegates view was that the post should go to Ismāʿīl al-Azharī. Mubārak Zarūq justified this position

---

[5] Buth Diu joined the fourth and all subsequent meetings.

[6] Gordon Ayoum joined the fifth and sixth meetings.

by listing "all the posts that al-Azharī shouldered after the departure of the English" – and he noted his parliamentary majority. He was seconded by Ibrāhīm al-Muftī, who said that al-Azharī was "fully aware of the developments and circumstances of the liberation of the country ... He is the best head for the national government, as its job is to continue the progress towards liberation that has been initiated by the present Government."

At the meeting of 15 December, the NUP representatives accepted a proposal from ʿAbdallah Khalīl about the composition of the national government, provided that al-Azharī was its Prime Minister. Khalīl's proposal was that the Cabinet would have 15 ministers, in addition to the PM himself: eight for the coalition partners, six for the NUP and one for the Front Against Colonialization. Khalīl suggested that thsee 15 nominated ministers would then choose the Prime Minister – and if they disagreed they should resort to Parliament. The meeting was adjourned before agreement was reached on the Cabinet's composition or leadership. Saturday 17 December was set for a resumption of the meetings. But even as the 15 December meeting was still in session in the Committees' Room of the Senate, Ismāʿīl al-Azharī entered the House of Representatives with a surprise that stunned everyone – including his senior Party colleagues.[7]

iii. The decisive event

British documents reveal that Sir Alexander Knox Helm had expressed a wish to retire in April 1956 and that that Foreign Office accepted his view that his successor should not be British but neutral. The Governor-General argued that his departure would remove the last trace of British domination, create the free and neutral atmosphere, defuse the impact of Egyptian propaganda and settle the issue of the supreme command of the Sudanese Armed Forces. Scandinavia and Switzerland were considered as nations that might provide a new Governor-General.[8]

---

[7] Yassin, *Mudhakkirāt*, pp. 306-7.

[8] National Archives, Kew, FO 800/662 (The Papers of Sir [Alexander] Knox Helm): Foreign Office telegram No. 2978, dated 8 December 1955, addressed to Cairo and repeated to the Governor-General; also ibid., Governor-General to Secretary of States for Foreign Affairs, 24 November 1955.

On 12 December, however – three days before Knox Helm was due to leave Khartoum for a short Christmas holiday in the UK – London announced officially that the Governor-General had expressed a desire to resign 'for personal reasons'. Furthermore, Trevelyan in Cairo had already informed the Egyptian Prime Minister that the British Government was prepared to accept Sir Alexander's resignation – and that London did not intend to nominate another British candidate to replace him. The British announcement went on to say that Britain was 'in communication with Egypt over the steps to be taken regarding the post of Governor-General, having in mind the requirements provided for in the Anglo-Egyptian Agreement that there should be a 'free and neutral atmosphere' during the remaining period of self-determination."[9]

Sir Alexander Knox Helm

In an unpublished note written just four days later and entitled 'The End of the Condominium in Sudan', Knox Helm said the press announcement about his resignation was not even shown to him before its publication; even after its publication, he did not receive it directly but through Philip Adams, the British Trade Commissioner in Khartoum. He

[9] Ibid., Foreign Office to UK Trade Commissioner, Khartoum, 12 December 1955.

was shocked as the announcement focused on his supposed wish to resign:

> In the years to come, interest would rest on the role which I had performed in the last weeks and months of 1955 as the last Governor-General, especially as the Foreign Office had announced that I had asked to be retired and many people believe that. This is not the position. I had never expressed such a wish, then or at any other time. In fact I was extremely happy in Sudan and I would have remained there gladly.[10]

The British had two reasons for creating a vacancy in the Governor-General's office: first, to prepare the stage for the Sudanese to declare their independence from within Parliament; second, to refute Egyptian claims that London intended to have independence declared in parliament precisely to extend the Governor-General's term after independence and during the period when a new constitution was being drawn up – as well as keeping the supreme command of the Sudanese Armed Forces under his control. It is clear – as acknowledged by Adams in Khartoum – that the surprise announcement of the Governor-General's imminent departure greatly speeded up the self-determination process because it motivated the Sudanese to focus on their constitutional future and not on internal intrigues for positions and political power.[11]

iv. A sudden statement

In Chapter 15, we described how Ismāʿīl al-Azharī's Government was returned to office on 15 November 1955 by a majority of just two votes. Still, al-Azharī showed little enthusiasm for the establishment of a national government in which he might not be the Prime Minister – and so be denied the honour of taking centre stage on the historic day of independence. John Duncan, an assistant to William Luce in the

---

[10] Ibid., 'The End of the Condominium in Sudan', unpublished article dated 16 December 1955.

[11] Ibid., FO 371/113602 (Future of British Officials in the Sudan Civil Service): Adams, UK Diplomatic Mission, Khartoum, to Selwyn Lloyd, Foreign Office, 6 January 1956.

Governor-General's office, wrote later that "[t]he defeat of the NUP became a matter of time, but Azhari was determined that he alone would stand at the head of the government on the day of his country's independence and that the credit would accrue to his party."[12]

Ismāʿīl al-Azharī's then decided to play the decisive card. At Prime Minister's Questions in the House of Representatives, he announced, with no prior notice, that on Monday 19 December he would table a motion declaring the independence of Sudan:

> The task of my Government is limited to the completion of Sudanisation and it is completed; to evacuation and it has been done; and then to uniting the Sudanese around complete independence and this has been done as well. Nothing is left except declaring it from within this House. Next Monday, God willing, I hope that the esteemed members of this House, Government and Opposition would not miss out on picking this tempting fruit.[13]

With this al-Azharī outperformed the opposition. At the British Trade Commission, Philip Adams wrote later: "They might be able to outvote Azhari in the House and indeed had probably hoped to defeat him again on the budget. But they could not vote against such a motion as he was proposing to bring forward. Azhari had seized the initiative and no longer needed a coalition with any particular faction in order to achieve his immediate aim, namely the emergence of an independent Sudan."[14]

At midnight on 15 December, Sir Alexander Knox Helm departed from Khartoum, flying to London on Christmas leave, after which he would never return to Sudan.

---

[12] JSR Duncan, *The Sudan's Path to Independence* (Edinburgh: Blackwood, 1957), p. 202. See also Daly, *Imperial Sudan*, p. 390.
[13] Bashīr, *al-Jalāʾ wa'l-Istiqlāl*, p. 55.
[14] National Archives, Kew, FO 371/113602: Adams to Selwyn Lloyd, 6 January 1956.

v. Four resolutions passed by the House of Representatives: 19 December 1955

On Monday 19 December 1955, four motions – agreed by Government and opposition – were tabled in the House of Representatives. The bills were drafted in Arabic and English by William Luce, his assistant John Duncan, the Governor-General's legal adviser Jack Mavrogordato, key Sudanese party leaders and the Clerk of the House, Muḥammad ʿAmir Bashīr Fawrāwī. By agreement between Government and opposition, back-benchers from both sides of the House took turns to table and second the bills.[15]

The motion given priority was "That the House is of the opinion that claims of the Southern Members of this Parliament for a Federal Government for the three Southern Provinces be given full consideration by the Constituent Assembly." This was done to secure the vote of Southern members to the motion declaring Sudan's independence.[16] However, drafting difficulties arose in the text of the motion for independence. The wording of the original Arabic draft read: "Full independence of the Sudan has become an established fact". Luce discussed this matter with Government and opposition, and it was eventually agreed to alter the wording to read that: "Sudan is to become a fully independent sovereign state".[17] However, the representatives of the Government and opposition amended the wording of the English version of the motion as agreed with Luce but kept the original Arabic version in its original wording: 'has become'. Luce noticed this subsequently and said that he had been double-crossed by the Sudanese. He noted that they were "trying to have it both ways by playing to the gallery in the Arabic version and observing propriety in the English version."[18]

The motions about the federal government and declaration of independence were passed unanimously. So, too, was that proposing a Constituent Assembly to draft and approve the Sudan's final constitution

---

[15] Bashīr, *al-Jalāʾ wa'l-Istiqlāl*, pp. 57-9.

[16] Daly, *Imperial Sudan*, p. 392.

[17] National Archives, Kew, FO 371/113625 (Political relations between UK, Egypt and Sudan): Luce to Foreign Office, 17 December 1955.

[18] Luce to Lampen, 24 December 1955, in Sudan Archive, University of Durham (Luce Papers), SAD.829/6/86-8.

and electoral laws for future parliaments. As for the motion proposing a committee of five members to exercise the powers of the head of state, it was passed by a majority vote Ḥassan al-Ṭāhir Zarūq of the Front Against Colonialization objected to some of the nominees for membership of the Committee. Agreement was reached on the membership of two independents, Aḥmad Muḥammad Ṣāliḥ and ʿAbd-al-Fatāḥ al-Maghrabī, and a Southern representative, for which Siricio Iro was nominated. The NUP representative was Aḥmad Muḥammad Yāsin.[19] For the opposition, the Umma Party nominated Ibrāhīm Aḥmad but al-Dardirī Muḥammad ʿUthmān requested the approval of Sayyid ʿAbd-al-Raḥman al-Mahdī to occupy the Umma's seat; his request was accepted.[20]

Ḥassan al-Ṭāhir Zarūq objected to the inclusion of ʿAbd-al-Fatāḥ al-Maghrabī and Aḥmad Muḥammad Yāsin. The masses of workers and farmers, he said, had not been consulted and the Front Against Colonialization which was the only advocate for their rights. The only criterion, he added, by which an individual should be judged for the most important positions was their patriotic past and their struggle for the freedom of their country. This should be the benchmark for any nominee for a senior post related to the country's independence. Indeed, there should have been a plebiscite to choose those who would represent the head of state. With this in mind, he proposed to add two nominees: Aḥmad Kheir and Aḥmad Mukhtār. The proposal was rejected and the motion proposing the five-member committee was passed by majority vote.[21]

vi. Passing the interim Constitution

In a joint session on 31 December 1955, the House of Representatives and the Senate passed an interim Constitution for Sudan. Mubārak Zarūq, the Majority Leader in the House of Representatives, explained the circumstances which led to proposing an interim Constitution: the need to fill the constitutional vacuum left by the end of

---

[19] National Archives, Kew, FO 371/113625: Luce to Foreign Office, 18 December 1955. See also Ḥamad, *Mudhakkirāt*, p. 247.

[20] Reminiscences of ʿAbd-al-Raḥman ʿAlī Ṭaha, in Ḥamad, *Mudhakkirāt*, p. 247.

[21] Bashīr, *al-Jalāʾ wa'l-Istiqlāl*, pp. 81-3.

the transitional period; and the need to accelerate recognition of Sudan's independence by Britain and Egypt. Replying to a question about the sources of the interim Constitution, he said that the shortest route was an amendment of the Self-Government Statute to conform with the evolution of Sudan as a sovereign democratic republic. The Governor-General had been replaced by a Supremacy Commission; undemocratic powers had been removed, while some minor amendments necessary for a democratic regime had been made. Any controversial amendments would be forwarded to be considered by the Constituent Assembly.

Ḥassan al-Ṭāhir Zarūq MP for Graduates Constituencies and a prominent politician of the Front Against Colonialization noted that the interim constitution made no allusion to the Constituent Assembly, and that this would cause a serious gap in it. Zarūq set out certain principles which should be reflected in the interim constitution: that the constitution should stem from the interests of the people, and the apparatus of the state must be democratic and accountable to the representatives of the people. Amongst those principles were also the freedom of thought, the freedom of faith and the freedom to embrace political ideas and to practice them.

Ismāʿīl al-Azharī and Condominium representatives

Zarūq further observed that Article 5 of the Second Chapter of the Interim Constitution overlooked some of the public freedoms, like the right to stage peaceful demonstrations, the right to privacy of communication and the freedom of movement. He then drew attention to the phrase in the last part of Article 5 which reads: 'within the limits of the law'. He said: "We have learnt from the experiences of the last two years of the colonial era that this phrase was used for the curtailment of the rights and freedoms guaranteed by law."

Perhaps the most outstanding aspect of Zarūq's statement before the House of Representatives was when he asserted that a basic principle of constitutional jurisprudence ordains that: "Any constitution in which the people do not participate in drawing up through their elected representatives would not be an expression of the will of the people; and we cannot ask them to respect it or to abide by it."[22]

[22] Ibid., pp. 87-9 and 93-7.

EPILOGUE

The Constitution of the National Unionist Party stipulated that the Party's core aim was to put an end to the Condominium regime and establish a Sudanese Government in union with Egypt. The principles of such a union were to be defined after self-determination. Contemporary documents reveal that neither the party's spiritual leader, Sayyid ʿAlī al-Mīrghanī, nor its president, Ismāʿīl al-Azharī, were in fact genuine advocates of union with Egypt. As early as August 1953, Sayyid ʿAlī had told John Kenrick, an adviser to the Governor-General, that the 'old slogans of unity' and 'one crown' were dead: the Sudanese nation wanted independence and they would get it. When independence was achieved, the Sayyid added, Sudan would enter into relations with other territories – and no doubt those arranged with Egypt would be close. Sayyid ʿAlī also told Kenrick on 23 May 1954 that the 'crucial fact' was that the Sudanese wanted to govern themselves in every aspect – and would reject all forms of subordination. Sayyid ʿAlī was then denying contemporary claims about a federal union between Egypt and Sudan and the merging of their armed forces and foreign policy.

As for al-Azharī, he told William Luce in an off-the-record conversation a few weeks after being elected Prime Minister that his aim was the 'total independence' of Sudan. Thus he proved the truth of what had been claimed: that union with Egypt was never a genuine aim of the Ashiqqāʾ Party; it was, rather, a tactic to get rid of the British. As al-Azharī put it to Luce, "most people in the country have for some time felt that it would be easier and more practical to ally themselves temporarily with Egypt in order to get rid of the English. But that did not mean that they wished to put themselves under the Egyptians."

In fact, union with Egypt in all its manifestations was never a widespread popular demand. Even after the Sudanese people opted unanimously for total independence, advocates of unity with Egypt invented a distinction between a 'separative independence' and a 'connective independence'. In many instances, when Muḥammad Nūr al-Dīn repeated that distinction, MPs in the House of Representatives would break into open laughter.

It is evident that the British Government outplayed the Egyptians in their management of the self-determination process. After a period of suspicion, animosity and tension, the Governor-General and his aides managed to build bridges and maintain a cordial working relationship with al-Azharī and his Government. Thanks to a high level of professional diplomacy, the British Government was able to achieve its aim: for Sudan to become independent and free from Egyptian domination. In Egypt, meanwhile, the revolutionary government's dream of achieving a link with Sudan remained, even after the removal from office of Ṣalāḥ Sālim and Gamāl ʿAbd-al-Nāṣir's decision to taking charge of the Sudan Affairs portfolio – right up to the eve of independence.

As independence became a more and more likely outcome, the British Government saw fit to curtail the self-determination process. That was why London proposed to Nāṣir on 1 October 1955 that he accepts the principle of Sudan's independence and allow the current Parliament in Khartoum to draw up a new constitution. Nāṣir, of course, resisted – just as he did later when rejecting another proposal for the Parliament of the day to decide self-determination – even though he believed that prospects of a real union were non-existent and that Parliament fully supported independence. The only remaining – and honourable – justification for his position was that he could not publicly abandon those Sudanese who were still in favour of a link with Egypt.

After Egypt concluded the Czech arms deal, London decided that the best way out might be for the Sudanese to take things into their own hands. So Britain proposed to al-Azharī that Parliament should decide on self-determination. Had it not been for the disagreements between Government and opposition, this could have been realised as early as 3 November 1955. The Egyptian Government vehemently refused the declaration of independence by the current Sudanese Parliament. Then it sought to present Britain with a a *fait accompli* by unilaterally inviting the International Commission which would supervise the self-determination process to convene, with a view to frustrating the attempt to declare independence by the existing Sudanese Parliament. Had the Commissioners assembled, the process of self-determination would have had to run the full course, as provided for in the 1953 Agreement.

The British Government then played its ace: to forsake forever the office of Governor-General – a different kind of *fait accompli*. It thereby negated the Egyptian claim that the British aim was to retain the Governor-General after the declaration of independence by the Sudanese Parliament and during the process of constitution making. By vacating the Governor-General's post, the British set the scene for the Sudanese to take over the self-determination process in Parliament, which indeed they did.

In sum, Nāṣir's 23 July Revolution Government failed to make linkage with Egypt an attractive option – just as the monarchical Egypt had failed to annex Sudan to the Egyptian crown.

The preoccupation of the ruling and opposition elites with national self-determination blinded them to any meticulous consideration of either the Southern Liberal Party manifesto, issued in January 1954, or the proceedings of the 2nd Juba Conference of October the same year. Had they done that, they would have realised that the Liberal Party aimed, *inter alia*, at the economic and social development of disadvantaged regions, including the South, the Fur, the Funj, the Nuba and the blacks of Sudan.

Benjamin Lwoki conveyed the resolutions of the 2nd Juba Conference to the Co-Domini, the Governor-General and the Prime Minister of Sudan, attaching a message expressing the wish of Southerners to put an end to Northern encroachment into the South. Lwoki added that the disparities between North and South could only lead to one of two things: federal union between the two or, if this were to be unacceptable to the Northerners, a divided Sudan, with each state independent of the other, just as Pakistan had seceded from India in 1947.

Even after independence, no evidence is available that the ruling class in Khartoum considered thoughtfully the proceedings of the Constituent Assembly's first meeting, held on 22 May 1958, to debate the recently completed April 1958 draft of the Constitution. Though the meeting is outside the chronological, i.e. pre-independence, period of this book, parts of its proceedings and resolutions can be found in the Appendices, since they are closely related to the historic decision taken by the House of Representatives on 19 December 1955. Included in that decision was a promise that the prospective Constituent Assembly would give 'due consideration' to the Southern demand for a federal government for the three Southern Provinces. Sorrowfully, the April 1958 draft Constitution reneged on that promise. It was devoid of any provision on the federal status of the three Southern Provinces. Predictably, the reaction of the Southern MPs was swift and angry.

Franco Wall Garang said that Sudan's independence would not be stable unless the situation in the South was stable – and if the demand for federation was not met, the Southerners might demand other things which were hitherto not required.

Father Saturnino Ohure of the Southern Sudan Federal Party threatened that if the demand for federation was not met, Southerners would seek 'another route' to attain their demands. Both MPs rejected the adoption of the Constitution by majority vote. Garang added that, "as long as the sun rises from the east, the Southerners will never be a majority in Sudan." Father Satarnino followed up by warning that, if the Constitution was endorsed by the majority and the Southerners remained a minority, the problem of the South would never be solved. Yet Northern politicians failed to heed this warning of an imminent danger – let alone think about initiating some kind of national melting pot project.

Sudan achieved its independence with an interim Constitution drawn from the Self-Government Statute – and a promise to the people that an elected Constituent Assembly would draw up a permanent Sudanese Constitution. More than half a century had elapsed since Sudan's independence, but this promise is yet to be redeemed.

A cynic might wonder how one could possibly think of a 'national melting pot' and a permanent Sudanese Constitution when independence has brought us nothing but a vicious cycle of short-lived democratic governments and coups d'etat, from which the Sudanese people reaped neither material sustenance nor safety from fear.

APPENDIX 1

Agreement Between the Government of the United Kingdom of Great Britain and Northern Ireland and the Egyptian Government Concerning Self-Government and Self-Determination for the Sudan

Cairo, 12th February 1953

The Government of the United Kingdom of Great Britain and Northern Ireland (hereinafter called the "United Kingdom Government") and the Egyptian Government,

Firmly believing in the right of the Sudanese people to Self-Determination and the effective exercise thereof at the proper time and with the necessary safeguards,

Have agreed as follows:

Article 1

In order to enable the Sudanese people to exercise Self-Determination in a free and neutral atmosphere, a transitional period providing full self-government for the Sudanese shall begin on the day specified in Article 9 below.

Article 2

The transitional period, being a preparation for the effective termination of the dual Administration, shall be considered as a liquidation of that Administration. During the transitional period the sovereignty of the Sudan shall be kept in reserve for the Sudanese until Self-Determination is achieved.

Article 3

The Governor-General shall, during the transitional period, be the supreme constitutional authority within the Sudan. He shall exercise his powers as set out in the Self-Government Statute with the aid of a five-member Commission, to be called the Governor-General's Commission, whose powers are laid down in the terms of reference in Annexe I to the present Agreement.

Article 4

This Commission shall consist of two Sudanese proposed by the two contracting governments in agreement, one Egyptian citizen, one citizen of the United Kingdom and one Pakistani citizen, each to be proposed by his respective Government. The appointment of the two Sudanese members shall be subject to the subsequent approval of the Sudanese Parliament when it is elected, and the Parliament shall be entitled to nominate alternative candidates in case of disapproval. The Commission hereby set up will be formally appointed by Egyptian Government decree.

Article 5

The two contracting governments agree that, it being a fundamental principle of their common policy to maintain the unity of the Sudan as a single territory, the special powers which are vested in the Governor-General by Article 100 of the Self- Government Statute shall not be exercised in any manner which is in conflict with that policy.

Article 6

The Governor-General shall remain directly responsible to the two contracting governments as regards:

(a) external affairs;

(b) any change requested by the Sudanese Parliament under Article 101 (1) of the Statute for Self-Government as regards any part of the Statute;

(c) any resolution passed by the Commission which he regards as inconsistent with his responsibilities. In this case he will inform the two contracting Governments, each of which must give an answer within one month of the date of formal notice. The Commission's resolution shall stand unless the two Governments agree to the contrary.

Article 7

There shall be constituted a Mixed Electoral Commission of seven members. These shall be three Sudanese appointed by the Governor-General with the approval of his Commission, one Egyptian citizen, one citizen of the United Kingdom, one citizen of the United States of America, and one Indian citizen. The non- Sudanese members shall be nominated by their respective Governments. The Indian member shall be Chairman of the Commission. The Commission shall be appointed by the Governor-General on the instructions of the two contracting Governments. The terms of reference of this Commission are contained in Annex II to this Agreement.

Article 8

To provide the free and neutral atmosphere requisite for Self-Determination there shall be established a Sudanisation Committee consisting of:

(a) an Egyptian citizen and a citizen of the United Kingdom to be nominated by their respective Governments and subsequently appointed by the Governor-General, together with three Sudanese members to be selected from a list of five names submitted to him by the Prime Minister of the Sudan. The selection and appointment of these Sudanese members shall have the prior approval of the Governor-General's Commission;

(b) one or more members of the Sudan Public Service Commission who will act in a purely advisory capacity without the right to vote;

The function and terms of reference of this Committee are contained in Annex III to this Agreement.

Article 9

The transitional period shall begin on the day designated as "the appointed day" in Article 2 of the Self-Government Statute. Subject to the completion of the Sudanisation as outlined in Annex III to this Agreement, the two contracting governments undertake to bring the transitional period to an end as soon as possible. In any case this period shall not exceed three years. It shall be brought to an end in the following manner. The Sudanese Parliament shall pass a resolution expressing their desire that arrangements for Self-Determination shall be put in motion and the

Governor-General shall notify the two contracting governments of this resolution.

Article 10

When the two contracting governments have been formally notified of this resolution, the Sudanese Government, then existing, shall draw up a draft law for the election of the Constituent Assembly which it shall submit to Parliament for approval. The Governor-General shall give his consent to the law with the agreement of his Commission. Detailed preparations for the process of Self-Determination, including safeguards assuring the impartiality of the elections and any other arrangements designed to secure a free and neutral atmosphere, shall be subject to international supervision. The two contracting governments will accept the recommendations of any international body which may be set up to this end.

Article 11

Egyptian and British military forces shall withdraw from the Sudan immediately upon the Sudanese Parliament adopting a resolution expressing its desire that arrangements for Self-Determination be put in motion. The two contracting governments undertake to complete the withdrawal of their forces from the Sudan within a period not exceeding three months.

Article 12

The Constituent Assembly shall have two duties to discharge. The first will be to decide the future of the Sudan as one integral whole. The second will be to draw up a constitution for the Sudan compatible with the decision which shall have been taken in this respect, as well as an electoral law for a permanent Sudanese Parliament. The future of the Sudan shall be decided either:

(a) by the Constituent Assembly choosing to link the Sudan with Egypt in any form, or

(b) by the Constituent Assembly choosing complete independence.

Article 13

The two contracting governments undertake to respect the decision of the Constituent Assembly concerning the future status of the

Sudan and each Government will take all the measures which may be necessary to give effect to its decision.

Article 14

The two contracting governments agree that the draft Self-Government Statute shall be amended in accordance with Annex IV to this Agreement.

Article 15

This Agreement and its attachments shall come into force upon signature.

Annex I

Terms of Reference of the Governor-General's Commission to be set up under Article 3 of the Agreement between the United Kingdom and the Egyptian Governments concerning Self-Government and Self-Determination for the Sudan.

1. It shall be the function of the Governor-General's Commission to consider the matters put before them by the Governor-General as defined in the following paragraphs and to notify him of their consent or otherwise.

2. The powers of the Governor-General as set out in the following Articles of the Self-Government Statute shall be exercised by the Governor-General subject to the approval of his Commission:

Article 31, Article 40 Section (2), Article 44 Section (4), Article 45, Article 53, Article 56 Section (1), Article 57 Section (8), Article 75 to 86 inclusive, Article 100, Article 101 (2), Article 102 (1) and Items 1, 2 and 3 of the Second Schedule, Part II.

3. In the absence of any member or members of the Commission they will be replaced by alternate members. These alternate members will be of the same nationality and will be appointed in the same manner and as far as possible at the same time as the members they are nominated to replace.

4. All decisions of the Commission shall be taken by majority vote.

5. The Commission shall draw up its own rules of procedure.

6. The Pakistani member shall act as Chairman of the Commission. Salaries and allowances of the members of the Commission shall be assessed by agreement between the two Governments and the Sudan Administration. The Sudan Government will pay the expenses of members of the Commission travelling within the Sudan in the course of their duties and supply the necessary offices and secretarial staff.

Annex II

Terms of Reference of the Electoral Commission set up under Article 7 of the Agreement between the United Kingdom and Egyptian Governments concerning Self-Government and Self-Determination for the Sudan.

1. Its functions shall be to examine and, if necessary, revise the draft electoral rules and thereafter issue rules for the forthcoming elections so that they may be held as soon as possible, and as far as practicable simultaneously throughout the Sudan.

2. It shall decide on the qualifications of voters in Senate elections, and on the indirect election constituencies for the House of Representatives. It shall also decide on the number of seats, not exceeding five, in the Graduates' Constituency.

3. It shall supervise the preparation for and the conduct of the elections and ensure their impartiality.

4. It shall submit a report to the two Governments on the conduct of the elections.

5. It shall draw up its own rules of procedure and methods of work in order that it may effectively carry out the duties stated above and shall, if need be, appoint sub-commissions for electoral constituencies.

6. The decisions of the Commission shall be taken by majority vote.

7. Elections shall be direct in every case where the Commission decides that this is practicable.

8. Salaries and allowances of the members of the Committee shall be assessed by agreement between the two Governments and the Sudan Administration. The Sudan Government will pay the expenses of members of the Committee travelling within the Sudan in the course of their duties and supply the necessary offices and secretarial staff.

Annex III

Terms of Reference of the Sudanisation Committee set up under Article 8 of the Agreement between the United Kingdom and Egyptian Governments Concerning Self-Government and Self-Determination for the Sudan.

1. The duties of the Sudanisation Committee shall be to complete the Sudanisation of the Administration, the Police, the Sudan Defence Force, and any other Government post that may affect the freedom of the Sudanese at the time of Self-Determination. The Committee shall review the various Government posts with a view to cancelling any unnecessary or redundant post held by Egyptian or British officials.

2. The Committee may co-opt one or more members as it deems fit to act in an advisory capacity without the right to vote.

3. The Committee shall take its decisions by majority vote. The Committee's decisions shall be submitted to the Sudanese Council of Ministers. If the Governor-General does not agree with any such decision or with the views of the Council of Ministers, he may with the approval of his Commission withhold his assent, and, in the event of disagreement between the Governor-General and the latter, the matter shall be referred to the two Governments. The Commission's decision shall stand unless the two Governments agree to the contrary.

4. The Sudanisation Committee shall complete its duties within a period not exceeding three years. It shall render periodical reports to the Governor-General who shall consider them in conjunction with his Commission. These reports with any comments thereon shall be transmitted to the two Governments for such joint action as they may consider appropriate. The two Governments shall give every possible assistance for the completion of the Committee's task.

5. Salaries and allowances of the members of the Committee shall be assessed by agreement between the two Governments and the Sudan Administration. The Sudan Government will pay the expenses of members of the Committee travelling within the Sudan in the course of their duties and supply the necessary offices and secretarial staff.

APPENDIX 2

Parliamentary Under-Secretary Appointees, December 1954

Education	Muḥammad Karrār Kajur (Amar and Bishārīn)
Local Government	Teifūr Muḥammad Sharīf (al-Dāmar)
Interior	Faḍlallah ʿAlī al-Tūm (Kabbābish)
Transport	al-Majzūb Ibrāhīm Faraḥ (Shendi)
Mineral Resources	Akeej Khamees Rizq Allah (ʿUwīl West)
Agriculture	Idrīs al-Zeibaq (Taqalī North)
Mechanical Transport	Ibrāhīm al-Ṭayyib Badr (Kāmlin)
Defence	Aḥmad Idrīs Abū al-Ḥassan (Merowe)
Justice	Muḥammad Harūn Tīma (al-Jawāmaʾa West)
Stores and Assignments	ʿUmer Ḥamza Muḥammad Aḥmad (Rural Khartoum North)
Trade	al-Marḍī Muḥammad Raḥma (Berber)
Social Affairs	ʿAbdallah Muḥammad al-Tūm (al-Madīna al-ʿArab)
Works	ʿAbd-al-Nabī ʿAbd-al-Qādir Mursal (Renk and Malakal)
Finance	Muḥammad Jubāra al-ʿAwaḍ (Kassala)
Health	Ḥassan Muḥammad Zakī (al-Funj South)
Animal Health	Yūsuf ʿAbd-al-Ḥamīd Ibrāhīm (Zālenjay North West)

APPENDIX 3

First Meeting of the Constituent Assembly to Draw up a Permanent Constitution for Sudan: 22 May 1958

On 7 July 1956, a coalition government was formed by the Umma Party and the newly-formed People's Democratic Party. This government, headed by ʿAbdallah Khalīl, selected a 46-member national committee to draw up a permanent constitution for Sudan. Members included experts in constitutional law, public figures, representatives of political parties, and representatives of the Workers' Federation' the Gezira Farmers' Union, the Lawyers' Syndicate, the Press Association, the University Graduates' Union and the Chamber of Commerce.[1]

The full list comprised:

Abū-Shāma ʿAbd-al-Maḥmūd; Aḥmad Kheir; Aḥmad Suleimān; Aḥmad Yūsuf Hāshim; Istānsalūs Pyāsāma; al-Dardīrī Aḥmad Ismāʿīl; Al-Ṣāʾim Muḥammad Ibrāhīm; Amīl Qurunfilī; Bashīr ʿAbd-al-Raḥīm; Bashīr Muḥammad Said; Buth Diu; Pauline Aler; Jābir ʿUthmān (Gezira Farmers Union); Ḥussein al-Sayyid; Ḥussein al-Hindī; Ḥussein ʿUthmān Wannī; Khiḍr Ḥamad; Ziyāda Arbāb; Fr Saturnino Lohure; Sarūr Ramlī; Saʿad al-Dīn Fawzī; Sayyid Aḥmad ʿAbd-al-Hādī; ʿAbdīn Ismāʿīl; ʿAbd-al-Raḥīm Aḥmad; ʿAbd-al-Raḥīm al-Amīn; ʿAbd-al-Qādir Ḥussein; ʿAbdallah al-Ḥassan; ʿAbdallah Mīrghanī; ʿUqeil Aḥmad ʿUqeil; ʿAlī Bedrī; ʿUmar Bakhīt al-ʿAwaḍ; Mubārak Zarrūq; Muḥammad Aḥmad Maḥjūb; Muḥammad Adam Adham; Muḥammad al-Sayyid Salām (Workers' Federation); Muḥammad Ṣāliḥ al-Shinqītī; Muḥammad ʿAbdallah al-ʿUmrābī;

[1] National Archives, Kew, FO 371/119604: British Embassy, Khartoum, to Foreign Office, 1 October 1956.

Muḥammad Fāris Ḥussein; Maḥmūd Muḥammad Ṭaha; Muhī al-Dīn alb-Bireir; Makkī Shibeika; Makkī ʿAbbās; Mīrghanī al-Nuṣrī; Mīrghanī Ḥamza; and Yūsuf Shibeika.

Bābikr ʿAwaḍallah, Speaker of the House of Representatives, was chosen as President of this National Constitutional Committee, with Aḥmad Kheir as his Deputy. Its first meeting, convened on 22 September 1956, was addressed by the Prime Minister and the Minister of Justice, Ziyāda Arbāb, who informed the gathering that Parliament would continue to sit until the end of 1956 and that it was hoped that elections for the Constituent Assembly would be held in March 1957.

APPENDIX 4

Draft Constitution Before the Constituent Assembly, April 1958

The Minister of Justice presented the draft of the April 1958 Constitution before the Constituent Assembly at its first Session on 22 May 1958. The first Chapter of the draft Constitution stipulated the following:

> "Sudan is a unified parliamentary democratic republic.
> Sovereignty in the Republic of Sudan belongs to the people who exercise it in accordance with the provisions of this Constitution.
> The provisions of this Constitution shall prevail over all existing and future laws.
> Arabic is the official language of the state.
> Islam is the official religion of the state."[1]

The Constituent Assembly passed six decisions jointly submitted by the Government and the opposition as agreed. Among the decisions passed was the decision that the Constituent Assembly would consider the draft Constitution prepared by the National Constitution Committee and submitted by the Minister of Justice on Thursday 22 May 1958, as well as the decision to refer the draft to the Constitution Committee for consideration and preparation of a report thereof in the shortest possible time. It is noteworthy that latter Constitution Committee was composed of forty members of the Constituent Assembly.

---

[1] *al-Lajnat al-Qawmīa li al-Dustūr al-Jamhūrīat al-Sūdān* (*The National Committee for the Constitution of the Republic of Sudan*) (Khartoum: McCorquodale, 1958).

Southern representatives in the Constituent Assembly objected to the draft constitution because it failed to provide for the issue of federalism and demanded its inclusion. Muḥammad Aḥmad Maḥjūb, the Majority Leader, explained that there is a misunderstanding and that the Constituent Assembly is entirely free to modify, reject or replace the draft. He said that if the Committee (i.e. the forty-member Committee) issues a report on federalism, it shall be submitted to the Constituent Assembly which will either accept it or reject it if the best interests of the country so require, according to the majority view.

Franco Wall Garang, Representative of the 15th District (Wau), rejected the approval of the Constitution based on the majority view and said:

> "As long as the sun rises from the east, the Southerners will never be a majority in Sudan. If that draft is the basis for discussion, we shall have nothing to do with it, because it neglected the main demand of the south. I declare here that the independence of Sudan will not be stable if the situation in the south is not corrected.... We hold no evil intentions against the independence of Sudan which we love and care for as any of you. But we want it to be a real independence rather than a falsely colourful one. We want to obtain our rights as a nation in the independent Sudan."

At the end of his speech, MP Garang said:

> "We are now standing on the brink of an abyss. The Federation is a sensitive issue. And if the demand for it is not met, the Southerners might demand other things which were hitherto not required."

Father Saturnino Ohure, Representative of District No. 80 (Torit Latoka), refused the claim that the proceedings of the National Constitution Committee were unanimously blessed. He explained that he was representing the Liberal bloc in the Committee meetings and did not agree with the findings of the Government and the opposition and demanded the insertion of an amendment providing for the federation.

When that was rejected, he withdrew together with his colleagues. He added that Southerners boycotted the National Constitution Committee, and as a result the work done was only carried out by part of the Committee's members.[2]

Saturnino went on to say: "The meeting of the proposed Constitution Committee (i.e. the forty-member Committee) would face a severe test when Southerners come and demand the federation, for when that request is rejected, Southerners would be left with no choice other than to withdraw. Approving the Constitution at that time would not be a legal action. Southerners will thus seek another way to achieve their demands. We are tired of the words 'due consideration' which were mentioned in the previous Parliament's decision. Many promises have been made to discuss this matter. Amending this draft will be futile. We must first consider the type of government which we desire: Is it the rule under a united Sudan or some form of federal government? "

Saturnino added that: "The south has a cause. And it is a just cause ... because the South wants to administer its own domestic affairs after the failure of the Northern administration which replaced British rule, and its inability to do the work... The clearest evidence supporting the position of the south is the rebellion that broke out three years ago. Southerners were dissatisfied with their condition and tried to get their rights the way they deemed fit. The rebellion occurred at an hour of rage and persistence. But I do believe that there are legitimate and legal means to achieve any goal. Therefore, I do not endorse the rebellion. It was recently discovered that among the causes of the rebellion is the behaviour of Northern merchants and officials in whose hands rested a responsibility which they failed to manage properly. Thus, the rebellion took place and developed into a revolution, which resulted in the loss of the lives of many innocent Northern women, children and men. This is just one face of the problem. The other face is that Southerners were prosecuted by a judiciary, of which Northerners constituted one hundred percent. As a result a large number of Southerners lost their lives or were imprisoned."

---

[2] *al-Ayyām*, 23 May 1958.

Father Saturnino concluded his speech by saying: "If we are going to rely on the issue of majority while Southerners are few, we will never solve the Southerners' problem."

Southern members subsequently withdrew from the Constituent Assembly meeting. Then they issued a statement saying that the Constituent Assembly should have considered first the question of federation between the South and North, pursuant to the previous Parliament's decision on 19 December 1955. They further said that they do not want to set up obstacles, but they will not discuss or consider any draft constitution or agree on a constitution not based on a federal union.

BIBLIOGRAPHY

1. Books in Arabic

ʿAbd-al-Khāliq Maḥjūb. *Lamahāt min Tārīkh al-Hizb al-Shūʿi al-Sūdānī* (*Glimpses from the History of the Sudanese Communist Party*). 3rd edition. Khartoum: Dār al-Wasīla Printing and Publishing, 1987

ʿAbd-al-Laṭīf al-Baghdādī. *Mudhakkirāt* (*Memoirs*). Cairo: al-Maktab al-Miṣrī al-Ḥadīth, 1977

ʿAbd-al-Raḥman ʿAlī Ṭaha. *al-Sūdān li al-Sūdānīn* (*Sudan for the Sudanese*). Khartoum: Khartoum University Press, 1992

ʿAbd-al-Raḥman al-Rāfaʿī. *Thawrat 23 Yūlyū 1952-59* (*The 23 July Revolution 1952-59*). Cairo: Dār al-Maʿārif, 1989

Aḥmad Ḥamrūsh. *Qiṣṣat Thawrat 23 Yūlyū, al-Juzuʾ al-Thālith: ʿAbd-al-Nāṣr wa al-ʿArab* (*An Account of the 23 July Revolution, Part 3: ʿAbd-al-Nāṣr and the Arabs*). Cairo: Arab Institute for Study and Publishing, 1976

Aḥmad Ibrāhīm Abū-Shouk and al-Fātiḥ ʿAbdallah ʿAbd-al-Salām. *al-Intikhābāt al-Barlamanīa fī al-Sūdān 1953-1986* (*Parliamentary Elections in Sudan 1953-1986*). Omdurman: ʿAbd-al-Karīm Mīrghanī Centre, 2008

Aḥmad Muḥammad Yāsin. *Mudhakkirāt* (*Memoirs*). Omdurman: Muḥammad ʿUmar Bashīr Centre, 2001

Aḥmad Suleimān. *Mashaynaha Khutan* (*Steps We Took*). 2 vols. Khartoum: Dār al-Fikr, 1986

ʿAlī Muḥammad Bashīr Mūsa. *Tārīkh Niqābat al-Sikka al-Ḥadīdīa 1906-1961* (*A History of the Railway Union 1906-1961*). Khartoum: ʿAzza Publishers and Distributors, 2007

Amīn al-Tūm. *Dhikrayāt wa Mawāqif 1914-1969* (*Memories and Situations 1914-1969*). Khartoum: Sudanese House of Books, 2004

Bashīr Muḥammad Sa'īd. *al-Za'īm al-Azharī wa 'Uṣruhu* (*al-Azharī the Leader and His Era*). Cairo: Modern Printing, 1990

Fadwa 'Abd-al-Raḥman 'Alī Taha. *Keifa Nāl al-Sūdān Istiqlālahu* (*How Sudan Attained its Independence*). Omdurman: 'Abd-al-Karīm Mīrghanī Centre, 2008

Faisal 'Abd-al-Raḥman 'Alī Ṭaha. *al-Ḥaraka al-Sīyāsīa wa al-Ṣirā al-Maṣrī al-Briṭānī bishān al-Sūdān: 1936-1953* (*The Sudanese Political Movement and the Anglo-Egyptian Conflict Over Sudan: 1936-1953*). Omdurman: 'Abd-al-Karīm Mīrghanī Centre, 2004

Ḥassan Makkī Muḥammad Aḥmad. *Ḥarakat al-Ihkwān al-Muslimīn fī al-Sūdān* (*The Muslim Brothers Movement in Sudan*). Khartoum: Institute of African Studies, 1982

Jamāl al-Sharīf. *al-Sirā al-Siyāsī ala al-Sūdān 1940-2008* (*The Political Struggle for Sudan 1940-2008*). Khartoum: Mint Printing, 2008

Kāmil Maḥjūb. *Tilk al-Ayyām, al-Juzu' al-Awwal* (*Those Days, Part 1*). Khartoum: Dār al-Balad, 1999

Khidir Ḥamad. *Mudhakkirāt: al-Ḥaraka al-Waṭanīa al-Sūdānīa: al-Istiqlāl wa mā Ba'duhu* (*Memoirs: The Sudanese Nationalist Movement: Independence and Beyond*). Khartoum: East and West Publishers, 1980

Muḥammad Aḥmad Maḥjūb. *al-Dimūqrātīa fī al-Mīzān* (*Democacy in the Balance*). n.p.

Muḥammad 'Umar Bashīr. *al-Jalā' wa al-Istiqlāl* (*Evacuation and Independence*). Khartoum: Dār al-Sūdānīa li al-Kutub, 1975

– –. *Tārīkh al-Ḥaraka al-Waṭanīa fī al-Sūdān 1900-1969* (*The History of the Political Movement in Sudan 1900-1969*) Beirut: Dār al-Jīl, 1987

Muḥammad Sa'īd al-Qaddāl. *Ma'ālim fī Tārīkh al-Ḥizb al-Shiyū'ī al-Sūdānī fī Nisf Qarn* (*Landmarks in the History of the Sudanese Communist Party over Half a Century 1936-1955*). Beirut: Dār al-Fārābi, 1999

– –. *Tārīkh al-Sūdān al-Ḥadīth 1820-1955* (*A History of Modern Sudan*

1820-1955). Cairo: Amal Publishers and Printers, 1993
Muḥammad Suleimān. *al-Yasār al-Sūdānī fī ʿAsharat Aʿwām 1954-1963* (*A Decade on the Sudanese Left 1954-1963*). Wad Medani: al-Fajr Library, 1967
Muḥsin Muḥammad. *Miṣr wa al-Sūdān: al-Infiṣāl* (*Egypt and Sudan: Separation*). Cairo: Dār al-Shurūq, 1994
Mūsa ʿAbdallah Ḥāmid. *Istiqlāl al-Sūdān: Bein al-Wāqʿīa wa al-Rūmānsīa* (*Sudanese Independence: Between Realism and Romanticism*). Khartoum: Arab Cultural Capital Documents, 2005.
Muṣtafa al-Saʿīd. *Mashāwīr fī Dirūb al-Ḥayāt* (*Trips Along the Roads of Life*). Khartoum: Sudanese Mint Printers, 2007
Qāsim Amīn. *Itifāqīat al-Sūdān fī al-Mīzān* (*Sudan's Agreement in the Balance*). n.p.
Najda Fatḥī Ṣafwa. *Min Nāfidhat al-Safāra: al-ʿArab fī Dhūʾ al-Wathāʾiq al-Briṭānīa* (*From the Embassy Window: The Arabs as Shown in British Documents*). Riyadh: n.p., 1992
Rifʿat al-Saʿīd. *Tārīkh al-Ḥaraka al-Shiyūʿīa al-Miṣriyya* (*A History of the Egyptian Communist Movement*). 3 vols. Cairo: Dār al-Amal li al-Ṭabāʿa wa'l-Nashr, 1987
al-Ṣādiq al Mahdī (ed.). *Jihād fī Sabīl al-Istiqlāl* (*Jihad in the Cause of Independence*. Khartoum: Government Press, 1965

2. Articles in Arabic

Jamāl ʿAbd-al-Jawād. *'Miṣr fī al-Sīyāsa al-Sūdānīa'* ('Egypt in Sudanese Politics'). *al-Mustaqbal al-ʿArabī* 97 (Beirut, September 1985): 68.
Muḥammad Abū al-Qāsim Hāj Ḥāmad. *'ʿAqabāt al-Taṭawurar al-Siyāsī wa al-Dustūrī fī al-Sūdān 1956-1986'* ('Obstacles to Political and Constitutional Development in Sudan'). *al-Khalīj*, 3 January 1987
Najda Fatḥī Ṣafwa. *al-Sūdān ʿala ʿatabat al-Istiqlāl'* ('Sudan on the Verge of Independence'). *Arab Researcher* (January/March 1986): 110

3. Books in English

Daly, MW. *Imperial Sudan: The Anglo-Egyptian Condominium, 1934-*

1956. Cambridge: CUP, 1991

Duncan, JSR. *The Sudan's Path to Independence*. Edinburgh: Blackwood, 1957

Grafftey-Smith, Laurence. *Bright Levant*. London: John Murray, 1970

Hawley, Donald. *Sandtracks in the Sudan*. Norwich: Michael Russell, 1955

Hill, Richard. *A Biographical Dictionary of the Anglo-Egyptian Sudan*. Oxford: Clarendon Press, 1951

Johnson, DH (ed.). *British Documents on the End of Empire, Series B, Vol. 5, Sudan Part 1: 1942-1950*. London: Institute of Commonwealth Studies, 1998

– – (ed.). *British Documents on the End of Empire, Series B, Vol. 5, Sudan Part 2: 1951-1956*. London: Institute of Commonwealth Studies, 1998

– –. *Federalism in the History of South Sudanese Political Thought*. London: Rift Valley Institute, 2014

MacMichael, Harold. *Sudan Political Service 1899-1956*. Oxford: Oxonian Press, 1958

Mahmoud Salih (ed.). *The British Documents on the Sudan*. 13 vols. Omdurman: 'Abd al-Karīm al-Mīrghānī Cultural Centre, 2002

Mavrogordato, Jack. *Behind the Scenes (An Autobiography)*. Tisbury: Element Books, 1982

El Amin, Mohamed Nuri. *The Emergence and Development of the Leftist Movement in the Sudan during the 1930s and 1940s*. Khartoum, KUP, 1984

Muddathir ʿAbd al-Raḥīm. *Imperialism and Nationalism in the Sudan: A Study in Constitutional and Political Development 1899–1956*. Oxford: Clarendon Press, 1969

4. Articles in English

Adamthwaite, Anthony. 'Overstretched and Overstrung: Eden, the Foreign Office and the Making of Policy, 1951-5'. *International Affairs* 64/2 (1988): 241-59

Daly, MW. 'Principal Office-Holders in the Sudan Government, 1895-

1955'. *International Journal of African Historical Studies* 17/2 (1984): 309-316

Fadwa A.A. Taha. 'The Sudanese Factor in the 1952-53 Anglo-Egyptian Negotiations'. *Middle Eastern Studies* 44/4 (2008): 603-31

Faisal Abdel Rahman Ali Taha. 'Some Legal Aspects of the Anglo-Egyptian Condominium over the Sudan: 1899-1954', *British Yearbook of International Law* 76/1 (2005): 337-82

Hill, Richard. 'A Register of Named Power-Driven River and Marine Harbour Craft Commissioned in the Sudan 1856-1964'. *Sudan Notes and Records* 51 (1970): 131-46

Rolandsen, Øystein H. 'A False Start: Between War and Peace in the Southern Sudan, 1956-62'. *Journal of African History* 52/1 (2011): 105-23

Selak, C.B. 'The Suez Canal Base Agreement of 1954'. *American Journal of International Law* 49/4 (1955): 487-505

Wakoson, Elias Nyamlell. 'The Sudanese Dilemma: The South-North Conflict'. *Northeast African Studies* 9/3 (1987): 43-58

5. Newspapers and magazines in Arabic

a. Egypt

al-Ahrām 1954: 12 January, 1 February, 22 April, 8 November, 20 December, 21 December

1955: 14 April, 19 May, 20 June, 5 July, 11 July, 16 August, 6 September, 17 September, 23 October, 24 October, 30 October

al-Jamhūrīa 1955: 24 October, 4 December

al-Muṣawwar 20/1597 (May 1955)

b. Sudan

al-Ayyām 1951: 27 February

1954: 19 January, 28 February 1954, 2 March, 27 March, 31 March, 4 July, 5 July, 2 September, 13 September, 19 October, 10 November, 16 November

1955: 24 January, 26 January, 4 February, 7 April, 8 April, 21 April, 16 June

1958: 23 May

al-Istiqlāl	1955: 23 June
al-Nīl	1955: 4 May, 15 June, 18 June, 29 October, 4 December
al-Rāyī al-'Am	1954: 19 January, 1 September, 7 October, 16 November, 16 December, 27 December
	1955: 9 August, 10 August, 15 August, 27 October, 15 November, 29 November, 4 December, 7 December, 8 December
Ṣawt al-Sūdān	1955: 14 November, 6 December
al-Sūdān al-Jadīd	1954: 14 May, 26 October
	1955: 15 November
al-Umma	1955: 13 October

6. Published official documents in Arabic

a. Cairo

al-Sūdān: al-Kitāb al-Akhḍar (*Sudan: The Green Book*). Cairo: Cabinet Office, 1841-1953

b. Khartoum

al-Lajnat al-Qawmīa li al-Dustūr al-Jamhūrīat al-Sūdān (*The National Committee for the Constitution of the Republic of Sudan*). Khartoum: McCorquodale, 1958

Minutes of the House of Representatives: Session No. 32 (16 August 1955; No. 33 (22 August 1955); No. 34 (29 August 1955); No. 36 (5 November 1955)

Taqrīr Lajnat al-Thaqīq fī al-Itirābāt bi Janūb al-Sūdān fī Agustus Sanat 1955 (*Report of the Commission of Enquiry into the Disturbances in Southern Sudan in August 1955*)

7. Published official documents in English

a. Khartoum

Constitution of the Republic of the Sudan, April 1958 (National Constitution Commission). Khartoum: McCorquodale, 1958

Report of the Commission of Enquiry into the Disturbances in Southern Sudan during August 1955. Khartoum: McCorquodale, 1956

Sudan Government Gazette No. 445 (1924)

b. London

Agreement Between the Government of the United Kingdom of Great Britain and Northern Ireland and The Egyptian Government Concerning Self-Government and Self-Determination for the Sudan. London: HMSO, 1953

Hansard, 27 January 1947, vol. 432, cc. 616-20

Supplementary agreement between the Government of the United Kingdom of Great Britain and Northern Ireland and the Egyptian Government for the establishment of an international commission to supervise the process of self-determination in the Sudan and exchange of notes modifying the Anglo-Egyptian Agreement of the 12th of February 1953 concerning self-government and self-determination for the Sudan. London: HMSO, 1955

8. Unpublished official documents in English

a. The National Archives, Kew

i. Colonial Office

CO1069/14 (Colonial Office/Sudan)

3: Sudan Elections for Self-Government

ii. Foreign Office

FO 93/32 (Protocols of Treaties/Egypt)

102: Agreement and Exchanges of Notes. Self-determination for the Sudan

FO 371 (Political Departments/Egypt and Sudan)

73471: Communism in the Sudan

80352: Communism in the Sudan

96913: Anglo-Egyptian negotiations for self-government in the Sudan 96916: Anglo-Egyptian negotiations for self-government in the Sudan

102711: The Mixed Electoral Commission and the General Elections in Sudan

102753: Agreement between Egypt and UK on the Sudan: efforts to achieve implementation

102925: Proposed establishment of liaison officers of foreign governments in Khartoum

108311: Annual political reviews for 1953 on Egypt by HM Ambassador, and on Sudan by UK Trade Commissioner in Khartoum

108320-6: Political developments in Sudan during 1954

108328: Sudan: Two-monthly political intelligence summaries covering period November 1953 to September 1954

108330: Nominations for membership of the Sudanisation Committee

108331-2: Establishment of the Governor-General's Commission in the Sudan

108340-1: Activities of the Sudanisation Committee

108343: Appointment of a Public Service Commission under the Sudan Self-Government Statute

108344: Minutes of conversations of various senior Sudanese Ministers with UK Trade Commissions, Khartoum and with Minister of State for Foreign Affairs, Selwyn Lloyd, during his visit to Khartoum

108348: Communism in Sudan

108377: Instructions issued by the FO for the British member of the Sudanisation Committee in Khartoum

108378: Future policy of HMG toward the Sudan

108380: Conversations on political matters affecting relations between UK, Egypt and Sudan

108381: Political relations between Egypt, Sudan and UK: fears of chaos or administrative breakdown in Sudan

113581-5: Political developments in the Sudan during 1955

113589: Communism in the Sudan

113596: Departure of Sir R. Howe as Governor-General of Sudan

113602: Future of British Officials in the Sudan Civil Service

113609-19 and 24-5: Political relations between UK, Egypt and Sudan

113697: Mutiny in South Sudan

113783-4: Self-determination for the Sudan: decision to hold plebiscite

119604: Internal political situation in Sudan, about to become an independent sovereign state

FO 800 (Foreign Office/Private Offices/Various Ministers' and Officials' Papers)

662 (Papers of Sir [Alexander] Knox Helm)

iii. Prime Minister's Office

PREM11/777 (Prime Minister's Office/Situation in Sudan)

CC15(54) 3: Egyptian Ministerial visits

9. Unpublished private documents in Arabic

Umma Party statement, 6 September 1955

10. Unpublished private documents in English

a. BBC Monitoring

7 January 1955

b. Sudan Archive, University of Durham

J. Carmichael Papers: SAD.993/1/33-5

J.W. Kenrick Papers: SAD.815/4/1-22

T.R.H. Owen Papers: SAD.350/10/1-192

W. Luce Papers: SAD.829/5/1-40 and 6/1-93

J.W. Robertson Papers: SAD.519/10/1-7

c. Miscellaneous

Badal, Raphael Koba. 'British Administration in Southern Sudan'. PhD, University of London, 1977

INDEX

Kenrick, John: 11, 98-100, 214
Khalafallah Khālid: 13, 15, 18, 89, 92-3, 101
Khalīfa Abbās al-ʿUbeiḍ: 19
Khalīfa Maḥjūb: 152
Khartoum District Garrison: 160
Khatmīa: 13, 16, 24, 27, 58, 60-2, 78, 87, 89, 92-4, 192-3, 195
al-Kheir Muṣtafa: 103fn
Khiḍr Ḥamad: 12, 16, 18, 194, 203, 226
Kinyeti River: 154
Knox Helm, Sir Alexander: 11, 128, 151, 171, 174-5, 177-81, 185, 189-91, 196, 206, **207**, 209

Liberal Party: 10, 30, 66, 68, 76, 109, 115, 121, 156, 185, 186, 195, 203-5, 216, 229
Liberal Unionists Party: 12-14, 115, 131
Lindsay, William: 32, 44
Lokoya: 152
Lolik Lado, Chief: 67, 152
Luce, William: iv, v, 11, 14, 16, 28-9, 59-60, **61**, 62-4, 92-3, 96, 98, 101-2, 113, 120, 151-2, 168-9, 178-80, 187, 196, 208, 210, 214

Mahdī: 11
Maḥjūb Muḥammad Ṣāliḥ: 132fn
Maḥmūd al-Faḍlī: 143-4
Maḥmūd Fawzī: 77, 201
Maḥmūd Muḥammad Ṭaha: 12, 227
Malakal: 71, 153-4, 225
Māʾmūn Ḥussein Sharīf: 41-2
Maridi: 70, 155
Mavrogordato, John: 11, 32, 210
Mian Ziauddin: 4
Milner, Lord: iii
Mīrghanī Ḥamza: 4, 5, 13, 18, 89-90, 92-3, 101, 121, 185, 203, 227
Monckton, Walter: 139
Mongalla: 71
Morgan, Marco: 73
Morris, Willie: 55

Nile Valley Unity Party: 12-14, 78, 80, 115
Northern Province: 16
Nuba: iv, 10, 69, 73, 74, 216
Nutting, Anthony: 77, 80-1, 111, 164

Pakistan: 4, 7, 28, 75, 125, 127, 167, 182fn, 216, 219, 223
Paulo Logali: 10, 68
Penny, J.C.: 15
Perkins, Warwick: 15
Point Four Program: 22, 104, 121
Post and Telegraph Workers' Union: 136
Progressive Democratic Party: 135
Public Service Commission: 142, 144, 146, 220

Qaḍārif North: 193fn
Qāsim Amīn: 6-7

Radio Omdurman: 156, 157
Railway Workers' Union: 6
al-Rashīd al-Ṭāhir Bakr: 120
Republican Socialist Party: 4-5, 12, 121, 185, 203
Revolutionary Command Council (RCC): 12, 31, 34, 115, 170, 174
Riches, Derek: 24, 48
Rifʿat al-Saʿīd: 130
River Transport Workers' Union: 136
al-Rufāʿ: 193fn

Saburi: 71
Ṣalāḥ Sālim: 12, 32-3, 37, 77, **79**, 81, 90, 92, 108, 115, 150, 163-4, 170, 187, 215
Ṣāliḥ ʿUrābī: 130
Salva Kiir Mayardit: 151fn
Sandon, Harold: 130
Santino Deng Teng: 18, 92
Saturnino Ohure: 217, 229
Sarūr Ramlī, Chief: 68, 226
Saturlino Oboyo: 155
Schwartz, Hillel: 131fn

Tewson, Vincent: 139
al-Tijānī al-Ṭayyib Bābikr: 129fn
Torit: iv, 6, 8, 74, 150, 151-2, 155, 195fn, 229
Trade Commission/er (UK): 19, 22, 23-4, 26, 48, 55, 76, 85, 93, 107, 138, 140-1, 207, 209
Trades Unions Congress (TUC): 139-40
Trevelyan, Humphrey: 150, 163-4, 170-2, 175, 177, 183, 187-9, 201, 207

al-ʿUbeiḍ: 17, 19, 194
ʿUmar Muḥammad Saʿīd: 103fn
ʿUmar Muṣtafa al-Makkī: 103fn
al-Umma: 178-80
Umma Party: 4, 11, 15-16, 18, 24-30, 32-3, 37, 40-3, 48, 50-4, 56-8, 60, 62-3, 66, 81-2, 88, 91, 102, 104, 117, 119-21, 125-7, 137, 141, 174, 178, 180, 185, 203, 211, 226
Union of Sudanese Students in Egypt: 131
United National Front for the Liberation of Sudan: 8
United Southern Party: 10
University College Students' Union: 102, 117
Upper Nile: 8, 64, 67, 70-1, 76, 154
Uqeil Aḥmad Uqeil: 18
ʿUthmān Muṣtafa Urtatāshī: 193fn
ʿUthmān Sid Aḥmad: 103fn
ʿUthmān Yūsuf Abū-Bakr: 143-4

Watson, James: 43
Wau: 153, 229
World Health Organisation: 20

Yaḥya al-Faḍlī: 18, 138-40, 178, 194fn
Yāqūb ʿUthmān: 29
Yambio: 155-7, 159
Yei: 8, 155
Yūsuf ʿAbd-al-Qādir: 193fn
Yūsuf al-ʿAjab: 121, 185, 203

Zakaria Jambo: 143
Zakarīa Muhī al-Dīn: 116, 183

Made in the USA
Columbia, SC
09 September 2022

66467818R00146